THE SUMMER WALKERS

Travelling People and *Pearl-fishers*
in the *Highlands* of *Scotland*

THE SUMMER WALKERS

Travelling People and Pearl-Fishers
in the Highlands of Scotland

TIMOTHY NEAT

CANONGATE BOOKS LIMITED

DEDICATION

This book is dedicated to my great friend Hamish Henderson,
and in memory of the storyteller Ailidh Dall.

First published in 1996 by
CANONGATE *BOOKS*
14 High Street
Edinburgh EH1 1TE
Scotland

Text and illustrations © Timothy Neat 1996
Salathiel's Song © Sean Rafferty, reproduced by kind permission of Carcanet Press
The author has asserted his moral right

ISBN 0 86241 576 4

British Library Cataloguing-in-Publication Data
A catalogue record for this book is available
on request from the British Library.

The publisher gratefully acknowledges subsidy of
the Scottish Arts Council for publication of this book.

Text and layout designed by Mark Blackadder

Printed by Snoeck, Ducaju & Zoon, Ghent, Belgium

CONTENTS

ACKNOWLEDGEMENTS

I would like to thank the Travelling People of Sutherland and Ross-shire for their friendship and all the help they have given me in writing this book. In particular I would like to thank Alec John Williamson, Essie Stewart, Eddie Davies, Gordon Stewart and their families. These are their stories. This is their book. I would also like to thank Duncan Williamson, Willie and Bella MacPhee, Jane Stewart, the Stewarts of Blair and James Stewart of Kemnay. I have endeavoured to present the many-faceted Shakespearean richness of Highland Traveller life in a way that is informative and true to life.

I wish to thank Hamish Henderson, whose pioneering work with the Travellers has been so important and so inspirational to the Traveller People, to many, many people in Scotland and to me. I could not have written the book without his support, advice and encouragement. In 1976 we made a film entitled *The Summer Walkers*. This book is another chapter in a professional collaboration which stretches back across thirty years.

I would also like to thank Stephanie Wolfe Murray for her impassioned commitment to the subject and the project, Jamie Byng, Neville Moir, Dr John MacInnes for his precision of mind, Allan MacDonald for his wonderful ear, Margaret Bennett, John Berger, The School of Scottish Studies, Carcanet Press for Sean Rafferty's 'Salathiel's Song' from *Collected Poems*, 1995, Scottish Television, The Festival de Cinema de Barcelona, Peter Adamson, Sheila Douglas, James Cairncross, Richard Harries, Howard Jones, my own family, and everyone at Canongate.

Photographs are printed with the permission of Alec John Williamson (AJW), Essie Stewart (ES), Eddie Davies (ED), Willie MacPhee (WMac), Hamish Henderson/Bobby Botsford (HH. BB), Jane Turriff (JT), Willie Morrison (MOR), Timothy Neat (TN), Anne Sleigh (AS), Jean Mohr, and *The Herald* (GH).

PREFACE

'The Summer Walkers' is the poetical name that the crofters of the north west Highlands give to the Travelling People – the Tinkers, hawkers and horse-dealers who, for centuries, have passed through their villages buying, selling and entertaining. These Scottish nomads are not Gypsies. They are indigenous, Gaelic-speaking Scots who, to this day, remain heirs of a vital and ancient culture of great historical and artistic importance to Scotland and the world beyond.

The Summer Walkers presents a contemporary 'group self-portrait' of Highland Traveller life as remembered today. It is a book of vivid stories, poetry, song, and factual record. It explores the Travellers' ethnic origins, customs, superstitions, craftwork, their secret 'cover tongue' known as the 'Beurla Reagaird', and their traditional work as pearl-fishers.

Since the 1950s, mass-production, good roads, the motor car, the welfare state have forced rapid changes on the Traveller community. Tinsmithing is a dead craft, horse-dealing a thing of the past, hawking now done by catalogue and supermarket but many older Travellers were brought up in tents and until recently made their living 'on the road'. This is the story of men and women who experienced at first hand the harsh realities of nomadism in the isolated and inhospitable landscapes of Sutherland and Ross-shire. Many Travellers have a remarkable capacity for almost total recall of past experience which makes them living witnesses to the unique cultural history of Scotland's Travelling clans.

The Summer Walkers documents Traveller experience largely through the spoken word – part of a living oral literature which is now recognised as being a key ingredient in one of great folk traditions of Europe. The Highland Travelling People are heirs to what is clearly a very ancient culture: their contribution to the contemporary musical folk culture of Scotland is out of all proportion to their numbers. They bridge time and space like art itself.

The Highland Travellers should not be confused with Gypsies, nor with tramps or pedlars: they live in family groups, many carry the great clan names – Stewart, MacDonald,

Cameron, MacAlister, MacGregor, Macmillan. As an Aberdeenshire Traveller said in the fifties, to differentiate himself from an eccentric Irish tramp 'Charlie Doyle's not one of us. Charlie Doyle just lives frae day to dae – but we,' meaning the Travellers, 'live entirely in the past'. They have a turn of phrase, pride in their archaic lifestyle and traditions. They maintain fierce allegiance to the places where they know their ancestors to have lived. Memory, familiarity, kinship are of central psychological importance: a harsh life has become a proudly born addiction.

In Gaelic the Travellers were known as the *Ceardannan*, the Black Tinkers, and recognised as a tribe, separate to the settled population. Who are these Travellers, where do they come from, where are they going? The name 'Tinker' has become a term of abuse and is not used within the group. Originally it did describe one aspect of the group's historical work – they were itinerant metalworkers, tinsmiths, but the word has become a label of contempt and as Alec John Williamson says, 'If somebody calls me a Tink today – that's fighting talk!' For much of the twentieth century the *Ceardannan* in the Highlands continued to make their living as horse-dealers, light-metal smiths, hawkers, and seasonal labourers. They have also served in the army, made music and told stories; some continue the ancient practice of pearl-fishing (fine pearls being found in the freshwater mussels, once common in certain Scottish rivers). Today, all like to be known as 'the Travelling People'.

The worldwide interest in Celtic music has ensured that Traveller culture has recently developed a renewed and more public vitality but there can be no doubt that the old way of life is passing – probably for ever. Since the Second World War the number of Travellers out 'on the road' in the Highlands has been in continual decline. Generally described, there are, perhaps, twenty thousand Travellers in Scotland but the number still living a traditionally semi-nomadic lifestyle, mostly in caravans, will be less than five thousand: while the number living the old migratory lifestyle in bow-tents, is now probably less than fifty. Many of the old ways are no longer economically viable, or socially tolerable – either to the Travellers themselves or society at large. Some Travellers have moved onto specially designed municipal sites – others have moved into houses and live lives almost indistinguishable from the settled population.

Thus the old traditions are remembered and honoured but disappearing fast. This book aims to document aspects of that life while still fresh in the minds of individuals who spent extended periods of their lives on the road. *The Summer Walkers* concentrates its attention on the Travellers of the two great north western counties of Sutherland and Ross-shire. Here Traveller life long retained its archaic grandeur, a puritan simplicity, a martial ardour – all personified in Alexander Stewart of Lairg, blind 'Ailidh Dall'. He was tinsmith, piper, soldier, singer and story-teller, a Homeric, Ossianic figure much loved in Sutherland, a deeply religious man of whom Scotland can be proud.

His granddaughter, Essie Stewart, is one of the central characters in our story. The Stewart clan, centred around Lairg, was the prime Traveller clan in Sutherland; in Ross-shire the Williamsons, based around Ardgay and Edderton, were pre-eminent. These two families have inter-married over many generations, and amicably shared their trading territories. In recent times both the Stewarts and the Williamsons have married out into the Davies family, travelling pearl-fishers from Dornoch.

Alec John Williamson of Edderton married Mary Davies in 1954. Essie Stewart married the pearl-fisher, Eddie Davies, in 1958. All spent their youth and much of their young adult lives on the road. Today only Eddie Davies still travels regularly but all have surprising stories to tell. Essie Stewart's step-brother, Gordon Stewart, speaks of his work as a tinsmith and horseman; and the book draws in various Travellers from further afield, including Duncan Williamson from Argyll, and Willie and Bella MacPhee from Perth.

A central chapter in the book incorporates memories and evaluations from Hamish Henderson, the outstanding poet/folklorist of twentieth-century Scotland. His 'discovery' of the vast repertoire and wonderful quality of the oral and musical tradition carried by the Travellers has been of great significance – and helped spark in Scotland a cultural renewal of the kind Picasso released in the visual arts of Europe when he recognised the power of African sculpture in 1906.

The Summer Walkers does not deal with music but it does present a selection of the songs and stories which have been for centuries such an integral part of life for the Highland Travellers. The majority of these were, of course, originally created and presented in the Gaelic language. This book is designed for the English reader but the deep roots that Traveller culture has in Gaelic culture should be recognised as integral to its existence.

The book presents a little known subject in a vivid and original manner. Travellers tell their own very personal and often moving stories but the book also raises issues of wide-ranging interest: it explores the process of oral transmission, the Travellers in written literature, the origins of the Travellers, and the reasons why the psychological and cultural characteristics of these 'outsiders' have provided a strange new fulcrum to Scottish national tradition.

Part One
The Travelling People

Essie Stewart

THE BLIND MAN'S DAUGHTER

Hushie, hushie, dinnae fret ye
The Black Tinker winnae get ye

Mare's milk – being forced to drink mare's milk as a cure for whooping cough – that's the first thing I remember. It was my uncle, Angie Williamson, did the milking. We met him camped with his mother, Curly Kate, out at Stoer in Sutherland. He had a crippled back and stood just four feet tall. It was thin, very thin, like skimmed milk, sweet-tasting. You had to drink it warm, straight from the pail, that's what he said. My mother dipped a tin-cup and made me drink. It was frothy, almost a yellow-gold. April 1946 it must have been, my fourth summer on the road. I had been very ill through the winter, first whooping cough, then pneumonia. We had a house but we made our living selling, so when the weather broke we had to get out. There were only the three of us – my mother, my grandfather and me: although I was still ill, I couldn't be left behind. I don't know whether it was the road, good luck, fresh air, or the horse milk, but here I am, large as life, half a century on.

Above. School photograph of Essie Stewart aged nine, 1950. (ES)

Opposite. School photograph of Essie Stewart aged fourteen, 1955. (ES)

Stoer is a small township in the parish called Clashnessie. The Travellers often camped out there. It's where my aunt Christina Stewart was born, so she was always known as Essie. I was named Christina after her and, like her, I've always been known as Essie, though I was born, I think, in Tain. My aunt Christina, married Lindsay Williamson. They had five children but every one of them died. They were first cousins.

My own mother's name was Jemima Paterson. My father was a colour sergeant in the army, stationed at Tain. I think he came from Elgin in Morayshire. His name was Gordon Bremner. I've never met him, nor heard a single piece of news about him. If he's alive, he'll be close on eighty now. My mother was a domestic servant at Edderton, in Easter Ross. I was illegitimate.

Previous page.
Joanne Stewart by the stove of her bow-tent, Sutherland, 1957.
(HH, BB)

My mother gave me away, just hours after I was born. That was 1941. She died very young, of TB I've heard, before the end of the war. I was offered first to my aunty Essie but she was pregnant and arranged that I should go to her cousin, Mary. It was all unofficial. I came with a letter from my mother saying that I was 'given to Mary Stewart of Remarstaig, Lairg, in the county of Sutherland'. And that was that. For years I kept the letter but now, I have to say, I don't know where it is. Mary Stewart was a single woman of thirty-three, she lived alone with her father, Alexander Stewart – blind Ailidh Dall.

As a child I knew none of this. Neither my mother nor my grandfather ever spoke of who I was, or where I came from and it did not occur to me to ask. But one day, playing with a girl from Edderton, out of spite I was told that my mother, Mary, was not my real mother. I was about ten. I was deeply upset. I still don't know the full story, but I do know my mother's mother was a Williamson, a Traveller woman, whose family lived in Tain. They had the ragstore there. They were the 'Bowlie' Williamsons – settled Travellers – they took in rags, rabbit-skins, woollens, in exchange for china ornaments and things that other Travellers, on the road, would sell to crofters all over Sutherland. This grandmother married a local man, one of the Patersons, and my mother, Jemima, was their daughter. So, by blood, I'm less than half a Traveller – but I lived the Traveller life from the day I was born till the day I married, then for twenty-five summers I was out on the road as wife of the pearl-fisher, Eddie Davies. Nearly fifty years on the road I had, now I live down here in Inverness, battered like my Ford Sierra – 129,000 miles on the clock!

The Stewarts of Lairg were a very old Traveller clan. We had relations in Perthshire, in Aberdeenshire, in Skye, but my own family were all born and bred in Sutherland or Ross-shire: that was home ground. We would go up to the horse fairs in Thurso, but Caithness was MacPhee territory. We'd go west as far down as Polbain, every year, but my family never went beyond Ullapool, and in the east I've never heard of the Stewarts crossing the Struie – not in the old days, not for trade. Our winter base was Remarstaig, three miles out of Lairg – that's a very old market town – from Lairg our roads spread out all over the north.

It must have been about a hundred years ago that the Stewarts took over a piece of ground, between the railway line and the road, at the top of the pass from Lairg to Golspie on the North Sea coast. Three small houses were built, but and bens with tin roofs. The land was ours – by habit and repute! It's a bleak, cold, windswept spot; over a thousand feet above sea level. No rates. We got water from a burn and there was a well for the horses. Our house had walls of brick and mortar but the other two were wood. Aunt Joanne lived in one with her son Gordon and her aged mother Black Anne. Peter Stewart and his wife lived in the other. They were to have a big family of seven children.

As well as the railway line, there was a siding alongside the houses. Because we were right at the summit of the pass, trains needed a place to draw in if they ran out of steam. Most of them had two engines on for the climb but they'd still run out of steam. That's what we liked them to do. We loved the railway and used to run down to the cutting and look down at the engines, shout to the drivers and wave to the passengers. I loved the smell of the steam and smoke. Over the years we got to know most of the engine drivers. The firemen would kick out coal – huge slabs of boiler coal – and we would take them home like prizes, hunks of whale meat! They were local men from Golspie, Rogart, Brora, and very good to us. Best of all was Norman Brunton, he used to stack it up! Have it all ready on the plate and kick it out as he went by. They would blow long blasts on the whistle to let us know they were on the way. But not if they saw the horses in the field. They knew horses. Everybody knew horses in those days. Grandfather knew the time of every train by heart; when he was blind it was the trains told him the time. The passenger carriages in those days were all Pullmans – brown and yellow-gold they were. We loved the railway men.

My mother Mary was known as Michie because she'd been born at a camp site at Migdale, at the edge of the oak forest. She was, people say, no

Opposite., Traveller camp, c. 1930, Elphin Bridge, Ross-shire (birthplace of the blind story-teller, Ailidh Dall). The old lady in the cart is Curly Kate, the man is her crippled son, Angus Williamson. On the left is a traditional bow-tent; in the background, Suilven, the famous 'sugarloaf' mountain. (AJW)

Studio portrait of Ann Stewart and Mary Stewart, c. 1916, grandmother and mother of Essie Stewart. (AJW)

direct relation of mine, but her mother was the very image of me. Alec John Williamson has a photograph of the two of them – my adopted mother's mother's face, her eyes, her mouth, are just like mine. She died of TB at the age of twenty-seven while my grandfather, Alec Stewart, was away in France. Michie was nine when her father returned after the war. She took over the house. She hardly went to school; she had to look after not only her father but also his mother, Old Suzie. She was blind. She died in 1936 aged ninety-one, by which time my grandfather was also going blind. It was cataracts. Three generations of that family went blind but all of them lived to a great age. Each one of them was a story-teller. Blindness and stories were things I knew well.

Alexander Stewart, Ailidh Dall, that means Blind Sandy, was born in 1882. He was my grandfather but he was more like a father to me. He came from a family of seven. He had no schooling. As a young man he was a tinsmith, and a much respected horseman, he did four years in the artillery, he was a very good piper and a singer. He couldn't read or write. He, and the Williamsons of Ardgay, were the last of the real old style Travellers in the north west and they were very well liked and very well thought of: It wasn't 'the Tinks', we were. The Stewarts were known all over Sutherland and in 1955 Hamish Henderson from the University of Edinburgh came to our camp at Brae Tongue to record my grandpa, and people say he was the best Gaelic story-teller ever recorded on the mainland of Scotland. He used to sleep in a long nightshirt and I would sleep between him and my mother, both at home and in the tent.

Every summer we would set out for five or six months on the road with the horses, dogs, one to three carts, our big bow-tent, and two or three bantams for eggs. Sometimes two or three families would travel together, sometimes our family would travel alone. But always in those days there were other Travellers to meet at the camping places. I first travelled out to the west when I was just three months old. During the Second World War we were one of the very few families that travelled, so there was good business to be done. By that time Ailidh Dall could no longer make tin, so everything depended on my mother selling round the doors. She took whatever was wanted and needed bringing in – overalls, trousers, shirts, socks, underwear, needles, pins, brushes, combs, frock-coats for the women. All the Highland women wore them then – with the flower patterns on. She would take orders, or know from years of selling what particular crofters, shepherds, keepers would be wanting. Most of the women were so pleased to see her. They would meet perhaps two or three times a year and many of them would see few other folk. There was real isolation in the Highlands then. We were friends and very welcome – we were travelling shops ahead of time! There were still very few cars in the forties.

On the road I normally had to stay behind at the camp to look

Stewarts on the road in Sutherland, 1957. Mary Stewart, Essie riding a half-hidden horse, Black Anne in second cart.
(HH, BB)

after my grandfather, do the washing, tend the horses, prepare food, but one week, not far from Scourie, right out on the west coast, several of the Traveller families had camped together, so I didn't have to stay behind and I went out hawking with my mother. I really liked to go out with her. I remember going up to the house of a woman my mother knew very well, whom she had visited once or twice a summer for thirty years. But this day she was not in, she was out, and her daughter, a beautiful girl of about eighteen answered the door. On her arm she had a baby, just a few months old. I was about seven then and she let me hold the child, a little girl. She had red curls. We had a cup of tea. As we were about to leave, the girl looked at my mother and said 'Do you want her? If you want her, you can have her.'

Mother asked how old she was and why she wanted to give her away. 'Ten months,' she said 'I'm not married. Mother doesn't want her, I don't know what I'm to do with her. Please, please Mary take her with you.' My mother was tempted, I'm sure. 'It's a pity it's a girl. I already have a daughter.' That was me. 'But had it been a boy', she said, 'I would have been pleased to take him.'

I remember looking at my mother and nodding and smiling and trying to persuade her to say 'Yes, yes, we will take her.' I would have loved to have had a baby brother, or a sister. I was often very lonely. I remember the girl pleading, 'Mary, please take her, she's good, she's very good.' But mother suddenly went to the door and said, 'I can't take her, it'll be all right, in your heart you love the child, it'll be all right.' But as we went down the path across

the field away from the house the girl followed us with the baby on her arm saying over and over again, 'Why not a girl Mary, why not a girl?' She was crying. On and on she went, 'Why not a girl Mary, why not a girl?' At the gate to the road we stopped. I whispered to my mother, 'I'll look after her, Ma.' I began to cry as well, 'Why can't we have her? Why can't we have the baby?' But mother was firm, she said that she was getting old and couldn't take another child at her age. As we walked away, I remember she took my hand and said 'You must not look back till we've passed the shop.' But I did and she was still at the gate, crying and crying.

Next year we heard that two shepherds, who lived alone with their sister, had taken the child. In her teens she got troublesome. What happened to her I don't know but she must be a woman in her late forties now. At that time I didn't know about my own adoption – but looking back – giving children away must have been common in the Highlands, right up until the 1950s. I know myself, five people, alive today, who were given away as children to the Travellers. There were so few of us, we needed new people, and for the country folk there was nothing easier, nothing better, than giving unwanted children to Travellers. My step-brother, Gordon Stewart, he was adopted. He says if the Stewarts hadn't taken him in, he would have ended up on the dunghill! They say the Gypsies steal children! It was not stealing – but like us – the Gypsies must have been given children. We gave lives and homes to many an unwanted child who might have died, been killed, put into institutions – or today, of course, not seen the light of day.

At the camp, or at home in wintertime there was always work to do. I was Cinderella. And Gordon, he was 'Jack the Lad'! It was always, 'do this, do that, mind Peter's bairns . . .' I was loved and cared for right enough, we were well looked after but looking back I see I never knew a normal childhood—there was so little play, no leisure time, always jobs to do. But, I have to say I was happy, I had a happy childhood. We were very poor most of the time but we had good times. Gordon and I were very close. He was my step-brother. He was twenty-two months older than me – but me the boss! We grew up together. We were a two-man band! Firewood, water carrying, feeding and cleaning the horses – they were the big jobs. As soon as we got back from school it was work – fetch the water, clean the horses, feed the horses, stack the firewood, carry the peats and coal. After tea there was the washing-up, and leading the old man down the road or round the camp.

We did not much like school, at least at first. We felt no need for school. By the time I started down in Lairg I had spent six summers with horses, travelling, selling, camping out in all weathers. We spoke Gaelic. We had a secret language. We knew the world! What need had we of school, or

Top left. Essie Stewart, her mother Mary Stewart and grandfather Ailidh Dall, with three of the children of Peter and Chrissie Stewart, Sutherland, 1957. (HH, BB)

Top right. Peter Stewart with baby, Sutherland 1957. (HH, BB)

Bottom left. Essie playing accordion, with Mary Stewart, by cart with tarpaulins and sticks for the family tent, Altnaharra, 1957. (HH)

Bottom right. 'Black Anne' Stewart in her bow-tent with two of her grandsons, Sutherland, 1957. (HH, BB)

books, or English? We were proud to be the Stewarts; known all over Sutherland like nobody else. 'What care we though we be sae sma – the tent will stand when the palace shall fa!'

School was a foreign place to us. We walked three miles down and three miles back each day. The teachers were very, very strict in those days, but I have to say they were good. My primary teacher was Miss Fraser, we had a Miss MacLean from Lochinver, there was a Miss MacDonald from Melness. They all spoke Gaelic. In the secondary school there was Mrs Jaffrey and Miss Gray, they are the two I remember. Mr Humphries was the headmaster. We got no persecution as Traveller children. None. And as I went up the school I enjoyed it. The fact that Gordon and I got six months off each summer – to travel – was a cause of envy among the other children but we had no trouble and I did quite well. I would read the letters for the old folk.

Gordon and I got to be very good with the horses. Some years we'd come back in the autumn with half a dozen. We'd ride through Lairg and up the hill. Before winter they'd be sold on, of course, and we'd keep just one good horse for going out again in the spring. But I mind years when we'd be so short of money, or feeding, that we'd have to sell our own horse to see us through. I remember one very hard year. By the spring we'd sold the horse and were completely out of money. We had to get out on the road to earn cash but had no horse to get started! Ailidh Dall was too proud to ask for money, or a horse, from anyone up at Remarstaig, so we took him down to Duncan MacPhee at Lower Torroble to borrow twenty pounds. He got the money and we got a horse in Dornoch. But then the weather hung on, very very harsh; the snow was still deep on the ground up around Altnaharra so we decided to go west. It was just the three of us. We camped a few nights at West Shinness, and Michie started going round the houses but the weather stayed bad – wind, rain, snow. We didn't carry feeding for the horse so after a few days we knew we'd outstayed our welcome. You couldn't go on asking the crofters for hay you couldn't pay for, so as soon as the rain stopped Old Sandy said 'Break camp – let's take the road!'

It's wild mountain country to the west of Loch Shin and we went out into the wind. At Fiag Bridge it started to snow. It was so cold no one could sit for a rest in the cart, we had to keep moving – the old man was getting on and I was just seven or eight. Michie was leading the horse, Granda holding on to the back of the cart and me walking behind him, holding his coat. I remember our fronts plastered thick with snow. We got to Overscaig – that's about eight miles. We uncoupled the horse and brought it round by the cart with its back to the wind and mother scraped the snow as fast as she could, so we could heave up a lean-to against the back end of the cart.

Top. Ailidh Dall overseeing the establishment of a new campsite, Caithness, 1957. Essie Stewart carries one of the bowed hazel sticks which give tents their rib-cage structure. (HH, BB)

Middle. Tarpaulins being laid out ready to be placed over the stick skeleton of the tent. (HH, BB)

Bottom. Essie and her mother Mary Stewart complete the tent, bad weather closing in. (HH, BB)

Then we tried to make a fire. We always carried plenty of old paper, so we soon got a great blaze going in the stove, but we didn't have any sticks! Mother and I searched all round and dug in the snow but all we found was a few sodden pine roots and the fire went out. I started to cry with the cold. Then grandfather had an idea. He told us about an old shepherd, Davie Storrie, who lived across the other side of Loch Shin at Creanich. He used to have his coal delivered on the Overscaig side and come over, by rowing boat, once a fortnight to get what he needed. Granddad said this coal was in an old quarry about three hundred yards away so he stuffed the last of the paper up inside his jumper and mother and I went off to look for the coal. We found the quarry and dug in the snow till we came to the coal and filled a basket. Then back we came. Once the fire was going and we'd all got warmed up a bit, mother set off again, this time for the Overscaig Hotel. After a while she came back with a gill of whisky for Sandy and a stone of hay and some oats for the horse. Whether she paid for it, or was given it, I don't know.

It was well dark by now but we'd got the lean-to snowproofed and the tin stove was glowing red-hot! Granda gave Michie a shot of his whisky, we ate bread and marge, and then huddled together to sleep. I remember Granda telling us about a man whose horse died in a snowstorm – so he cut it open and climbed inside to keep warm till the morning! We slept very well and next time we saw Davie Storie we made up for the coal.

Two days we were stuck at Overscaig, then we went on to Achfary – we knew we'd get help there. We were in quite a bad way – so when I saw the flag flying up over the castle, I shouted to Granddad, 'The flag is up!' and he said 'It'll be all right now.' The flag meant the Westminsters were in residence. And before the tent was up Hughie Morrison, the chauffeur, came down to the camp in a Rolls Royce with a box full of dry clothes and food! And we asked how he knew what was needed and he said that the Duchess had seen us come into the campsite and asked who we were. 'I told her,' he said 'it must be Mary Stewart and Blind Ailidh Dall, and she said "I'll make up a box – and you take it down when you're passing." ' And in ten minutes the box was there by the front door and Hughie brought it down straight away. There were even chocolates in it. That was the kind of people they were. The Achfary kitchen was ordered never to refuse food to the Travelling People. There was a French chef who would heap up our baskets full with delicacies. Coming back in the autumn I've seen our carts leave Achfary with the venison tied on with ropes. So much.

At Remarstaig we had a wireless which ran off accumulators but piping, story-telling, ceilidhing, they were the only entertainments until Gordon and I started going to the pictures in the Drill Hall in Lairg. Out on the road, ceilidhs would break out every time several families met up at a big campsite. The local people would come down and join in, especially up at Melness, and at Kinlochbervie we had huge ceilidhs. Ailidh Dall would play the pipes, there would be singing, melodeons, tin-whistle sometimes, dancing, stories.

By ourselves, after supper, there'd be chit-chat round the fire then someone would say 'Come on Sandy, tell us a story!' and after a bit he'd start. Some of the stories were very long but he was such a good story-teller – he had them word-perfect—each time word for word near enough the same: except sometimes he would deliberately surprise you with a change. He told them slow, so you had to think up or remember what was coming next – though they ended up always the same they'd always be interesting. We loved them like songs or nursery rhymes. He learned most of them from Old Suzie his mother – he never read a book in his life! I have my mother's birth certificate and grandfather's signature is just a little cross, beside which the registrar has printed out 'Alexander Stewart, Tinsmith' and written 'his mark'. It was memory he had; having told a story in Gaelic he could tell it all again in word-perfect translation for the English speakers.

Ossian was one of my favourites, and *Am Maraichre Mairnealach,* the one about the snake. That was a story from Old Suzie. She was born in 1845 so she must have learned her stories from people born in the eighteenth century. In three tellings those stories go two hundred years. The Travellers die off young – or live to be very old!

Some of Ailidh Dall's stories were true stories – about what he'd done, some were about life in the old days, and some were the big songs and stories from long ago. He had many, many stories about horses. It was with horses he worked during the First War in the Royal Artillery. He used to tell us about a cockney sergeant that he had, Sergeant Dutton, from Shepherd's Bush! A cocky little man he didn't like. But Sergeant Dutton kept a pet monkey called Jacko, which had become the regimental mascot. He used to bring it out tied to a long tether and when the men gave it scraps to eat, granda said it would leap up onto the roof of the tin shed and eat the bits and scratch itself and throw its droppings at the soldiers! Even when the shells were whistling overhead.

My grandfather had good sight in those days. It was only after he was demobbed that he began to lose his sight and in 1926 he went to Edinburgh for an operation on one of his eyes. For eighteen months, my mother used to say, he could thread the smallest needle in her purse but then, suddenly, that eye went blind. Because of that, when the other eye began to go, he refused to go to the doctor. He used to say, 'I'll let nature not the doctors rule my life!' And that eye went very slowly. When I was a small girl he could still tell dark

*Chrissie Stewart with six of her
seven children, Sutherland, 1957.
(HH, BB)*

from light and see people move across a window or a door but for the last
twenty years he was totally blind. Out on the road he'd hold a leather strap
behind the cart. He knew where he was by the sounds and by the steepness of
the road. He could walk all day. He got a blind person's pension of five shillings
a week, then when he reached seventy he got his old-age pension.

Mother was a lovely singer. She didn't tell the 'big stories' like my
grandfather but she liked to tell stories about us, about her own family, the road
– and we'd all be out there in the west with a beautiful white horse, a perfect
cart, the weather fine and she'd tell us how, after a good day round the houses,
we'd all be going swimming and have a picnic down by a burn, and we'd go
back to the tent to find a feast – the like of which would please a king! She liked
to give us parts in her stories and we'd be doing great deeds – like heroes –
coming back to the camp laden with meat and boxes of honey and chocolates.

At home our cooking was all open-fire cooking. We didn't have
an oven till after I left home. Then mother got a Trueburn Stove for safety
reasons. Grandfather loved the fire but there came a time when he could not
be left alone with a free-burning fire. It was soups, stews, potatoes, tea, we
lived upon. The potatoes were boiled in their jackets, summer and winter, and
the skins fed to the dogs, with scraps. We boiled the kettle on a hook. There
was a cauldron and iron saucepans suspended from hooks above the fire. When
I was about fourteen mother got herself a metal stand on which the pots and

The cart and bow-tent of Ailidh Dall, Mary and Essie, Sutherland, 1957. (HH, BB)

pans could rest, but this tended to get things burned down one side – so the firestand was little used. Our cooking was very simple, mostly frying and boiling. Saturday night was Dumpling Night. Cloutie dumplings were our weekly treat. Mother would steam them in a muslin cloth – a handful of this and a handful of that – raisins, carrots, treacle, syrup, flour, mixed spices, water, dollops of fat, sugar. During rationing my mother always swapped her clothing coupons for sugar for the tea, 'We dinnae need new claes,' she'd say 'but a' the Stewarts ha'e had a sweet tooth since the Flood!'

At Remarstaig we had a dry toilet in the stable, a plank with a hole above a pit, but on the road it was always 'wherever' – as long as it was downstream of the well and the tent! For washing we would use a bowl, a piece of soap, a towel – or a pool in the burn. In a heatwave we children would find a pool and bathe. I never learned to swim but we'd play for hours in a good stream. We always put on bathing costumes, even if the nearest house was seven miles away. My first costume lasted years and years, wool it was, with green and yellow stripes. A woman in Strathnaver gave it to my mother. She had been a stewardess on one of the great ocean liners in the twenties: it must have been thirty years old when I got it but it was good quality wool. I would have been the very height of fashion if I'd been a friend of Mrs Simpson and the Prince of Wales! It fitted very well – I was a big eight-year-old – big in the thorax. The only problem would be midges if there was no wind.

I had some basic sex instruction at school, but sex was something never discussed at home. We all lived on top of one another, everything was very proper, very old-fashioned. I knew practically nothing about sex till I got married at seventeen. For my mother, the subject was taboo. It was something we never spoke about. There was never a man friend after I came along – she didn't have sex before she went into her grave. First she had looked after her grandmother, Old Suzie, then she cared for her father and me. It was understood in Traveller families that one of the daughters would stay behind and look after the parents. That was my mother. She died of cancer of the breast, aged sixty-six, three years after the death of her father.

Marriage was not a problem for me – but marriage was a problem for the Travellers, at least up in Sutherland. Travellers did not marry outside the Traveller clans – and there were less and less Travellers. I can see now – there was bad health and infertility, interbreeding. The Travellers in Sutherland were very religious and very proper; for them it was marriage, or nothing. I could name you a dozen of my relations who did not marry. Johnnie Williamson of Ardgay, he proposed to my mother but she refused him. He was a relation but he was a very eligible man. Would she take him? No! With me and Grandfather she already had a family. She was a person who did not seem interested in sex. Johnnie must have been – but all he did was live to a great age and leave a small fortune! His brother Peter did not marry. His sister Katie did not marry. Just one sister in that family married. That was Ina, she married Brian Stewart, but she married so late that they had no live children. Their only daughter was adopted, like me. I have a love letter that shows my mother was courted by an English packman during the thirties, before I was born. He sold very good quality goods. He was a mountaineer and used to collect eagles' eggs for sale. It was still legal to take eagle eggs in the thirties. His name was Brown. Try as he would he could not persuade my mother to leave home. It was a beautiful letter he wrote, with drawings of horses. But she wouldn't leave her father you see and she didn't want to go down to London. He said she loved her horse more than him. My mother kept that letter all her days. We have it yet.

Myself, I started going out with Eddie Davies when I was sixteen. I had known Eddie since I was a small girl; his sister, Chrissie, was married to Peter Stewart and lived next door to us at Remarstaig. Eddie and his family would come up to see them. The Davies were all pearl-fishers, they travelled all over the north. We would meet them on the road. Eddie had a car. He was twelve years older than me, so when Eddie started writing letters and wanting to see me, I didn't tell my parents. But they found out and they weren't very happy. Michie sent Eddie packing with a flea in his ear, but later on after I'd started work in Lairg, we began walking out and going to the pictures. It was domestic work I was doing and I was bringing in good money – so when they got to hear about what was going on they weren't keen that I should take off but I was sixteen then and Ailidh Dall spoke with Eddie and very soon we were married.

The wedding took place in the Free Kirk in Lairg. Gordon was best man. My grandfather gave me away. Then we went up to Remarstaig for a big reception. Granddad played the pipes, there was plenty dancing, drinking, singing. It was September and in the early evening Eddie and I set off for the west in his A40 van. It happened that the Williamsons, Johnnie, Katie and Peter, were camping at Rosehall so we offered them a lift. They'd come in for the wedding and had to get back. On the way we had a puncture! We had no puncture kit so Eddie stuffed the tyre with grass and on we went. By the time we got to Rosehall it was dark. Katie said she'd make us supper and Johnnie and Peter persuaded us to stay the night with them. Thunder was coming, they said. We got our bell-tent up, then Eddie opened up a half-bottle. The Williamsons weren't big drinkers but we had good crack around their stove in the big galley, then we all went off to bed.

Early next morning, we woke to hear Katie calling 'Will you be having a cup of tea?' and into the tent she came. 'It's hot,' she said, 'but I think the milk is on the turn.' On the turn! It was round the bend! As soon as she was gone, we poured it in the grass. We stayed three nights with the Williamsons then drove on to Lochinver. It's a lovely campsite at Rosehall between the stone walls and the big Caledonian pines. They say the Duke of Sutherland ordered the walls to stay well to the side of the road – to allow the Travellers to keep camping the site. It's one of the few places left to us now. Well, that first night was the first night I'd ever spent away from Ailidh Dall and my mother and after that I became Essie Davies, the pearl-fisher's wife.

Wedding portrait, the Free Kirk, Lairg, 1959, Gordon Stewart (best man), Eddie Davies, Essie Davies, and Phammie Davies (bridesmaid). (ED)

Eddie Davies

THE PEARL-FISHER'S SON

Tinkie, Tinkie tarrie bags
Go to the well and wash your rags

I am the last – because I am a Traveller and a pearl-fisher. I am the last Traveller on the road in Sutherland – all these glens I travel – the Shin, Strathnaver, Glen Oykel, Lochinver, the Conon. I fish the rivers all summer through, depending on the weather. No tent these days – no family – no dough! I sleep in the car, or on the ground. I have my can, my memories – a can or two! My life is now all memories. I had a beautiful wife and lovely family. I drink and smoke, too much, they say! Just my eldest daughter, Sandra, still lives at home with me.

None of the children smoke. Very sensible. My mother was a heavy smoker – she died when she was seventy-five. My father was a heavy smoker and a heavy drinker – he died when he was ninety-three. Grandfather was the same – he died aged eighty-nine – but my great-grandfather, he was what you call a binge drinker – month on month off! Smoked like a chimney and lived to ninety-six! Myself, I've just signed on for another thirty years – I'm sixty-five. Good stock we are, the Davies.

Eddie Davies I was christened, by the monks, at Fort Augustus. My son Edward, is the fifth Eddie Davies in a row – ex-Royal Marine, ex-salmon poacher, ex-deer poacher, he's twenty-nine. He used to go out poaching with that man called 'Star'. You will have heard of him, best shot in Sutherland – till, they say, he lost his nerve. But he's still the best. The Sheriff Court in Dornoch was burnt to the ground the night before they were up for trial! They say it was drug dealers from Aberdeen but everything was put back months by that. It wasn't them like, they wanted it over and done with. It was bad for them. Made them look bad – going up to the court and finding a

Eddie Davies at Lower Torroble, 1995.
(TN)

smoking ruin! They've calmed down now like – I'm hoping Edward'll take on the pearl-fishing – seventeen years, every summer, he was on the road with me, as a boy. But there's no money in it, not for a man who likes to spend. Where's the spondulicks? That's what I say. With me it's a joke like but everyone else – they're after the money.

'Big rat, stoat, weasel!' The Davies family is very superstitious. If you heard that – you'd turn back in the road. See a person with red hair – that was bad luck – go somewhere else. If you saw a minister, it was the same. Red hair, bad luck – that's what we'd say – even though Jesus Christ himself had hair that was auburn red. It mattered very much with us what you first heard, or first saw, in the morning.

'Big rat, stoat, weasel!' See one, hear the word, and that was that! Sometimes I'd say it for devilment! 'Big rat!' If the pearl-fisher, Bobby Campbell, heard those words – what a curse he'd give! Not a river would he enter, not a mussel would he cut, until a night had passed. My father, he would just change plan. If he was heading for the Naver, he'd go up to the Mallard, if he was set for the Mallard he'd go back down to the Naver. Unlucky names. Unlucky things. It was like a wind that blew – settled what you did that day. Nor did we like to hear the name MacPhee, not in the forenoon – it was a jinx!

I have this psoriasis. As you can see – my face, my neck, my hands, my feet. But I was a good-looking bloke when I was young – you know that. I'm like that man in *The Singing Detective*! Dennis Potter! Name like that, he must have been a Tink! I come of mixed blood myself – half Highland Traveller, quarter Irish Traveller, one eighth English Gypsy and one eighth Welsh ram. But born and bred in Sutherland three generations – this is my country. I'll stake claim against the Duke himself! It was my great-grandfather came from Wales. He was the first Davies in Sutherland, but there's plenty of us up here now. We multiply as the Bible tells us do.

Old man Davies was, my grandfather said, an apprentice plasterer. He went up to London and it was there he met his wife. She was of the Gypsy people. They had two boys, Willie and Edward. Then something happened and he took to the road – debts, feud, murder, I don't know – but he left London and came up here; took Shank's pony and got a job with Lord Lovat at the castle in Beauly. He worked as handyman and the boys went to school with the Lovats; there was a private school there in the castle. One day he was working high up on the walls when he sees this man come up to speak with Lord Lovat. He was a pearl-fisher. And my grandfather saw Lord Lovat pass three gold sovereigns across and say 'Come back with a match for this, and any more like those you brought last time.' Three gold sovereigns! For a single pearl! And he was working for a shilling a day! He climbed down his ladder

Stewarts fishing the Ythan in the 1930s. (TN)

from the wall and as the man was leaving, Davies spoke with him.

And this pearl-fisher told my great-grandfather about the river mussel and the Scottish pearl. He said he was fishing the Beauly river and he took out a handful he had left in his pocket – beautiful, all colours, shapes – and he laid them, warm, in the old man's hand. Davies fell in love. A few days after that he packed in his job at the castle and took to the road, again. It was a pearl-fisher he would be and the boys went with him. They were about eight and ten. That was 1870, or thereabouts. They fished the Beauly river, then the Conon, then they came up to the Sutherland rivers and this is where we stayed.

Left. Eddie Davies by the Naver, Rhifail, Sutherland, 1995. (TN)

Right. The Laxford bridge, Sutherland. The Laxford is a famous salmon river and a traditional pearling river for the Davies family. It was close to this bridge that Eddie's great-uncle Willie died in 1901, and here that his father, Edward, came to collect parcels from the Durness coach. Snow-covered, the massive rock face of Arkle rises in the distance. (TN)

He gave his life to it. They'd camp by the rivers and they met in with the Travelling People. They were very well liked and the boys would stay with the Travellers while their old man went on alone, staying in the shepherds' houses and in the Model Lodging Houses. He'd spend a month on the road, working the rivers, then go down to Inverness to sell the pearls.

As time went on the old man would make his way and the boys would make their way, more and more. Sometimes he'd drink for a month, till he was penniless, then back to the river he'd go – fish long days into the night – way out in the wilds – living rough. There was a good market for pearls in those days, but he was like the oilrig workers today—work and spend. It was a hard life but a healthy life. I never saw him and I don't have a photograph – he died in the year of the National Strike, in Inverness, four years short of his hundredth birthday. White hair, like Merlin, they say he had.

My grandfather, Edward, I mind very well. He used to fish all summer up here, then wander down to Aberdeenshire for the winter. He was a man good with his hands. He'd be mending machines, riddles and sieves. He made wire baskets, potato baskets, flower baskets, wooden flowers, wire flowers and he made puzzles. And I've done all that myself, like. He travelled round the farms, round the bothies, selling his wire puzzles to the bothie loons, or the cornkisters as we would say, and they'd pay him to teach them the secrets, or he'd swap a good puzzle for a sack of tatties, or a sack of neeps to take home. He met his wife down there in Aberdeenshire, Margaret O'Neill. She was a hawker, one of the Irish Travelling People, and they got married in Inverurie.

They had seven sons, and six girls, I think, still-born. Why it was the girls that died I don't know. I mind my father tell of when his mother bore a still-born bairn at Laxford Bridge, by the shepherd's house near the camping place at Stack, underneath the mountain. It was a great river for pearls, the Laxford – I'm in it yet. And that day, my grandfather asked my father, he would be about seven at the time, to go down to meet the Durness coach at Laxford Bridge. And there he was given a parcel wrapped up in brown paper with string. He didn't know what it was. It was light, but too big to put under his arm, so he put it on his head and walked back to the camp. On the way he suddenly became curious and wondered what was in the box. He thought it might be something to eat. But when he opened the parcel, it was a wee coffin. It was for the still-born baby and next day my father said, the old man walked all the way down to Scourie with that tiny coffin 'under his wing', as he used to say, and the minister buried it there in the graveyard at Scourie. And after that the doctor came back up with them to the shepherd's house to tend to my grandmother.

My great-uncle Willie, my grandfather's brother, the one that walked up to Sutherland from London when he was a boy, he also died at Laxford Bridge. Willie had gotten married to a Williamson from Tain but he spent a lot of time fishing the Ythan, and the Dee and the Don, in Aberdeenshire and it was down there that he got ill. He went into Aberdeen Royal Infirmary and they told him he had cancer and just a year to live – so he came back up here and went on fishing, best he could. When he knew the end was near, he invited all the Travellers and pearl-fishers to meet him at the Laxford Bridge. He liked it there. And they had a great party. Oh he was weak and frail – but he had money about him, and he had a lovely horse and cart and he sent the youngsters down to Scourie to come back loaded up with booze and food. It was summertime so there was only an hour of darkness and the party went on all through the night and in the morning he was gone. They went looking for him and they found him dead, inside his tent. That was in 1901. He was thirty-two. They took his body down to the graveyard in Scourie but they burned the tent and built a cairn of stones above the spot where he died. It's still there to this day among the bracken. There must be more than two hundred stones. When a Traveller died in his tent they would build a cairn so that no one would then come and camp where the dead man died. In Gaelic they call death 'the day of the mountain'.

All the Davies went into the river from about the age of five. So my grandfather had seven boys fishing for him. In 1926 my father and mother ran away together. She was seventeen and he was eight years older. She was Tina, a MacAlister, from Dingwall. They were a wild people, the MacAlisters when they got the booze! Real tinks you might say! When they heard that the young lass was away with the pearl-fisher, Davies, they said 'The bastard! We'll kill the bastard!' Even though the MacAlisters knew my father well! And Katie Williamson went up to them and told them 'That's a nice young chap to run away with.' That didn't matter! Their blood was up! The girl was away and they would get her back! It was a hue and cry. The MacAlisters were going to kill them! That was 1926, the year his grandfather died.

It was in Oban that they fell in love. They knew there'd be trouble, so they made a run for it. They went east, way over the bridlepaths, they were not heard of for three weeks, they went away over the mountains, up past Fort William and landed up in Speyside, where my father built a wee stick tent and started fishing. The Spey was always a good river for us like – but the floods came and they went on down to Tomintoul where his father's father used to winter and it was there that they were caught up with. But it was not the MacAlisters who found them!

It's a funny thing but once they'd got away over the mountains the MacAlisters seem to have forgotten all about them. Flare-up, flare-down that was the MacAlisters. Maybe it was a way of making sure youngsters stuck together – because one night together was seal for a lifetime. Marriage rules were very strict among the Travellers, and strictly broken you might say! No, it wasn't the MacAlisters that found them, it was the Davies! It was my grandmother and all her family that found them – and my mother was about six months pregnant. 'When did you get married like?' they asked. And of course they weren't married. Oh it was a terrible thing not to be married in those days! And my grandmother, Maggie, said 'You'll have to get married. You'll have to go away somewhere and come back married. If your grandfather finds out you're not wed with a bairn, there'll be a row worse than the MacAlisters!'

It was wintertime and they were making money gathering rabbit-skins, so they wandered on across the hills to Laggan, near Kingussie and they took his brother Tommy with them, to help with the snaring. They set up camp in a wood, and the two of them went to see the minister and asked to get married. And he said they had to be there for three weeks, so that he could read the banns and see the registrar and all that. It was February. There was snow on the ground. Down there it's a cold, cold country, high up with no sea, but they had to stay on. There was a big blow and half the trees in that wood got flattened – but they had to stay on for the wedding. And it's a strange thing – they hadn't told Tommy that they were going to get married, so he asked 'What are we staying down here for – why don't we go back to Tomintoul and get in a house?' So father told him he was waiting on a man bringing in a horse! Now that was a lie, but he wanted to keep Tommy with him, you see, for company

and safety; he didn't know what the MacAlisters might do, and the gamekeepers could be vicious in those days – and he needed to have someone to keep on at the rabbits.

Anyway, the minister arranged for them to see the registrar. He was a kindly man and he had a very nice wife, and they asked my father and mother to come down to the house two hours before the wedding was to start. So they did and they were asked into the house and there they got a bath and the registrar's wife had laid out a beautiful wedding dress for my mother and a good suit for my father. And because the banns had been read – all Laggan turned out for the wedding. It was in that wee church by the bridge at Laggan, and the minister blessed them and the whole village was there when they came out on the step – and it was snowing – and they cheered them and flung confetti at them in the snow. Oh they were a fine-looking young couple. No photographs, of course, but the wedding ring was a thick bit of copper wire, beaten and polished by my father, and in the village hall there was a wedding tea set out for them. And after that they went up to the registrar's house and changed back into their old clothes and went up to the wood where they told Tommy that they had got married and showed him the certificate. They were fifty-seven years together. That was Laggan.

So they were wed and on the 19th May, 1927, my sister Lena was born in a tent above Loch Ailort overlooking the Isle of Skye. They'd walked twelve miles over the mountains from Moidart to Loch Ailort, carrying all their stuff, when mother felt the pains coming on and she went into labour. They weren't alone. Some of his people were with them, but it was a difficult birth. After a day and a half my father had to get help and he set off for Arisaig, which was nine miles away, to get the nurse. Two miles along the road he saw a bike outside a house, so went to ask if he could borrow it. It was a woman's bike. But the woman, when she heard the news, said 'You must take it!' And he pedalled down into Arisaig where he found the nurse. Then she got on her bike and they both cycled back to Loch Ailort.

Now it was late on the second day. The nurse thought my mother was going to die, so she got my father to race off again – for the doctor in Mallaig. His name was Dr Silver. What a shock my father got – he was black as the ace of spades! He stood in the door and said he couldn't come till he'd been paid. He was an African. He was very good like, he knew his job, but he said he had to be paid before he set off. Luckily, my father had put aside two pounds ten shillings for the confinement. So he paid the man on the spot. Then he left the bike by a garden wall and rode back in the car with Dr Silver who saw the baby safely born. Lena grew to be a big handsome woman. She's Lena MacNeill today. Lives in Bonar Bridge, seventy years of age. My father says she was very well looked after the week she was born – the nurse came back twice to bring clothes for the baby and all the things my mother needed.

Dr Silver! You see a black man in the Highlands was a rare sight in those days. There's only three or four today. I heard that poet, Iain Crichton Smith, was having a breakdown in a hotel in Glasgow. Mental breakdown. He was very bad, it was two o'clock in the morning. His wife, Donalda, phoned for a doctor. As the clock struck three, there was a loud knock on the bedroom door and a huge black man stood there, panting! 'My name,' he said 'is Emmanuel!' Crichton Smith thought he'd died! Died and gone somewhere else. He got sent straight up to Lochgilphead – the loonie-bin. That was his name, Emmanuel! After that they say Crichton Smith never looked back, and nor did my mother.

Eighteen months later my sister, Chrissie, was born during a thunderstorm in a miniature caravan, in Raffert, Morayshire; and I was born at Dornoch, Sutherland, November 1930. I came very fast. My father was away at Rogart, selling things around the houses, and he was looking at a pony that the Post at Rogart had, and when he got home he heard a cry, all his people were there before him, and I, his first-born son, was born. I was born while he was buying a horse in Rogart! He came into the room where my mother lay, and in her arms he saw his first-born son. The tears came down his face. Seven pounds I weighed but father used to call me the four pound kid! This was because he knew the Postie wanted four pound ten shillings for the pony – so he'd only taken up four pounds to Rogart! That's what he offered and that's what he paid for the pony. And we both arrived on the same day.

Next year we set off for Ireland and that little pony went all the way down to Stranraer with us. We were going to go across with my father's brothers – for a month's fishing. They had good carts but on the road they didn't pass us and in Stranraer we couldn't find them. We waited three days. My father couldn't go on to Ireland alone, not with a wife and three small bairns and hardly a penny; so he turned back at Stranraer and we didn't go to Ireland. They did the dirty on us. They never left the Highlands! Father swore he'd never speak to them again. That was 1931.

It was a long road home. I remember my father telling me how by the time we got to Drummelington the shoes on the pony were thin as a silver sixpence – and it cost seven and six for a new set of shoes! So he decided to divest himself of capital! He would sell the last two pearls he had – two flat-bottomed, button pearls, to get new shoes for the horse to get us home. Passing a big house, he saw a woman working in the garden. She was wearing one of those wide-brimmed straw-hats. He asked her if she wanted any garden-work or weeding done. She said, 'No thank you, I like to do my own gardening.' She was a lady like, a toff-woman, as we would say. He wished her 'good day' and said that he would travel further north before looking for a camping place. He liked talking with educated people. Then she said, 'You're not from these parts?' 'No,' my father said, 'I'm a pearl-fisher – I've come down from the far north, from Sutherland.' 'A pearl-fisher!' she said 'I've heard about the river pearls but I've never seen a pearl-fisher.' 'Well,' he said, 'you're seeing one now! I may not be very good to look at, kinda raggy-tattered . . .' but she butted in and said, 'Do you have any pearls?'

'Oh yes,' says my father, 'but only two, two button pearls from the Highlands.' 'How much do you want for them?' she asked. They were white pearls and very near to a match. He gave them her. She looked at them. 'Five pound' he said. He had to think fast. And she said 'I'll take them for five pounds.' Five pounds! More than the price of the pony! He said, 'Thank you Ma'am, you'll find them, I'm sure, to be very fine pearls.' And he wished her well and went on his way. Five pounds! We went to a blacksmith and put on shoes – bought food and drink – new clothes – went on up Loch Lomond-side like kings!

North we went till we hit the Conon river and started fishing at a place called Moy, Moy Bridge. And who should my father see in the river but his brothers – fishing! He shouted down at them. 'You bastards! Get off this river! We don't want no pearlie bastards here!' He was angry like – about Stranraer – but they made it up. 'A good sale is a wonderful healer', I've heard him say that. My father had, what you call, the gift of the gab! He had a way about him. He could put things over, knew how to sell, he liked to sell to the nobility, to colonels, to ladies. They did not look at our clothes, or correct our speech, it was not in them to try to make us feel inferior. They could pay the price of pearls and he would talk with them.

Eddie Davies fishing the river
Evelix, Sutherland, 1995. (TN)

Tinkie, Tinkie, tarry bags
Go to the well and wash your rags!

That was what the children sang when first we went to school. I've even sung it myself! It was a little school called Kilmore – three miles out of Oban, down in Argyllshire. And it was a hard time we had of it. We had a caravan down there. There were two big ragstores in Oban, and my mother loved it over on the west, but my father, he preferred the east coast where he could work on the big farms in the winter. And when the war came in 1939 we came back to Dornoch permanent like. My father was afeared he would be called up and he didn't want the family left down there in Oban, so he got a job in the wood and we came back to Sutherland. You see, my father was only thirty-nine but he'd done two years in the First War and knew how things could go on. The Travellers had a rough time in Oban.

I mind my teacher in Oban, Miss Campbell saying to me, 'Eddie, you must be civilised, now you're over here in the west.' But when we came back to Dornoch, Mrs Mathieson, she wouldn't take us at all! She came from Muir of Ord and she didn't like the Tinker People – so my mother had to go to the minister and beg him to get us into the school. She relented like, but that school was full of big bullies – we called them brunkies, mewks – big things who ate big breakfasts in the morning while we had just half a can of milk and a piece. We were very hard up in the war, with father cutting wood, just two pounds a week is what he got. We had no horse, no car, near enough no fishing but father got us a house – he built it himself, just in behind the wee Tin Temple, the Free Presbyterian Kirk, in Dornoch. We got a piece of land with a fifty-year lease, from Provost Murray. The Murrays had made millions in the Slave Trade in Africa. He gave us the ground, as he'd given ground to the kirk in earlier days. It was the first Free Kirk in Scotland and people used to come from all over the west, for communion, and all the ministers had the same name – MacLennan. It got blown down in 1950, now they've got a brick and cement kirk. A big backward step! To look at, like.

We hadn't been there a day when a crofter came up and said to my father 'I hope those bairns won't be making a noise on the Sabbath Day! Put them to church!' That was wee Humpy Geordie, Geordie Grant, he was a hunch-back. And twice a day we went to church, morning and evening. It was all in English like, not Gaelic but there was no organ, just the human voice and they would sing for hours. The presenter would start off OOooooooooooooooooiiiiihhhhhhiiooo! and the others would join in and we would get hiccups – we laughed till we cried but we never made a sound. Later we got to enjoy it; it took the animal out of us. No idolatry, no Virgin Mary, they didn't like Catholics – but they were very good people and they never classed us as different from themselves. But when I was in the RAF and the call came 'Catholics and Jews fall out!', I was off like a bomb!

The Second World War was six hard years for us, but it's a strange thing, we came out of that war – like everyone else – except the dead like. That war was good for the Travellers. It was the First World War did the big damage.

My grandfather was in the Scottish Horse, uncle Willie was in the Scottish Horse, and my father was in the Cameronians. He went out in 1916, when he was sixteen years of age. It was not easy to get into the Scottish Horse – that was a grand regiment – but our family was going to the big lodges and we knew the keepers and they got the Davies in. The pearl-fishers were very respected. Even though we went hawking the houses, they knew we were fit, they knew we knew horses and they needed good horsemen.

My grandfather was on the Somme but came back unscathed. My uncle Willie was wounded at Arras – one ankle was shattered, but he came back to the pearl-fishing and my father came back. He was a hard man to keep up with – walking. The Cameronians did fast marching, 160 paces to the minute I think it was and he got the habit. He was at Ypres and then at Passchendaele where he got a rupture, so he was transferred into the Black Watch, and then he worked as a stretcher-bearer with the Red Cross. He saw terrible things – the boys with their legs hanging off. Carrying them through the mud. Mustard gas smoking off their backs. He took it all. It was my grandfather got the crust to him, became the moody one, kept himself to himself, got tetchy like.

My father would pass the time of day with anyone, but grandfather, no, walk on was his style. Like a horse! No good mornings, no left or right – for months he wouldn't give the time of day to man or beast. His mind was somewhere else. Whether that was the war or something in himself we'll never know. Pearl-fishing can be a lonely business, gives you time to think, gives you many a cause to moan! There were times when I loved him and times when I was afeared of him. And a strange thing – he still had a cockney accent when we took him to his grave – he must have got it from his mother when he was just a bairn in London. That was 1956. He was very strict with all of us; 'fend for yourself' was the way of the world to him. We burned his house.

I mind him telling about a man he called Darkie MacGregor and where he came out of nobody knows. Very short, very dark, like a little Japanese – four feet nothing in his boots! Skinny, yellow in the face, ugly, my grandfather said. And he came up here to the north to fish. He was a pearl-fisher. He had fished the Conon and was fishing the Borgie when my grandfather came on him one day in the water. They got talking and he told Darkie that the Naver was a good river for pearls. But he didn't tell him that the bailiff on the Naver was Colin Fraser. Oooh a dangerous man if ever there was one! Now control on the Naver was always very strict, it still is very strict – nobody likes you to fish in the Naver! It's a big salmon river as you know, so you had to be out very early, five o'clock, and get an hour's pearl-fishing done before the bailiffs came on. Colin Fraser was the worst. He'd crucify anyone he found on the water. He'd shoot you as soon as look at you! But grandfather didn't tell Darkie that.

A few weeks later MacGregor moved on north and got round to the Naver and he was fishing one of the big pools – he couldn't go in very deep because he was such a tiny bloke – when up comes Colin Fraser with a shotgun. 'Get out of there!' he says, 'get out of there or I'll blow your head off!' 'Oh' says Darkie, standing up and putting shells in his bag 'you're going to shoot me? Wait till I get out then!'

'Come out you bastard,' shouted Fraser, 'I'm going to give you a kicking you'll never forget!'

Now, as MacGregor came out of the pool he didn't seem to get any bigger – and this surprised Colin Fraser. For a moment he was silent. Then he shouted, 'You look like a bloody monkey!' and he went up and towered over him and he spat it out at him 'No monkeys, no tinkers, no fishing the Naver!' And he swung a great blow with the butt of the gun but – bang! Wee Darkie was in between his legs and had Fraser on his back in no time! 'Get up!' said MacGregor, 'and fight like a man!' Now Fraser knew he had a fight on his hands so he picked up the gun and flung it high on the bank. He liked a good fight! Then he circled MacGregor and grabbed for his shoulder but Darkie was fast – he was like a black belt – and he flung the bailiff down on his back. On it went till Fraser ended up in the pool – and they say wee Darkie stood, with one foot on the bank and one foot on Fraser's head, and he asked the man very nicely, 'Now can a body fish in the Naver?' And he was going to drown the man! But Fraser gave in and MacGregor was allowed to fish the Naver any time after that. That Fraser was a pig brute of a man! And he never changed. He near enough shot my grandfather.

It was one morning, early, not long after the end of the First War, and grandfather was in the Naver, fishing, when down came Fraser with his gun. Davies was deep in the water using his glass and he didn't see him. So the bailiff fired the shotgun – just over his head – to frighten him. But Davies wasn't afeared of anybody – he looked up, slow, then turned and started walking towards Fraser. 'Fraser,' he said 'you've only got one shot left!' and kept coming towards him. 'Aye,' said Fraser 'but one's more than enough!' So grandfather stopped, and he took down his trousers. 'Blast away you cowardly bastard!' he said, and stood there half-naked in the water. And Fraser fired the second shot and the pellets bounced off the river just a man's length to the right of where my grandfather was stood. Well after that grandfather pulled up his trousers, turned round, and started fishing again! Fraser was reloading the gun when two

Overleaf. Duncan and Shaunas MacPhee (Stewart) pausing for a tea-stop at the Moine, on what the Travellers knew as the 'lang, cauld and hungry road' from Melness to Hope, Sutherland, 1939. (ES/AJW)

shepherds came up to see what the shooting was. Well, that put a stop to it—Fraser told the shepherds it was sport he was having and he laughed it all off as a joke!

Fraser did that! Even though he knew my grandfather had fished that river for thirty years! And everyone knew the Davies didn't take salmon. We made a good living – the rivers were our livelihood! Why would we waste time on a salmon when we could be getting pearls? My son Edward, he's the first one ever to have been up for poaching. It's not the Davies way, it's not the Traveller way – not up here like. But Fraser was a bitter man, he liked to throw his weight about, rule the roost, and that night my grandfather was in his tent when the policeman from Bettyhill came up on his bike. 'Davies,' he says, 'I hear you had trouble in the forenoon, I hear Colin Fraser's been using the twelve bore.' And the policeman told him that the two shepherds had come by and reported themselves witnesses to the scene with the gun. And the policeman told my grandfather, 'We can get him for this!' Fraser was a very unpopular man in Strathnaver, he was like that Patrick Sellar! But do you know this, though my grandfather hated that man, and he used to ramble on, delirious, about Fraser the year before he died, he told the policeman – he wanted none of it! He said he didn't even remember the incident! So they drank a cup of tea by the fire and the policeman went back to Bettyhill.

But it didn't end there, Colin Fraser got to hear about this. He knew it was a crime to fire a gun at a man like that. So he went looking for my father. And when he found him, he said, 'Aach Davies, I'm sorry about all that!' And my grandfather said, 'Mr Fraser, you should know not to raise your twelve bore at me – I stood against the Hun – I've seen young boys, over in France, getting blasted away half a dozen at a time. It'll take more than a few lead pellets or a bailiff's curse to move me off the Naver!' And he said, 'Mr Fraser, I was a pearl-fisher in the Naver before you saw the light of day and I shall be a pearl-fisher still when you lie in the ground!' And Fraser was quiet. Then grandfather said, 'You were just doing your job – but so was I!' And Fraser knew what he meant, and he said 'Davies, you know I've got a temper and you know there's pearl-fishers go after the salmon! But Davies, I'm telling you now – you're free to fish the Naver whenever you want. Just keep out of the pools!' And they both laughed. He'd been over in France himself – but he was a pig of a man! I think he took a shock and died, twelve years before my grandfather.

In the Davies family father was always the boss. Until it came to modern times and me, as you might say! Until the boys got married, or moved away from home, every pearl we found went straight to the father and he paid out what he thought was fair – for HIM! The Davies men kept their boys on reins that suited them and we didn't learn the trade of selling till we had to learn ourselves. They were difficult men, the Davies. My father could be a cantankerous old sod. Many was the time, when I was young, that I thought about running away from home – and I had plenty offers.

Duncan MacPhee asked me to go on the road with him, more than once he came down and asked my father if he would give me over to him. Oooh I liked Duncan very much; you see, he'd married his wife Shaunas when she was past childbearing and they had a nice wee house at Lower Torroble, half-timbered walls and a red tin roof. That's just along from the market at Lairg. Duncan was a MacPhee, had come down from Caithness. Shaunas was a Stewart, related to Ailidh Dall up at Remarstaig. She was a beautiful dancer, short and thick in the body, but light on her feet like a boxer, very strong calves. And a lovely voice she had and a brother who used to travel with them, Donald. More than a wee bit slow, Donald was. He never married but outlived them all and he died in Migdale, where my Sandra works, at ninety-three. Oooh they were a very friendly couple and when I was a boy, before the war, Duncan was always wanting me to go away with them, go on the road with them. 'Your family's too big, my family's too small!', that's what he'd say, and at home, coming back from the well with a big churn of water a yard at a time, I used to shout at my father 'I hate this – I'm going away with Duncan and Shaunas!' 'Away you go!', he'd shout back, 'he's welcome to you!' It was almost a quarter of mile we had to carry our water.

Out fishing in the summer we'd always be meeting the MacPhees and we'd go up of an evening and ceilidh with them. I'd sit there listening to them telling tales of the old days, me just a shy boy, not saying a word, getting a scone and my crowdie from Shaunas. I knew they liked me, and one night by the fire Duncan said 'Eddie, if you come away with us, everything I have will be yours, when I go like.' Oooh I was tempted – but Duncan was a man who could put the fear in you. He had a bit stubble on his face, white bristle, and a big moustache, and the way he looked at you – there was a look in his eye, you never knew what he'd do, or say, next – so I didn't go.

I mind us meeting the MacPhees up at Laid, on Loch Eriboll, at Eriboll farm. It's deep water there in the loch. We went to sleep in our tents and when we woke up there were battleships there, cruisers, destroyers anchored in a great row down the loch. That was the 2nd of September 1939. They'd come in to hide, waiting for the war. The Williamsons were camped not far along. There must have been four tents and seven yokes between us. We were boys then and we cheered and waved our bonnets at the sailors. They must have wondered who the hell they were fighting for!

All the MacPhees walk with a gait you can't mistake. Duncan walked stiff-shouldered – like a man from the Punjab, very oriental – but he was full of jokes. It was white lies he would tell. You wouldn't know whether he was telling the truth, or joking, or if he was serious. He'd be rubbing things in – in a jokey way – to tell the truth about things. One day he came to the house of a man who had passed away a few months before, up there at Durness, and he was talking at the door with the widow. 'Oooh!' he said, 'it's very, very sad about your husband.' 'Oh yes,' said the wife, 'it'll take me a while to get over it.' 'And where did you bury him?' he asked. 'Down at the old graveyard,' she said. And Duncan laughed and came back 'I thought the back garden would have been good enough for him!' And she said, 'Duncan, God forgive you for that!' But that's the kind of man he was. He was awkward and not afraid to speak the truth – because that dead man had led his wife a hard, hard life. He was alcoholic. Duncan could be cruel all right – they say the MacPhees are the hardest men in Scotland, with their fists and with their tongues – and that woman knew what Duncan meant.

Another time at Oykel Bridge, some MacAlisters from Muir of Ord came by Duncan's camp and they asked him if he had any peats for their fire. 'Och aye,' says Duncan, 'I cut peats here every year, see them stacked on yonder brae,' and he pointed to a big line of peat stacks on the skyline, 'Youse bring doon half a cairt for me, and youse can hae the rest for yourselves!' Of course, they weren't Duncan's peats at all, they were the crofters' peats! It was a joke, but the MacAlisters swallowed it and Duncan got his peats. He's buried now in the old graveyard up in Lairg and, I believe, there's a stone on his grave. Of course, when he said he'd make me his heir there was a twinkle in his eye. He knew he didn't have much, but he meant it! Duncan came out of Caithness looking for a wife, and he and Shaunas would have loved to have had a son but . . . When he died, some cousins came down from Thurso and took the horse, the carts and the valuables – but they left the house. It's still there with its red-painted roof. Whose it now is, I think nobody knows.

You know that old saying about the Travellers, 'We cheils and cuckoos are alike in many respects, but especially in character, everybody speaks ill us both – but everyone's glad to see us again!' Well that was the MacPhees and that used to be me – I don't think there's many too pleased to see me the day!

> For every gypsy comes to toon –
> Twa hens will go amissin' soon!
> Gypsy hair and devil's eyes –
> Ever stealin' – full o' lies!

You know that one? That's the Gypsy People! I've taken a peat or two, I've even taken a salmon or two, for the pot, but the Travelling People here in Sutherland were always very law-abiding, very proper, very religious, very

The derelict cottage at Lower Torroble, outside Lairg, where Duncan and Shaunas MacPhee lived each winter; and which Duncan said he would give to Eddie Davies when he was a boy — if he would leave his own family and come away with him, 1995.
(ES/AJW)

strict — they got on well with the local people. We had to. That was our business. Going round the houses, the womenfolk would always make sure they were clean and always be nice at the door. I've seen the women down at the burn; I've seen my poor mother say 'get away now' and clear us children out the tent, so she could wash and put a sponge between the sweaty bits. Coming from the camp we'd be reeking with the peat smoke and the wet but the womenfolk kept themselves clean as a pin. Round the camps you'd always see the washing hanging up on the line or on a bush.

      Out on the road, it was an inside fire that we had, a stove inside the tent, no open fire. I like an outside fire, but father used to say 'Look at this — a big hole in the ground!' And he made sure we'd leave each camping place just as we found it. Even the tinsmithing was done from the stove. Turfs would be cut where the stove was to stand and be placed back when the Travellers moved on. That was a rule for us, for the Stewarts, for the Williamsons but Travellers from Caithness, or coming up from the south, or off the boat from Stornoway — they could be rough and leave a pretty good mess. 'Kick you to death as soon as look at you!' that's what we'd say about the Caithness MacPhees. In the fifties some of them still wintered out in caves — but the Social Work came in. All those caves got condemned, that's what I heard.

      The last of the old-style Travellers on the road in Sutherland and Ross-shire were Katie Williamson and her two brothers, John and Peter. Just one big tent they had, big boughs, fine bedding hay — they'd leave a stove and boughs behind at all the big campsites and only take the covers on the cart.

They took their time. Katie would go round the houses. She had good stuff, very good stuff – shirts and trousers, and the men would look for a deal with horses. The Williamsons loved their horses. And they, like their fathers before them, would go to church in all the places where they set down a camp.

The Ardgay Williamsons last went out with horse and cart in 1978. Katie's still alive, ninety-one years of age. She's a great old woman. A good brain she has and a good heart. I mind the time when many of the crofters were very, very poor – and in the spring have hardly a penny to their name. And Katie – she'd just leave her stuff, 'I'll get the money anytime!', she'd say and keep a note inside her head, till she came round in the autumn, or Katie would wait a year and then even take her pay in milk, or oats, or a mutton shank. The Williamsons were good people, but never poor. They say you never see a poor Williamson in Ross-shire. The Williamsons were businessmen, they never wanted for a pound, always drove a hard bargain, always drove a good yoke.

When Johnnie died he left fifteen thousand pounds and more besides. They had a house at Ardgay. A very nice house but no conveniences. When Johnnie was getting on, I used to say, 'Johnnie, why don't you get a toilet in the house?' 'It's in the stone,' he'd say, 'I like to piss outside the house!' They all used to like to go behind a bush, do what they'd always done. I'd say, 'What

The Williamsons, the last 'old-style' Travellers on the road in Ross-shire and Sutherland – Peter, Katie and Johnnie Williamson, camped at Inchnadamph, by Loch Assynt, 1978. Katie, now ninety-one and housed in Ardgay, had a great reputation amongst the old crofters as a trader, while her brothers were well-kent horse-dealers. (WM)

about a wash-bowl with a running tap – hot water?' and he'd say 'We've got hot water on the stove.' And I'd say, 'What about a bathroom for the bad weather?' and he'd say 'Why should I need a bath now? After all these years? I've kept clean for eighty-one, I won't get dirty now!' The Williamsons were good people and very religious but it was save, save and never spend – that was the Williamsons. The Davies! We were spend, spend and spend again, look to the day and ne'er think of the morrow – and look at me!

My father got his first car in 1935. I got my first car in 1947. It was great for getting away to the rivers and taking out the girls, but I tell you this, there was always only one woman in my life – Essie Stewart. I met Essie first when I was just a boy of twelve and she a bairn. I started writing letters to her when she was thirteen and I was twenty-five. Her mother found out about it, and asked me to stop – me being an older man and that. Of course, they thought . . . but there was nothing like that about it. She was well-developed, but it was not a sexual relationship that we had. What a dressing down I got! That was Mary (Michie), Essie's mother – she was looking after her. Others used to call her Michie, but I always called her Mary – her proper name. She died in the room behind us here in Struie Place, breast cancer. If she had lived, Essie would not have left this house. Not left me, not left the bairns. She said she had this lump, and I said 'Mary, you must see the doctor immediately with that.' But it was too late – she died on Christmas Eve. Very private, the Travelling People. It was fate. Essie fell in love with another man and here we are . . .

After Mary ticked me off for writing the letters, I kept away from Essie for three years. But when she got to sixteen, we started going out – to the pictures down in Lairg. Secretly at first. No sex. I loved her very much and you don't . . . not when you love someone very much – at least not in those days. Today, of course, they're jumping into bed like flies! Oooh I was tempted, I was a young man, any fellow would be, but she'd say, 'Baaa – away you go! Davies behave yourself!' that's what she'd say and that was good enough – because I loved her so.

When she got to seventeen, I went to her grandfather, Old Sandy, Ailidh Dall, to ask him if I could take her out. You had to be a brave man to face Ailidh Dall! His blindness gave him power you see. He weighed a man up – like he was sounding him – like he was opening up the mouth of a stallion to check the teeth. Look right into you, that's what he did, even though he was blind! His words, when he spoke, came far apart, and he would pause – like a minister, reading the Bible. Make a big pause, before he went on.

It was dark in the house and I came before Ailidh Dall, like Isaac come before Abraham. Ooooh I tell you this, I was nervous. He knew my voice. 'Ah Eddie it's you,' he said, 'you've come back from the west.' And I told him about things in Lochinver and Scourie and Melness. That was the year the Stewarts stopped travelling, so he wanted to know how things were. Then I asked about Essie. 'I've something to ask you, Sandy,' I said. 'Oooh you've something to ask me?' he came back. 'Do you know that I'm taking your granddaughter out?' I said. 'Oooh' said Sandy, 'Eddie, you know I cannae see – but my hearing's not that bad!' Then he says, 'Look, she's the world to me but if you play the game and be a man you'll get my blessing. I hope she'll be the world to you. Where is she now?' 'She's speaking there with Ma along the road. Tell her to come,' the old man said, and he put his hand out to my arm.

Oh I was so happy then. And after she had come, I asked if I could take her out to Brora that very night. 'Take her anywhere you like,' Blind Sandy said, 'but play the game!' I knew what he meant – not to get stuck into her! That's me talking now, not me talking then! But I can tell you this, after speaking with Ailidh Dall and getting the big hurdle over, I felt like a bit of sex that night! But things were all different then. No television, no contraceptive machine in the toilets. Essie was innocent. 'Get away,' she'd say, 'away you go!' and I loved her for that. 'Give us a kiss,' I said on our wedding night – and it was something great.

We had our honeymoon at Rosehall. The van got a puncture and we had to stop – the Williamsons were camped there and they said 'Stay here with us,' and we stayed there for three days and three nights. Tatties and herrin' Katie cooked for us. I had a half-bottle. We passed it round. Johnnie and Peter had two bottles of beer. Twenty-nine years of age I was and she was seventeen – my lovely bride. I was so proud. Aaah good times, happy times. Essie was virgin on her wedding night and so was I.

It's all pine trees up there at Rosehall. The stars were out. It was the Duke of Sutherland ordered the trees to be kept and the roadside wide between the walls, just for the Travellers. That's about the last of the old camping places now. Democracy has fenced us off like dogs!

For our honeymoon we went on down to Lochinver. It was holiday but I went out fishing in the Kirkaig river – and every pearl I found I gave to her who I was now so proud to call my wife. I was very old-fashioned in those days and much worse now that I'm getting old.

Next spring we got a caravan above the road at Rogart, where my father bought the pony on the day that I was born! The wild goats used to come down from the cliffs. Great big horns, the little kids, the nanny goats, all colours, we used to watch them from the window. I taught Essie about pearls, about the rivers, about what to look for, about selling. We worked the farms – harvest, tatties, neeps, hedging, ditching – Essie did it all with me; she could

Essie Stewart's grandfather, the blind story-teller, Ailidh Dall, to whom Eddie Davies went to ask for Essie's hand in marriage, 1957. (HH, BB)

trim a blackthorn hedge just like a man. Stooking we would do – a pound an acre's what we got. You'd still hear the corncrakes then! Fencing, drystane walls, antique water-troughs we'd find and sell – money in the hand we had, we'd go to hops at Lairg, at Dornoch, Brora. That's where the last wolf got killed and where the last witch in Scotland lived before they brought her down to Dornoch to be burned.

Money we had in those days. We'd go to the pubs, have meals out. We had the van. It was four years before wee Sandra came. Two and half pounds she weighed, no bigger than my hand for three months after she was born. Essie took the German measles. The baby came too soon. We didn't think the bairn could live – but she came through. And you should see her now – she's thirty-one. Twelve years she's worked up there at Migdale Hospital. Poor wee Sandra! She was so bright and tried so hard. It took the doctors seven years to find out she was deaf. She never heard a thing we said. It was not brain-damage held her back, stone-deaf she was. But she's come through. Next year she's getting married to a great young man from Invergordon – but for the now she's still here looking after me. She keeps me straight. She's bossy, but she has a goodness is its own reward.

I don't believe in 'Paradise Tomorrow', angels singing all that stuff but when the Jehovah's Witness people come, I tell them that I like to think of God – and we talk away for hours.

Alec John Williamson

SINGER OF THE FLYING CLOUD

I stand here a stranger
Where a heap of stones now lie
It was once a happy homestead
In the happy days gone by

My mother died on the Isle of Skye when I was four. We were down there among her own people at Broadford. She died on the Thursday and was buried on the Friday because of a heatwave – it was so hot we couldn't keep her body in the tent or have a proper wake for her. Just the one night we had. In the morning, my father and his brother went down to dig the grave. And they came back and put her in a coffin and carried her up into an open-topped bus, a canvas-topped convertible it was with everyone standing round the coffin, and they took her away to the cemetery. Although I had seen her go into the box and in the bus I expected her to come back that night, as she had always done. But she didn't come back. I slept next to my father. My mother's people said they would take me and my sister, Katie, but father would not hear of that and he brought us all back to Edderton. He used to sing a little rhyme 'Mother Midget' and although she was not a small woman as I remember her, when my father sang that song, I always thought about my mother.

Alec John Williamson, of Edderton, Ross-shire, at West Shinness in Sutherland, 1995. (TN)

There's a happy little woman
in the old oak tree
and she's sewing, sewing, sewing
through the sunny summer dee:
for her thread it is a hay wisp
and her needle is a thorn
and the naughtie little fairies
with hats and jackets torn
go to Mother Midget in the old oak tree

and she makes their clothes for nothing
— in the very latest way.

Oh Mother Midget is a marvel
she can do so many things
she can make a fairy's jacket
she can mend its broken wing
she can dress a grown-up fairy
for a party or a ball
she can make a baby fairy — a bib or overall!

My father did not marry again. My mother was his second wife. We settled down in Easter Ross and the last time my family travelled out to the west with a yoke, that's a horse and cart, was 1954. But I'm Highland *ceard* on every side — as far back as I go. My mother's great-grandfather, Alexander Stewart, was sent out to a penal colony in Australia, in the 1840s. His people came from the Outer Isles, they stayed in Stornoway on the Isle of Lewis. One night he went out to a shebeen, moonshining, looking for a bottle of whisky — which he got. Then he went back for another and the man in the shebeen said 'No more!' or something of the kind. A quarrel broke out. Alec grabbed the man by the privates and flung him out the door — he must have been a coarse kind of man! He didn't kill the gadgie — but he nearly did and he got taken in. He was convicted and sentenced to deportation to Van Diemen's Land. He had a wife and young family and next morning my great-grandfather, Charles Stewart and his brother, Alec, rose before it was light and went down to the jailhouse in Stornoway to see their father go. But they were told he was already down at the harbour; they then tried to make the pier but by the time they got down to the harbour, the boat was away and they never saw him again.

Not a word came back. But years later his family heard about a soldier, a prison guard out there in Australia, who'd come back to Stornoway — and he told a story about a prisoner he'd met who spoke the Gaelic. So my great-uncle Charles went to see him, and this soldier told him how there were great herds of cattle, white cattle, out in the desert and many of them died, and there'd be horns lying about in the sand. Big horns. One day he was watching this prisoner kicking a horn, when he heard him say to himself, 'If I was at home by the fire the night I'd make a bloody good spoon out of you!' It was Lewis Gaelic that he spoke! So that made our people sure it was Alec: horn-spoons were a trade for the *ceards* alone and a Stornoway *ceard*, they thought, must have been our man. That was the last they ever heard of him. It's his name that I have and my eldest son is Alec too.

One of the songs my father used to sing is called 'The Flying Cloud'. I don't know anyone else who has it. Some Travellers over in Muir of Ord know bits of it, I believe, but I'm the only one who has it all. It's about an Irishman – but it's my great-great-grandfather Alec Stewart who comes to my mind when I sing this song:

Oh my name is Edward Allan boys
As you will understand
I was born in the city of Waterford
In Old Eirean's happy land.

When I was young and innocent
At beauty I may smile
My parents doted on me then
For I was their only child.

They bound me to a tradesman
In Waterford the town
Sure they bound me to a couper lad
His name was William Brown.

I served my master faithfully
For eighteen months and more
Then I took a trip on the Ocean Queen
Bound for Barbados Shore.

When we arrived at Barbados Shore
We met in with Captain More
Proud captain of The Flying Cloud
A native of Stramore.

It's with him that we did all agree
On a slavering barge to go
To the burning shores of Africa
Where the sugar canes they grow.

It was eighty-five of those black slaves
From the native land we bore
Sure we sold them to the planters
To be slaves for evermore.

For rice and coffee fields to reap
Beneath that burning sun
We made many a wretch lead a poor led life
Beneath master's whip and gun.

The Flying Cloud she's a Spanish bark
She carries eighteen ton and more
She could easily outsail any bark
That ever left Baltimore.

For her sails are like the driven snow
Her name gives her aspect
It's eighty-five brass powder guns
She carries on her deck.

Oh many's the man was put ashore
And off to see his girl
When Captain More came back aboard
And said this to his men.

There's gold and silver to be won!
Let me be a shower of rain
We all agreed but five young boys
And then we turned again.

Oh two of them were Boston boys
And two from Baltimore
Sure the other of them was an Irish boy
From a town they call Tramore.

And I wish to my God that I had gone
Along with them ashore.

We hoisted up the pirate flag
We scoured the Spanish Main
We made many a widow and orphan
With sorrows to remain.

As we made them walk the plank
We gave them watery graves
For the motto of our captain was
'The dead can tell no tales'.

But soon a British man o' war set sail
With her dangerous sails in view
Sure she fired a shot across our bows
As signal to heave-to.

We happened to pay no notice boys!
And ran before the wynd
Till a bombshell split our quarter deck
And she came up behind.

We cleared our deck for action boys
As she rollied on her side
While all across oor quarter deck
Rolled o'er a crimson tide.

We knew that Captain More was lost
And eighty of his men
When a firebomb set our ship afire!
We were forced to surrender then.

'Turn oot, turn oot you pirate crew!'
We were bound fast in iron bands
For we sank and plundered many a bark
Down on the ocean strand.

It was drinking and bad company
That made a wretch of me
So come all you boys awandering take
But a curse to the pirate sea!

Sae fare you well the seas that toss
And the girl that I adore
The music of her charming voice
I'll never hear no more:

No more I'll kiss her ruby lips
Or squeeze her saft's I can
For I'm here to die a pirate's death
Ashore in a foreign land.

The Lewis Stewarts knew no English at all. They didn't have
horses, they had small boats and they went from island to island, working and
trading; sea-ceards, sea-tinkers, that's what they were. But then, Charles
Stewart married into my father's family and they moved to the mainland. It was
hard times. You could be transported for little enough in those days. Some
people were moved off the land – our people had no place on the face of the
earth. He was glad to come over. On the mainland if you couldn't find a crust
– you kept going! It was the Lewis Stewarts gave me the Gaelic. The
Williamsons were not Gaelic speakers, they came down from Orkney so I've
heard. A Williamson up there worked on the cure for smallpox, in the
eighteenth century that was – but whether he was relative of mine, I could not
say.

There was a lot of medicine in my family – cures and proverbs –
but it was horn was the big thing with us, before the tin came in. Tinsmithing
came in the nineteenth century with electro-plating; before that it was all horn
– spoons, powder horns, drinking horns, snuff-boxes. And before that it would

A nurse visiting a traditional
Traveller camp, on the edge of a
forest of Caledonian pines,
Sutherland (?), c. 1935. (AJW)

have been the old metal-work, copper, bronze, pewter, blacksmithing –
wrought iron, sword steel, that kind of thing. Our people got their horn from
the abattoir in Elgin. Good horns were put aside for us and others too no
doubt. Myself, I never worked in horn, but my father, my step-brother, my
brother Lindsay they all worked tin. Sheet-tin. It was manufactured down south
somewhere and brought up here by train. I worked tin when I was a boy, but
by the time I went into the army at eighteen years that trade was dead. But I'll
tell you this – a horn spoon is still the very best way to eat a boiled egg! My
grand-uncle, Angie Williamson used to say, 'He who discovers the use for
boiled-egg water – will do the world no harm!'

You've seen the photograph of Angie, some people say he was a
dwarf, but Angie Williiamson was not a dwarf. He was born as straight as you
or I – what happened was this. They were up Strathconon way, up about Moy,
in the wintertime. The parents were away and the children were all playing on
the big pond, sliding on the ice. They took Angie out with them. He would be
about two at the time, and he was wearing just a jumper and a little kilt. Of
course, he went out on the ice with the other children, but he was too young
to slide, and he sat down on the ice with his bare buttocks. He cried out, but
the other kids were playing and took no heed of him. At last his grandfather
came out and took the bairnie in beside the fire. But the ice had burned him.
He took meningitis and his spine got hooked up and he couldn't grow, so he
was a cripple but he was never a dwarf.

Angie Williamson was a good man of business. He was a very
clever man, he could make a deal, make tin, work a horse. And he had a fine
face, a bonnie-looking face and lovely curly hair. He died in 1963 at the age of
seventy. He'd taken a bad turn, had a stroke, way back in 'fifty-six, the time of
the Suez Crisis, and he was never the same after that. His speech was slurred
and he took bad spasms, it must have been to do with his shape, so for the last
seven years we looked after him. 'I was once,' Angie said to my father, 'as
straight as any of your own bairns.' And that was true. It was being down on the
ice that broke him.

The Travellers are very caring one for another. One reason why
my family went off the road was this – we didn't like to leave Angie behind,
alone, after his granny died. But, of course, the Traveller life itself was dying
then. The last time I went out was 1954, after I'd finished in the army –
National Service. I did my eighteen months, then went on the Reserve.
Achiltibuie, Ullapool, Durness, Tongue, and Reay in Caithness – they were the
last places we travelled to. The following year I got married, to Mary Davies.
That's Eddie Davies' sister. Being pearl-fishers they were out on the road every
year. She was a very beautiful young woman. Say what you like, the Davies are

a good-looking people. I'd been away on two weeks manoeuvres, down in Wales, so when I came back, I walked out to the west to find her. And there they were at Laxford Bridge. We ran away to Ireland. No reason to — we just wanted to go. Five months we were away — then we came back here to be wed, in the Registry Office at Tain. Seven children we have, four boys and three girls. And she's still a beautiful woman though, she says this herself, she's now got wrinkles where she shouldn't have wrinkles!

My father was born in Strathconon in 1887. If you come from Dingwall, heading out to Ullapool, you turn left up the glen at Muir of Ord. There's few enough inhabitants in that glen today — but there were plenty of people up there in his day. In a tent he was born. His name was Alec, like his father before him. First he married Elizabeth MacAlister. She was only twenty-five when she died. It was TB, and he lost a bairn as well. He was left with one son, James Williamson. Years passed, and he met in with my mother, Janet Stewart, her people still travelled the islands as his people had years back. They got engaged coming across on the boat from Uist to Skye and were married in Portree, in the summer of 1914. He went right through the war. He enlisted in the Cameron Highlanders. There was himself and his four brothers and his brother-in-law, they were all away at the same time. My father and one brother were wounded, another brother, Donald, was badly gassed, and my uncle Peter was killed. He was a groom. He was Mary's uncle too. We have his photograph and the big medallion everybody got, in the cabinet.

Going out to France, Peter was stationed in barracks at Bedford, in England, and the last postcard he sent shows the statue of John Bunyan in the square at Bedford. Now we don't know why he chose that card – but John Bunyan was what they called in those days 'a tinkler and brazier', and at home we used to read *The Pilgrim's Progress*, round the fire. It was only when John Bunyan got sent to prison that he learned to read and write. So maybe this statue appealed to Peter, or maybe he thought it would appeal to the people here, or maybe, Peter knew he would never see his home again, and he thought the Pilgrim would speak for him. Father knew page after page by heart. I still have some of it myself:

'As I walked through the wilderness of the world, I lighted on a certain place where was a den, and laid me down in that place to sleep; and as I slept, I dreamed a dream. I dreamed, and behold, I saw a man clothed with rags, standing in a certain place, with his face from his own house, a book in his hand and a great burden on his back. I looked and saw him open the book, and read therein; and as he read, he wept and trembled; and not being able longer to contain, he brake with a lamentable cry saying "what shall I do?" ' 'Well it was a postcard of John Bunyan, Peter sent from Bedford. We have it yet. He was twenty-two years of age. It was at Arras that he fell. He looks just like my son, Angus. He goes out pearl-fishing with Eddie Davies – and I was telling him just the other day, John Bunyan must have done some fishing in his time:

Opposite. Peter Williamson, Ross-shire Traveller, working as a groom, 1916. Within a year, Peter was killed at Arras, in France, on the Western Front. (AJW)

> You see the ways the fisherman doth take
> To catch the fish; what engines he doth make!
> Behold how he engageth all his wits;
> Also his snares, lines, angles, hooks, and nets;
> Yet fish there be, that neither hook nor line,
> Nor snare, nor net, nor engine can make thine:
> They must be grop'd for, and be tickled too,
> Or they will not be catched, what e'er you do.

How doth the fowler seek to catch his game?
By diverse means! All of which one cannot name:
His gun, his net, his lime-twigs, light and bell:
He creeps, he goes, he stands: yea, who can tell
Of all his postures? Yet there's none of these
Will make him master of what fowls he please.
Yea, he must pipe and whistle, to catch this;
Yet if he does so, that bird he will miss.
If that a pearl may in a toad's head dwell,
And may be found too in an oyster shell;
If things that promise nothing do contain
What better is than gold, who will disdain,
That have an inkling of it, there to look,
That they may find it . . .

My father was away four years but he came back and, with two wives, he had a well-spread family. They travelled between Ross-shire and Skye and all over Sutherland. I was the last to be born, in 1933. My father was only fifty-four when my mother died, but that was it for him. He did not think to marry a third time, he brought us up alone. It was himself who did all the cooking. We had a hut up above Edderton. It was a small house. He built it himself. And it was in Edderton we went to school: six months of school and six months off school, on the road. We got our certificate at Easter, then we were out till October, that was the law.

Tinkie, Tinkie, toadbags
Go to the well and wash your rags!

Sometimes the kids would shout that kind of thing – at school or playing out. It could be nasty – but often enough there was no real malice in it. 'Dirty hands make a clean hearthstane!' That's the kind of thing my father would say to us. 'Let others shout and call us swine! Jesus Christ was a carpenter – and his two hands were just like mine.' 'We may hae less, and be ill kent – but it's they hae more, will need repent!' Things like that he'd pass and he'd tell us about how, of the four nails set aside for the crucifixion one was stolen by a Travelling man . . . Small things there'd be, but in Edderton we had no trouble.

Tinkie, Tinkie, stink bags
Father drunk and mother a hag!

It could be bad but we were not persecuted – ooh I mind fights at school when a new boy came. That's the way it is up here. I've been in a few fights myself! But they weren't about me being a Traveller. There would have been fights if there were no Travellers for a hundred miles. This is mountain country! And I can tell you this – most people liked us – they liked us coming round – we were useful, we were company, we were honest. Look at old Katie Williamson – you could not find a more honest woman than she. The country people knew the old Travellers by name across the whole of Sutherland and Ross-shire. It was us kept the Gaelic going for many of them and that's a fact.

When I started school, at the age of five, I could say 'yes' and 'no' and that was all, everything else was Gaelic. But when I went into the higher classes and we studied grammar and all that – I was the best English speaker in the school. Recitation, composition, poetry, I liked all that. And I had a good hand there; the headmaster was a Lewis man, Murdo MacKenzie was his name. He encouraged me. He liked to speak to me in Gaelic. If he was giving me a rough time, he'd always speak in Gaelic! We got on very well.

The Williamsons were the only native Gaelic speakers in the school, but when it came to English composition – I always won the prize! They weren't big prizes – it was during the war. Maybe it would be a pencil with paint on. All the pencils were plain wood, utility things, so a painted pencil was a treat. Lines of gold, or a crimson end, or a pencil with a rubber on; that's what I used to win. Murdo MacKenzie was a very good teacher to me. His son was a pilot officer in the RAF. He was shot down over Germany and we were all very sorry in the school when we heard about it. His body was never found. Murdo had another son in the Navy, he was a doctor, but he came home to work in Tain. He's long retired now and Murdo's dead these many years. My own father was too old for service in the Second War. He worked first at the aerodrome down in Moray, then up here in the Ross-shire woods – with the Newfoundlanders. Oooh they were very good woodmen. It took some keeping up with them!

'You can take a Traveller off the road but you can't take the road out of the Traveller!', my father used to say. Six years we stayed at home, but that first spring, after the war, 1946, we went out to Skye as we'd always done, to see my mother's people. I was thirteen years of age and it seemed like the old ways were back for good. There were just the five of us, me, my two sisters, Cathy and Annie, Lindsay, my brother, and my father. Of course we'd meet other Travellers at the camping places. I've seen four or five yokes travelling like a wagon train – but the motorists didn't like big convoys of tinker carts. We slowed them up. All the roads were single track in those days and passing places few and far. So the wagon-trains died out after the war.

But big convoys weren't good for business; it was best for the Travellers to move in small groups. Selling goods – you needed to cut fresh ground, not follow on too close behind others in a similar trade. There was only so much trade to be had! The Highland population was still declining then. We had to turn our hands to anything that paid – but one thing we did, we still kept ourselves to ourselves. That's what the people up here wanted – to be left alone. We knew where we were wanted, what was wanted, and how to behave. I used to especially like Achiltibuie, Strathcarnaird and Ullapool. They were very, very nice people there, and I'll tell you this, many a pound we took out of them. But in the fifties, plastic came in, cars, buses, Fergi-tractors came – one tractor could be made to serve a whole community! That was good for the crofters but bad for us. Our business was horses, and tin and bringing in what people couldn't get out to get! In the fifties our business went down hill so fast you couldn't see the smoke! It was the motor-car that did for the Traveller life. In 1954 I wrote a poem:

> There's a tent around the corner
> On a stance that's spruce and trim,
> There's a tent around the corner
> And a hammering of tin.
>
> There's bairnies there from three to ten,
> There's lurcher dogs as well
> And horses tethered on the grass
> – and young ones for to sell.
>
> There's pails, jugs and basins
> And skillets by the score
> A basket full of washing
> And hardware from the store.
>
> The carts are highly painted,
> The harness fairly shines –
> Black Beauty's brass all spick and span
> – her shackles and her reins.
>
> Monday morning all dressed up
> To the market go in style
> We've classy horses for to sell
> And some just rank and file!

But time and the horse have now gone both
The craftwork and the tin
Black plastic and the motor-car
Have neither kith nor kin!

The camping stance is so forlorn
— no horse, no children's chatter —
The fence-posts stout, to keep us out
While the gadgie's sheep get fatter.

O for the days of the old, old ways
O for the seller, the buyer!
If I say this strife, is a much better life
Then God take my wife — I'm a liar!

The Williamson clan in convoy near Elphin Bridge, Ross-shire, 1947. In the background Meall Coire an Lochan. Johnnie Williamson stands with the first yoke, Peter with the second, Angie with the third.
(AJW)

It was a hard life, but we had good times. Out on the road we'd eat a lot of oatmeal, porridge, brose, skirly – that's oatmeal and onions, fried. You leave the onions till they're golden brown and then you put your oatmeal in, it's like a mealie pudding, a white pudding. Very good. In the spring when we were going off, the tatties would be poor, or gone, and you'd have to wait for summertime to get the new potatoes from the crofts out in the west. There were travelling vans for tins of meat, for sugar, biscuits and for tea. We ate rice puddings. We got a lot of fish – in Ullapool we could pick up heaps of fish for nothing – plenty fell from the baskets up on the pier. From the shepherds, we'd sometimes get mutton: at the backend, coming home, there'd be venison. We

The Ardgay Williamsons on their last trip out to the west, Loch Assynt, 1978 – Johnnie, Peter and Katie. (WM)

would come in by Achfary, the Duke of Westminster's estate; and there would be plenty of venison they gave away. I've seen us coming back with so much venison, it would not fit in the footbox — we had to tie it to the cart! In Edderton we'd give it round to other folk.

Going through the houses, milk and eggs would always come your way. And sometimes we'd be given oatmeal instead of money. We needed oatmeal for the horses. We'd steep the oats in a bucket of milk — maybe for about two hours — then we'd boil a kettle and mix the water in. That was very good for a horse — we called it 'The White Drink'. All Traveller horses got it. It had to be steeped and you had to get hot water on it. Then it was cooled with cold water. Other people didn't know the way of it. Our horses were well-treated. We could turn our hand to anything.

Once I was out hawking in Polbain and I came to the house of the man who did the salmon fishing, his wife was a Fraser, Abigail, as nice a woman as you'll ever see — very kind. Well she bought some things from me and gave me my tea and then she said, 'Is your father busy?' I said, 'He's always busy!' And she said her husband had an engine-cover needing fixing, 'Would father fix it?' So I took it up to the camp. It was a big job and our tin was just one sixteenth of an inch thick — too thin for a good engine cover, but sometimes you'd find a piece of tin much thicker than the others, so father went through all the sheets and found the thickest ones. And he made a new cover, using two or three of the thickest sheets. 'This'll cost her a bit!' he said. So when I took

Ina Stewart, wife of Brian Stewart, sister to Katie, Johnnie and Peter Williamson, camped at Tuiteam, on the river Oykel, 1957.
(HH, BB)

it back, I asked her for thirty shillings! A colossal sum for us in those days. That would be one pound fifty – or about thirty quid today! She paid on the spot and she asked me to get two more repairs done there and then. A good night we'd have after a day like that! Many a good singer we had in my family and some of the songs were bawdy songs! But no swearing. You might not believe that but that was it – no swearing.

The Travelling people up here, don't like swearing. There's a story about that, I got from my grandfather, on my mother's side. He was at Borve, on the Isle of Skye, with his family, at the camping place in the Skittery Wood, just north of Portree. That was a wood full of crows, in those days! Camping with them was Alistair Stewart, from Stornoway, and his family. Now Alistair had a retarded son, with a speech impediment; his name was Jacob and he was given to swearing and blaspheming.

One evening the boy went down, with my uncle Alec, to the burn for water – to cool the oats for the horses. As he stooped over the stream, the boy shouted, 'Stop that, stop that!' In Gaelic, of course. 'Stop that! You're slapping me!' And he ran back up to the tent, where his grandfather and my grandfather were smoking and talking. And he sat between them – cowering and whimpering and warding off the blows – as though he was being skelped! Then he jumped up like a Jack-hare and with a great volley of swearing ran out and between the two tents he was caught and lifted off the earth! The two men went out and looked up, for they heard a screaming high above them dying away. No sign of him. They told the womenfolk. They stayed up all night, until about two in the morning, when, out of the darkness, Jacob returned, all covered in glore. Shining wet, with black mud and peat in his hair, on his face, on his shirt, blood. He was in a terrible state. And he stood there by the fire and he stuttered out very slowly '*Botach, botach*; *geit, geit; peastar, peastar!*' which, being interpreted, means 'Man, cigarette, moustache'. Then he went on, 'Velvet jacket! Big split! Big man! He put me down – I put man down – he put me down – I put man down – BANG! Now I home!'

And that was it! What it was we'll never know. He was a boy of about fourteen at the time. What happened to him, where he went, with whom he went, how he got back, we'll never know! If his impediment was bad before, it was worse after that! But Jacob Stewart lived to a good old age. He settled down in a caravan, outside Inverness. He took to dressing smart – clean as a pin he was – a great man for kilts and cowboy outfits! He became very religious. And he never swore again till the day he died.

It's a strange thing – people talk about there being witchcraft among the Travelling people, but we always knew it among the country people. And I can tell you a true story about that. One day my two grannies went to a house in the Black Isle, hawking. They were just friends in those days – it was before they got married and got related. In the house was an old woman. She bought things from them and gave them a cup of tea. Then my mother's mother asked the old woman, 'Will you read my cup?' And the old woman took the cup and said, 'You're not married but you're courting a young man in the Queen's uniform and there's another man after you – but it's not him you'll marry.'

Now at that time the man who was to become my grandfather was a soldier in the Militia in Fort George and there was another man after asking for my grandmother's hand . . . Well it was the soldier she married. Now you'll say there's little enough witchcraft in that! And you'd be right. But then the old woman asked my other granny for her cup, and she studied the leaves and she said, 'There'll be water and mountains between yourself and your family. Every one of your sons you'll see again but there's one will not come back.' My granny was upset by this and she asked, 'Are you the woman made the dead herring jump oot o' the cart?' 'Who told you that?' the old woman snapped, 'I wouldnae do a thing like that – though sure eneuch my sister would!' And she went on, 'It's not in me to dae a thing like that – some things I dae, some things I willnae do and one there is who says, there's naethin' that I cannae do!' And on she went, 'If I saw two people walking down the road there – I could put trouble between them – sure as grass!' Well the grannies didn't stay long after that. They got out before the sister came home! And of course, one granny married her soldier laddie and when the Great War came, two of her sons went out and two came home. But the other granny had two sons went away to France – and only one came home. That was Peter, he stayed out there in Flanders Field. The waters and the mountains lie between. I don't know whether that was witchcraft, second sight, or what – but it was fact.

When the Travellers tell a story, sing a song, or speak about the old ways – we like to get the right way of it, get things straight as you might say otherwise the best of stories is a mess and it's easy enough to end up in the wrong pub without getting wrong directions! Ailidh Dall, up at Remarstaig, he was always very correct, very proper. I mind asking him in 1954, how long he'd been blind and he answered 'Alec John, it's twenty-four years since I saw a man but if you move away from the stove I'll know you're not standing in front of the fire!' He was wise in his affliction, and he was not a man given to complaining – about the war, about his blindness, about hard times. He played his pipes, he said his prayers and he told stories made you think. He told me about a man named Alec Stewart – he had the name himself – but it was not about himself that he spoke:

'Alec Stewart was a man had two grandmothers, one down there in Perthshire and one up here in Sutherland and both his parents were dead. He was a very clever man, and he walked between the two places, winter and summer, and one year he got married on the Isle of Skye. Because he was a knowledgeable man, people used to ask him questions. One day a man came up to him and told him about a woman who had borne a child with two heads. "Do you believe," he said, "that that child has two souls?" It was the mother's question that be brought. Well, Perthshire Sandy sat there by the road to consider this, and he answered the man with a question, "Can you tell me," he said, "were the two mouths breathing?" "Well," said the man, "I've travelled far and wide and asked many people this question and that's the best answer I've got." So the man went away to speak with the mother. And next year when Sandy came back up from Perthshire he sought out the man and asked him how the child was. "It died," he said, "but the mother told me you were right – God had breathed the breath of life and made two living souls." ' It must have been a case of combined twins, Siamese twins.

Our people were full of old sayings, rhymes and riddles. Most of the rhymes were in Gaelic, of course, and in the English language they lose expressiveness, but still you get the idea if not the whole message! If we were talking about some person with whom we'd lost contact, we'd say 'the stone that doesnae come our way will not likely cut my shin the day!' Of a girl who was getting on, and past the age of getting married, I've heard the parents say 'It's not the water willnae run – but the mill that willnae grind!' She was willing, you might say, but not the man! Then there was a son, went to live with his mother, after his wife died. But this mother was already living with her other son and his wife. One day somebody said to the young widower, 'So is it alone with yourself, your mother is?' 'Oh yes,' says the son, 'where else would I be?' And his brother's wife was listening and she said, 'Did you ever hear about the man who went for a bowl of meal? Well, he took a horse and he went for a bowl of meal. He put the bowl of meal on his back, went for the horse's back himself, then went back the way he came in! Well,' she said, 'that's him!', pointing at her husband's brother, 'he takes his bowl of meal and goes back the way he came!' That's like a riddle but I think we know what was going on!

My daughter, Christina, she's got a new one: 'President Clinton and the First Lady drove up to a gas station in Arkansas. When Mrs Clinton saw the attendant she whispered to the President, "I went to school with that man, in fact we went out together." "Fancy that," said Bill, "if it wasn't for me you might have ended up married to a gas station attendant!" and he sniggered the way he does. "Put it another way," said the First Lady, "if I'd married him – he'd now be President of the United States!" '

You have to remember a joke and get it right. You spoil a good joke or a story if you get it wrong. You have to practise. When it was winter-time, around the fire we used to practise – that's the place to practise or out in the fields, I've heard people sing in a field the same song over and over. Many a good man sings to himself and many a good woman sings songs to her man. There's no harm in repeating a good thing one hundred and fifty times! My son, Angus, he says he's practising to get married!

'There never was a slut but had a slit! There never was a daw but he had twa!' A daw's a lazy braggard! 'There's a very slippery stone on the door of the mansion house!' No great wisdom there, but it sounds very good in Gaelic! Its meaning is much the same as, there's many a slip twixt cup and lip. 'What is it God can never see?' Another like himself! Alexander, my eldest boy, he's got a good one – about the Devil. We've got many, many names for the Devil!

'Well it's about the Devil, when he made a bargain with three men, an Englishman, an Irishman and a Scotsman. He said "Each of you can have whatever you want for one year on the understanding that if you can't ask me one thing I can't do, you'll be mine, in hell!" The Englishman built himself a castle, the Irishman got a job in a brewery, and the Scotsman bought a big hotel in Florida! The year passed and the Devil returned with his question "What can I not do?" First the Englishman answered the knock at his door, he said, "Turn this castle into gold!" – and the Devil did that. So off to hell he went! Then the Devil phoned up the Scotsman in Miami. It was a mobile phone he had. And the Scotsman said, "Make me landlord of the whole coastline of

Florida before dinner and have Princess Diana, ready naked, on my four-poster bed . . ." and before he put down the phone it was done! So off to hell he went. Then the Devil went down to the brewery just as the Irishman was coming out singing drunk. And the Devil had only asked him "What . . ." when Paddy farted and said, "Catch that and tie a knot in it you bastard!" He knew what was coming you see! The Devil kens his ain as they say! That's how Murphy's got started!'

My wife, Mary, tells the story about the witch of Brora. All the Davies were brought up by the river Evelix over there at Dornoch, and it's there she was taken to be burned. She was the last witch in Scotland to be burned, and it wasn't very long ago.

'Her name was Janet Horne. She was a native of Brora. They say she was a backward child and she used to go about with her cat, singing to herself, and people thought that she was fey. And they started to watch her and they saw her picking flowers and plants and they heard her singing and they decided she was a witch – she was about sixteen years of age. So they stripped

Left. Mary Williamson, wife of Alec John and sister of Eddie Davies, Edderton, Easter Ross, 1995. (TN)

Right. Alec John Williamson with his dog, Jockie, 1995. (TN)

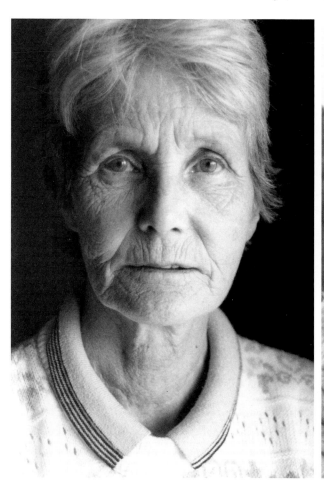

her bare naked and put her on a donkey and they took her all the way down to Dornoch. It took them two days to get her from Brora into Dornoch and she was brought before the court and tried and convicted of witchcraft. A stake was put up and a great bonfire made and she was tied to it and burned alive.

'It was a very cold morning, so that when they brought her before the sticks that made up the fire, she knelt down in her petticoat and put her hands towards where the flames would rise – as though she thought she could warm herself. She didn't know what was happening to her. They tied her to the stake and they burned her alive.

'She was never a witch! She was just a lassie lived out on the hill. Janet Horne her name was. She was just a lassie like my own lassies. It was the neighbours. It was religion. Stripped naked, they took her down on the back of a donkey! When I think of that – and when I think of her bending over the sticks to warm herself, it breaks my heart. They buried her in unhallowed ground, outside the wall of the town. There is a stone marks the spot, and one day when Eddie and I were young, we were hunting rabbits out there and we found the stone. And in those days you could still read the words carved on the stone. It was in among the whins. There were plenty of rabbits but after we found the stone we never went back in there. We could read you see and we ran for our lives! This is a poem we used to say at Camore school:

> *I watched her plucking cowslips*
> *I marked her where she stood:*
> *She never knew I watched her*
> *While hiding in the wood.*
>
> *Her skirt was bright as crimson*
> *And black her steeple hat:*
> *Her broomstick lay beside her*
> *– I'm positive of that.*
>
> *Her skirt was bright as crimson*
> *Her eyes were – I don't know –*
> *For when she turned towards me –*
> *I thought it best to go!*

First it was sacrifices, then it was witches, then it was the Burkers – but I'm not going into all that! I'll just tell you one last story my father used to tell. It's a true story, it's about the time my grandfather, that's my father's father, got drunk and the white mare got off her tether. He was about six at the time. This was down at Torrin on the Isle of Skye. All the Travellers liked to have a white horse, and you could get a high price for a white horse – the big houses liked to bring down the stags on a white horse. Well, my grandmother sent my father out after the white mare, but she could be a contrary beast and she wouldn't come. It was a very hot day. He followed the mare, calling her, running and creeping up on her for miles, and he got very thirsty. On and on they went till the white mare came to the iron gate across the road to the cemetery at Kilbride – and the mare went straight through the gate.

When the boy got to the gate he climbed over, not thinking at all, and he followed the horse on down to the loch. And there he saw two piglets playing on the shore. They scampered about and they came right up to him and then ran off again – right into the water. And the boy scooped with one hand and he drank from the loch and he stood there with his feet in the water, watching the piglets swim out into the middle of the loch and he was just about to follow them away, when he felt something warm come into his hand. It was the muzzle of the white mare. And my father climbed onto the white mare's back and they set off both, for home. Oooh he was very, very tired and when he came to the iron gate, the mare stopped and he got down and opened the gate and led the mare through. And there she waited while he closed the gate, and when he was mounted she brought him back to the camp. Well, his father was sober by this time and the boy told him the story about the gate and piglets swimming out into the loch and he said, 'That'll teach you to go wandering off on your own!'

Well it was a strange thing – the mare going through the gate and the piglets enticing him out onto the water like that but that graveyard was the very place where my father took his second wife to be buried, my mother. Forty-eight years after he went after the white mare, my father went down that same road, to the same cemetery, to bury my mother, through the same gate. That was another very hot day. And he stood, with all his family there, looking out over the same water.

Hamish Henderson

THE MAN WITH THE BIG BOX

'I hear they speak about our maker'

'Hamish's Great Discovery', that's what Calum MacLean the Gaelic folklorist called it. 'Drop everything,' he said, 'close down your desks, we must go now with the Travelling People!' Calum was my colleague at the School of Scottish Studies in Edinburgh, and this discovery was the realisation, that besides the ballad tradition of the Borders and north east Scotland, besides the multifarious culture of Scottish Gaeldom, a third great zone of Scottish folk culture exists among the Travelling People – Scotland's indigenous nomads. Indeed, at that particular moment in the early nineteen fifties, the oral literature and song of the Travelling People was, probably, not only the most substantially ancient but also the most vital of all Scotland's various, towering folk traditions – traditions which are of crucial national importance here at home, and matchless gems in the crown of international folk music.

As, historically, a non-literate group, the tape-recorder was crucial in bringing the art of the Travellers to the wider world. As a boy in Blairgowrie, I'd rubbed shoulders with the Travellers, at school I read *The Tinkler Gypsies of Galloway*, as a student, walking and biking in Scotland before the war, I had met Travellers who taught me songs but it was the tape-recorder which appeared before me, like a revelation, in Italy in 1950 that made me realise what could and should be done with such machinery, in Scotland. It could make permanent one of the most elusive and ephemeral of all art forms – traditional folksong – it could give back to the Scottish people what John Ruskin called that most solemn virtue of Scotland 'The domestic truth and tenderness breathed in all Scottish song'. And, of course, there's much more here in Scottish song than Ruskin dreamed of.

Hamish Henderson driving 'Piper', Isle of Barra, 1988. Photo; Jean Mohr.

Hamish Henderson tape-recording Gaelic stories from Alexander Stewart (Ailidh Dall), Sutherland, 1957. Am Bron Binn – 'The Sweet Sorrow' – the oldest of these stories, refers to 'Arthur King of Britain' and is, by origin, at least 1500 years old. (HH, BB)

Thus, when the School of Scottish Studies was established in the University of Edinburgh in 1951 the magnetic tape-recorder and living tradition were there at its heart. Calum MacLean, who had worked in Ireland for the Irish Folklore Commission, took responsibility for the Scottish *Gaidhealtachd* and I went out into the Scots speaking areas, especially the north east, where I recorded the great bothy songs and traditions of the farming community. And it was there that I became conscious, I was made conscious, of the magnificent folk riches lying, totally unregarded and essentially unknown, among that traditionally maligned group 'the Tinkers', the Travelling People. They are a small minority group, but they are a generous, frequently noble and aristocratic people tied together by kinship, lifestyle, and historical circumstance.

In 1953, enquiries in the old market place in Aberdeen led me to the great Jeannie Robertson. An event after which, neither I, nor Scotland, nor the world, were ever quite the same! She had genius of a high order – and she knew it. Jeannie was a settled Traveller in the prime of her middle age; a woman who had grown up on the roads of Aberdeenshire, and acquired a huge repertoire of songs, stories, riddles and anecdotes – which make her, like MacDiarmid in his different way 'a torchlight procession of one' through twentieth-century Scotland. A singer 'sweet and heroic' was Jeannie.

As if one such figure, with her brilliantly gifted relatives, was not enough, in 1954, in league with Maurice Fleming, I unearthed the multi-talented Stewart family in my native Blairgowrie. And the following year, half by chance, I met on the road, in the very far north the still nomadic Stewart

Hamish Henderson and Essie Stewart lash the arched sticks of the family bow-tent to her grandfather's cart. (HH, BB)

clan, of Lairg in Sutherland. Prime among them was the Gaelic story-teller, Alexander Stewart – blind Ailidh Dall – the patriarchal master of a Traveller family still living a traditional 'Tinker life' on the road. Trying to record, document and preserve the superabundance of oral and musical genius these discoveries revealed was like holding a bucket under the Niagara Falls.

Half by chance? It was less than half! The Sutherland Stewarts were distant relations of the Perthshire Stewarts, and they are closely related to the Aberdeenshire Robertsons and Higgins. It was not chance! This Stewart clan makes up one of the great musical dynasties of Europe and, in addition, my own family is half Perthshire and half Sutherland . . . I was drawn, naturally, into a network of families and onto a network of roads, drawn 'once again to our welcoming north'. Going then to Sutherland was coming home. My mother's family come down from the Gunns of Braemore.

As a folklorist, involved in collation in Edinburgh, I knew good work was being done – but I also knew there was so much more to do, fresh ground to cover further out. I was a fieldworker, not a librarian – I needed to meet people! My great lack then, as now, was money. Field trips had to be financed and source singers treated with every ounce of respect I could muster. And although I had status as a lecturer in the University of Edinburgh, there was practically no money to be had. Most years my best source turned out to be the Yanks. Alan Lomax, and a small host of others, began coming to Scotland at this time and I guided them to base. They helped me by sharing expenses.

In 1955 help came from another quarter, from England. Peter Kennedy, a folklore musicologist working for the BBC, came up to Edinburgh

Left. Hamish Henderson with Joanne Stewart, Sutherland, 1957. (HH, BB)

Right. Ghengis Khan arrives in Scotland! Hamish Henderson takes a turn on 'Maggie', Sutherland, 1957. (HH, BB)

with Tommy, his Welsh wife, and I 'hitched' a ride north with them. They were going up to Orkney, to record for the radio and the BBC archives. They came with a car, a caravan, and a small bairnie; they asked me to travel with them and introduce them to a few folk. I leapt at the chance! I had no car, and my motorbike, a hardy old Rudge Special which had served me so well after the war, when I was writing and teaching, was not the conveyance for a large taperecorder plus tent in the wilds of Sutherland!

The first place we stopped at was Perth. And there I went looking for an old Traveller I'd met in the berry fields, Henry MacGregor. I took pot luck and asked at a house where he lived – and we stayed for three hours! It wasn't his house but the folk there had heard of me, via my work amongst the berry pickers over at Blair – and a ceilidh broke out. We got a dozen good recordings then we went on to the real Henry MacGregor's and the same thing happened! Half his friends and comrades came over to ceilidh with us! Songs, music, liquor flowed all night . . . We had begun what Alan Lomax later described as 'the most productive recording tour ever undertaken'. He qualified it with the statement, 'up till that time.'!. But I don't know who has got more, better, since! Euphoria. Peter Kennedy knew he'd entered a gold mine but as the hours flashed by and the night grew wilder, both he and Tommy began to chaff at the bit. They had to get to Orkney to start work! And so it was all the way up. We drove through the Highlands shrouded in the spray of Niagara!

From Perth we detoured north east to Blairgowrie, where I introduced him to Alec and Belle Stewart; the family now known as the Stewarts of Blair. Later Ewan MacColl and Peggy Seager, and then Sheila Douglas, were to do intensive, scholarly research with the Stewarts. From Blair we took the back road west to Dunkeld and rejoined the A9. South of Newtonmore we found a huge Traveller encampment, then another at Kingussie, pearl-fishing the Spey. All Stewarts! Peter Kennedy was getting the impression that every Traveller in Scotland was a singer named Stewart – and in a way he wasn't far wrong! In Inverness we met more, and in Easter Ross we met Williamsons married into the Stewarts. The Williamsons are another widespread Traveller clan, carrying a brilliant, slightly different culture of its own. We might have stayed at Muir of Ord for a fortnight – but the Kennedys had to get to Orkney! On we went. My final throw was to persuade them to drive to Scrabster, via Lairg and Tongue, rather than north east via Golspie. That was an inspired ploy I've never regretted.

With the caravan in tow, we set out across the barren moorlands into the heart of Sutherland. The weather was dreich and it turned out that Tommy was prey to agoraphobia. She reacted very badly to what seemed like an endless expanse of peat-hag, barren deer forest and bleak distant mountains; eventually she began to get hysterical. Not only were we three adults and a baby but we also had with us a Northumbrian piper, Bob Rundle! I forgot to mention him, he came from Devon. He was very good, but all in all we were a desperate gang with a problem – agoraphobia outside and claustrophobia inside a steamed up car! It was like some televised family holiday turning to nightmare before your eyes; a cultural breakdown, Hell in a wing-mirror. Turn back, or go on?

Tommy was desperate to turn back before things got worse! It was not just the weather, or the mountains – Ben Klibreck can assume sinister form – but the mind. Having coming so far, however, I was determined to go on, and after a short stop, I persuaded Tommy, that to go back would be worse than to keep pressing on! 'If we go back now we will just see everything in reverse and still have the long drive to Scrabster to do!' Gilding the lily, I said 'If we go on, we'll quite soon leave these mountains and come down to the ocean and the white sands of the north.' Fortunately she bought this. We went on, and that evening we camped in a small quarry high on a brae above the sands of the Kyle of Tongue. It was late, it was drizzling, but the clouds were lifting and the light was still just enough there on the waters below for us to see 'the pale sands yonder'. And the tensions began to slip away. The shallow tidal waters of the Kyle can make the Caribbean look very much second-best, and next morning was perfect.

I rose from my tent and walked over the brow of the hill to look south across one of the great landscapes of Scotland: Ben Hope and Ben Loyal silhouetted above the small, illumined fields of the croft-lands. Suddenly my heart went cold – there, just below me, was a half-circle of tents with chimneys smoking – bow-tents – the domed, grey-green galleys of the Stewarts of Remarstaig . . . Those whom I was soon to know, as 'The Summer Walkers'. I might have been in Mongolia. I might have stood there any summer during the last eight thousand years and seen a similar sight. I know no more beautiful landscape in the world, no grander campsite under the stars. The Stewarts call Brae Tongue the King of Campsites. It remained Ailidh Dall's favourite camping place long after he went blind – until he died. No wonder.

I went back to tell Peter Kennedy what I had seen, and immediately returned to meet these Travellers whom we had struck by what seemed like chance. I had no idea then who they were, where they came from, what they might have been. At the edge of the camp was an old woman, washing clothes: I spoke with her and asked if anyone there knew songs or old stories. 'The old man has plenty,' she said and nodded towards one of the tents. This was the woman known as the *cailleach* – the old woman. Who she was, or where she came from I never found out. And then from one of the tents came a very old man, leaning on the arm of a boy of about sixteen years of age. This was Alexander Stewart and his nephew, Gordon Stewart. He was blind. We introduced ourselves and sat down in the heather at the strange, split mouth of his tent. We spoke in Gaelic. I asked the old man if he had old stories. He said he knew one or two. I asked him if I might record them on a machine. I said 'There's a man up on the hill who does not speak Gaelic but he has a machine that does!' He was silent for a while, then said 'I would – if it were any other day. Look what day it is!'

It was Sunday. This was Sutherland and the Sabbath kept as strictly as anywhere in all of Scotland. Maybe I'd forgotten but I knew I only had this one day before Peter Kennedy would move on so I immediately asked Ailidh Dall, 'Have you heard the word of God today?' He said he hadn't. It was the right question for Ailidh Dall was a devotedly religious man, who prayed twice a day and would conduct family services each Sunday. I told him I had a Gaelic New Testament up in my tent; that I would like to bring it back and read from it.

When I returned, the family gathered round and I read to them a chapter from St Matthew's Gospel – the one about scribes and Pharisees and hypocrites. It sounds very fierce and marvellous in Gaelic. The word of God was spoken, the ice well and truly broken! And it was not twenty minutes before we were recording Ossian stories in that beautiful, primeval, timeless landscape – among people James MacPherson might have met two hundred years before when he was searching out the substance of his great bogus epic. I pressed hard to get recordings that day – because the Kennedys were moving, within hours, to Caithness and would brook no more stops by me. And that was how I met the man whom Calum MacLean described as 'the best Gaelic storyteller ever recorded on the mainland of Scotland!' Ailidh Dall was a piper too of course, and a singer. But it was his stories, told with Homeric *gravitas*, that take the biscuit. I have never heard the haunting, slow, deliberate rendition of Ailidh Dall equalled for archaic authenticity. I held a bucket there, as it were, beneath the sky, a rusty can – to crystal water cascading down the cataract of day!

Essie Stewart was at the camp. A handsome girl of fourteen then. Riding a pony round the stakes where Gordon had tethered the horses. She played her accordion and sang her uncle Brian Stewart's English song, 'By Klibreck and Ben Loyal'. He was in Burma during the war. It describes so well the Traveller routes in the north west.

By Klibreck and Ben Loyal and the bonnie Kyle of Tongue,
That road we often travelled in the days when we were young:
There's magic and there's beauty in those hills when passing through
There's many miles from Lairg to the waters of Kylesku.

Chorus: Of all of bonnie Scotland I dearly love the west,
Its bens and glens in summertime, they surely are the best
For grandeur and for beauty in those hills when passing through
There's many miles from Melness to the waters of Kylesku.

By Craigie Pool and Loyal and the Coldbackie sands
I've thought of them when soldiering in far off foreign lands;
I dreamt I saw the sunset on the hill of Cashel Dhu
In fancy I was wandering by the waters of Kylesku.

There's beautiful Achfary on the shores of Loch More
Where winter waves are breaking like the seas on Skerray More;
By Laxford and Rhiconich and the bonnie cave of Smoo –
There's many miles from Durness to the waters of Kylesku.

By Ledmore and Loch Assynt, from Lochinver down to Stoer
You can view the wild Atlantic from its cold and rocky shore;
The clear and sparkling rivers here, where salmon are not few
There's many miles from Oykel to the waters of Kylesku.

After that, the Kennedys went on to Orkney. They did very good work up there, and I went back to Edinburgh. And that was it for me, in Sutherland, for two years! But what a taster I had had! And what a banquet, I knew, awaited me on my return.

In 1957 I organised a second, serious collecting trip to Sutherland. I planned it in harness with Bobby Botsford, an American scholar, with a Landrover, the perfect vehicle for those parts. He came, we saw, we conquered! He drove, he took some wonderful photographs, he returned south but left the Landrover there for me. Free range in Sutherland – what more could one ask?

We set out from Edinburgh in July, the two of us, plus a young student from Benbecula, Norman MacLean, whom I had met earlier that year at the National Mod, the Gaelic Music Festival, in Aberdeen. Norman was a native Gaelic speaker, a singer, a first-rate piper and general enthusiast, at that very moment developing an interest in the traditions that are the foundations of both his piping and his passion for the Gaelic language. Since then, Norman has become a household word in the *Gaidhealtachd*, comedian, poet, man o' pairts – he came as a student and left as a friend. He lugged the big recorder, which I had long lugged for myself, for Lomax and the rest, alone! Norman got on very well with Gordon, and with Essie – she was a very beautiful young woman. But he didn't stay long and Bobby Botsford had to go back early to

Hamish chats with Gordon Stewart who as a boy took care of old Blind Sandy, guiding him round the camp, morning and evening, 1955. (HH)

Edinburgh, to defend his thesis, and so there I was stranded with nothing but a Landrover and the Stewarts of Remarstaig! It was the cream of my life, the top of my life – those two months up there with the Stewarts, a four-wheel drive and a ridge-pole tent, out on the road three families strong, with horses, carts, with barefoot children and an old man telling Homeric, Ossianic tales – as though the Aegean were lovely as Loch Eriboll!

The first song I recorded from Ailidh Dall 'The Sweet Sorrow', *Am Bron Binn*, is one of the oldest songs in Europe. It tells of Arthur 'King of Britain' and makes a unique and direct link between the worlds of P Celtic and Q Celtic, the two great branches of Celtic language and history. To start at the beginning is always good but to get started in 500 AD was the stuff of dreams! Needing mains electricity, I set up my first 'studio' in the Tongue Hotel. We had a bit of trouble getting in! A residue of antipathy toward the 'Tinks' was still strong in the fifties. But the management came round, Ailidh Dall took a dram and another great collecting tour began. This time, a large proportion of all I gathered was in Gaelic and all the more precious for that.

Once more I was lucky, 1957 was the last year the Remarstaig Stewarts spent the whole summer on the road and for the only time in my collecting career I arrived on site, supplied with reasonable funds for my work. The School of Scottish Studies was a new institution. Funds were very difficult to come by but I knew that what I had to do was of such importance, that I decided, that year, to go straight to the top and request funds for 'A collecting tour of Sutherland' from the University of Edinburgh itself.

I went round to see Mr R O Curle, who was then the chief accountant, and I explained what I was going to do and how important it was, that things needed to be done, had to be done 'here and now'! And he gave me three thousand pounds. It was the first and last time that I got real funds for my work. I lived most of the summer sleeping out in my tent (keeping the money for more important things than hotel bills) and came back to Edinburgh that autumn, with hours and hours of what can only be described as priceless historical and cultural material. Curle sent me forth – and money made me free as a bird. The Stewarts were a tiny band, but both their lifestyle and their culture were affirmation of a major strand in Scotland's history, what Scotland was, is, and will be. They're in the archive now. Death hath no dominion! Curle's support allowed me to treat my informants with a little of the hospitality they deserved; to return a little of the hospitality they gave.

That year we all met up one evening at Altnaharra, beneath the spreckled, moonlit sides of the same Ben Klibreck which, two years before, had so frightened Tommy Kennedy. Now it stood like a benign pyramid above us. The Stewarts were camped just to the north of the Altnaharra bridge, in a grassy hollow by the burn, just a few yards from the standing stones that mark the centre of Sutherland. I'd written to Gordon Stewart at Remarstaig. I knew roughly where they'd be and our paths crossed almost immediately (speaking of which, it's a sad fact, that Calum MacLean, on various trips to the north, never managed to find them – the Stewarts travelled well-known routes but the timing of moves and detours were always decided by needs and the moment). From Altnaharra we travelled north, in convoy, to Brae Tongue, down to Coldbackie sands, on through Naver Bridge, Armadale, Bettyhill, Strathy, Melvich, to Caithness. We hawked, traded, tinsmithed and ceilidhed our way through Sutherland to Janetstown – where we turned back. The Stewarts never went further east than attendance at the horse fair there in Janetstown.

I remember at Janetstown, asking Essie, 'Why not go deeper into Caithness?' and she replied, 'Because, up to here, the people are Scots like us, and speak Gaelic.' It was a beautiful statement about the ethnic thing up there in the far north. The 'ethnic' border between Gaeldom and Norse settlement does not coincide with the county boundary between Sutherland and Caithness – it lies quite deep inside the latter. The frontier, to which Essie alluded with epigrammatic clarity, is a physical border, the river Forss, which over centuries has affirmed very ancient tribal, linguistic, religious and cultural division. To some extent the Forss still divides Scots/Gaelic society from Norwegian/English society. This clear boundary line can be contrasted with the English Scots border – where none of the classic separators apply. This national border is essentially a construct of history and cultural force – but none the less real for that – and it stands an exemplar for the future of nations.

Hamish Henderson and the now famous Gaelic comedian and piper, Norman MacLean, meet an old Traveller woman near Muir of Ord, Ross-shire, 1957. (HH, BB)

Nineteen fifty seven was a summer with a good deal of sunshine. We had wonderful times. I had the Landrover, I could drive where I pleased but I enjoyed joining in, working with the horses, putting up the big bow-tents, loading the carts for the road, being there to capture the essence of life as the Travellers lived it. I remember one milky white night when we were camped on a little plateau, high above a cliff looking out across the Pentland Firth. The tents were set out along a gently sloping piece of lawn-like grass above what seemed an endless sea of heather: Ailidh Dall was playing the pipes. Couples began dancing. An eightsome reel got underway. All the family joined in, and the lines of the dancers gradually widened and the couples swinging spread out in great parabolas down the slope and away into the heather. It was a night that will stay imprinted on my mind as long as I live. So far north in summertime the darkness is always incomplete; on a clear night one has to look hard to see the stars. I danced with Essie. She was sixteen then, with Mary her mother, with Black Anne, with her daughter, Joanne. The tents were humped round a semi-circle and at a short distance the horses watched us. With the heather in bloom, the perfume coming off 'the flower of the mountain' seemed to become substantial in the dewy air. I went back to my small tent thinking, 'Life is good – life is very good like this.'

One morning I decided to walk out to Kinloch, underneath Ben Loyal. I'd seen on the map 'Grave of Diarmid' and I wanted to find this grave. Being mythological places they're quite common! We have plenty of graves of Diarmid in Perthshire! It was hot. I walked a long way but did not find the grave; so I lay down in a small hollow among the birches and went to sleep. After a while I awoke aware of something beside me. I lay still and opened my

Norman MacLean with Traveller girls and Bobby Botsford, 1957. (HH, BB)

eyes without moving and there – at arm's length away – was a fawn, looking at me! It showed not the slightest fear. For some time we looked at each other and then, half playfully, it scampered off. By its size it must have been a roe deer fawn, not a red deer calf. I remember the broken sunlight on its spots. I returned to the camp.

Forty years have passed. I've still not found the grave of Diarmid but I remember Essie later showing me what she called the Stone of Ossian, *Clach Oisein*, by the camping place at Melness. And it was she who showed me the grave in which Peter, Alec John Williamson's brother, is buried in the graveyard there, having been brought by cart from the camping place at Kinloch, where he died of a fever at seven years of age.

Another day one of the young girls, one of Peter and Chrissie Stewart's daughters, came to my tent quite early with two water buckets and asked me to go down to the well with her. It was about a hundred yards down a winding path through the heather. She led and I followed. I had drunk nothing that morning. I was thirsty. I knelt and drank from my hand. The water, so dark in the well, so clear in the light, was nectar. I remember thinking this is the well at the world's end. We each filled our buckets, then walked back to the camp, she first, me four paces behind. Our feet were bare and up above, smoke was rising from the tent chimneys; the peat reek mingled with the ling and bog-myrtle. I turned and looked at Ben Loyal, at Ben Hope, at the winding river in the sands of the Kyle. And I thought of the words of Christopher Smart 'For in my heart I quested for beauty, but God, God, has sent me to sea for pearls.'

There is a Gaelic proverb 'Watch out for yourself – the law has come to Ross-shire!' It probably dates from about 1820. Fortunately the law had still not come to Sutherland when I arrived in the fifties! Biblical authority is something else. Sutherland has long been a stronghold of Old Testament Calvinism. I remember an elderly crofter at Melness saying of the Travellers, with deeply serious satisfaction, 'I hear that they are mentioning our maker.' The Sutherland Travellers were as religious as the country people themselves, and this meant a great deal to the crofting community.

During the seventeenth century the people of Sutherland were deeply moved by the piety of Cromwell's Puritan troops. There are stories of local people joining the Cromwellians on their knees in prayer. After the Battle of Dunbar when Cromwell triumphed over the forces of the Scots Estates, English power rapidly extended right up to Sutherland and one of his major generals reported, 'The justice of God has given these distant realms the true law and love of God.' That is something very different from the 'law' the men of Ross-shire feared in 1800. The welcome given to these English troops almost certainly owed a great deal to the fact that many north Highland Scots had just

Alexander Stewart, Ailidh Dall,
Sutherland, 1957. (HH, BB)

played a major part, on the Protestant side, in the Thirty Years War. Almost a quarter of Gustavus Adolphus' Swedish army was made up of Scots. One of my own ancestors, the giant Lachlan Gunn of Braemore, was knighted on the field of Breitenfeld by the Swedish King, Gustavus Adolphus: and great was the mourning in Sutherland when Gustavus was killed at Lützen in 1632. He was a hero and military genius of the kind that the Royal House of Stuart was no longer able to produce.

The primacy of the names Stewart and Alexander among the northern Travellers tells us something about Traveller allegiance, lifestyle and ambition, their royalism, stoicism, martial ardour, their sense of pride and propriety. One consequence being that there is much less overt bawdiness in the oral repertoire of the Sutherland Stewarts than there is elsewhere among the Scottish Travellers (Alec John Williamson being a Ross-shire man!). But that being said – in some of Ailidh Dall's stories, like *Ossian* and *Am Maraiche Mairnealach*, sexuality is given a wonderfully subterranean force which makes it all the more powerful.

Am Maraiche Mairnealach – 'The Weather-Wise Mariner' – is a great story that both Ailidh Dall and his nephew Brian Stewart used to tell: this is it, much as I remember hearing it at the foot of Ailidh Dall.

'Once long ago there lived a king – the High King of Ireland. He was married to a beautiful Queen and they had just one son but one day the Queen took a fever and died. Great was the mourning all over Ireland, but time went by and the king married again and the boy lived with his father and his stepmother. He was a big lad, well-built, handsome – and when he came of age, his stepmother took him aside and said, "I'm going to give you a very special present."

' "Oh!" said the boy, "I've never given you a present!" And this was true. But the Queen said, "that doesn't matter, soon you'll be a man and then you'll be leaving home." So she gave him a beautiful shirt, made of the finest silk; from China she said it came and the Prince ran his hand across the silk and said "I've never seen a shirt so fine or soft as this shirt."

'That evening, before the feast for the coming-of-age, the Prince dressed himself up in his finest clothes and put on his new shirt. So soft it was, and just a little tight that he said to himself, "fits me like they say a glove!" And he looked at himself in the bronze mirror by candlelight. Very handsome he was! And the shirt was crimson wrought with gold embroidery. "This is some shirt!" he said. Then he felt the silk tighten round his waist and up his back he felt a curling thing unfolding round his shoulder and coming up behind his head, all thick and smooth. He tried to grab behind his back and shouted out "What's wrong with this shirt!" He tried to pull it off – but the shirt was cutting tight into his back and had turned into a great hissing snake! "A snake!" said the Prince, "this is some present she's given me!"

'So the handsome Prince stood there like a hunchback, bent double he was, with a monstrous snake swaying side to side of his head. He locked his door and hid himself but nothing he did would shift the brute – so he crept along the darkest passages of the castle until he came to his father's quarters and the Prince told his father the story. And the King said, "That's some present she's given you! Only the hen-wife can cure a thing like that!"

'So the Prince went out into the night, to the hen-wife's house. It was a shack of sticks at the edge of the forest. And when the hen-wife saw the boy, she said "My poor lad! That's terrible, who was it put a thing like that on you?" "It was the Queen, my stepmother" said the Prince, "God curse her bones!" and he asked the hen-wife if she would cure him – or cut out the beast. 'The hen-wife said she knew only one person who could cure a monstrous snake like that: "There's a woman was a friend of mine – lives on the summit of the island standing in the waters of Loch Leug – she might cure you. But how to get there? That is the question?" And the old hen-wife turned to the cauldron that simmered on the fire and stirred the broth. "The only one who could get you there," she said, "is *Am Maraiche Mairnealach* and he's blind and deaf and he's not risen from his bed these last seven years!" But she poured the boy a bowl of soup and when he'd eaten, she took him to the door of the shack and pointed the way to an upturned boat where *Am Maraiche Mairnealach* lived by the loch. The boat was black with tar. The Prince knocked on the hull and as he bent down to creep inside, he banged the snake against the lintel. It was the prince who felt the pain! "That beast is right inside me now," he said.

'When his eyes had grown accustomed to the gloom, he saw, lying in a bed of dirty straw, the oldest man that ever grew white hair. "I am deaf and blind," the old man said, "but the ferry lies there on the shore. Seven years in sand and storm she's waited ye! If you can shift her you can have her. That's what I always say!" So the boy went down to the shore. He levered with poles, he dug out the sand, but try as he would, nothing would budge the ferryboat. So he went back to the upturned boat and stood at the door. "Won't budge!" said the boy. So *Am Maraiche Mairnealach* said to the Prince, "See if you can find my trousers? I've not had them on these seven years!" And the boy saw that the old man's dog was lying on the trousers just by the door. He kicked off the dog and he picked them up. "Enough of that!" the old man said, "It's the dog that keeps them warm!" And so he helped the old man into his trousers and the two of them went down to the shore where the ferryboat still lay in the sand.

'*Am Maraiche Mairnealach* now said to the boy, "What I need is my shoulder 'gainst the prow." And the Prince guided the blind man and placed his shoulder against the prow of the ferryboat – then the old man straightened his back, took a deep breath and gave one long steady shove. Into the sea the ferryboat went – three times her own length and rode there high in the water. "Some strength you've got!" said the Prince, and he helped the old man into the boat and they set sail for the island. "You'd best hide down there in the prow," said the old man, "a thing like that's best out of sight!"

'Sitting on watch, the woman of the island in the centre of Loch Leug, saw the mast of a ship on the distant waters – and she knew who it was. "Let them come from below, let them come from above, I see the mast of a ship like a tree, and in her rides a bull and a cow!" And she put on her best clothes and went down to the shore to welcome the ferryman. "Glad was my heart when I saw the mast-top of *Am Maraiche Mairnealach*," she said, "never did I think your last time was the last." And she gave him a great welcome and asked him what cargo he brought. "A cargo," he said, "of which you'll ne'er see the like! I bring you a cargo half-man and half-beast!" And then he got the Prince to stand up in the prow.

' "Never" she said "bring cargo like that! Is it man or a beast?

Never will a cargo like that tread these shores while I have a cat with four paws!" And she had a good strong cat! "Get yourself and that lad away from this place! If you or that beast touch sand on this isle I'll sink you like a stone in the sea!" "I had hoped," said the old man, "you'd heal the boy – but I see it's no use!" and he turned to the Prince and said in a loud voice, "It's worse than I thought – we'll just have to go home."

'Am *Maraiche Mairnealach* then pulled anchor and shouted to the woman "Farewell it is, this time forever!" The old woman stood on the sand watching and the blind man picked up two pails. "It's a long voyage we'll be having," he shouted "so the boy'll fill two pails with fresh water then we'll be away!" But as soon as the boy jumped down from the boat, *Am Maraiche Mairnealach* hoisted sail and with the wind across his bows sped clear of the island.

'The Prince dropped the buckets and ran, and he hid all day among the rocks and that evening he made his way to a spring outside the walls of a beautiful garden. The sun was still hot so he drank the cool water and lay down, very tired. He made himself comfortable on top of his hump and went to sleep. When he awoke he did not move, he felt somebody watching him. Through half-opened eyes he saw a young woman looking over the wall at him. It was the daughter of the woman who had forbidden him to set foot on the island! Looking down at the young man, she said to herself, "This is the most beautiful young man in the world!" And each fell in love with the other. But the Prince dared not move, and the maiden did not dare waken the sleeping Prince.

'Then the girl picked a plum that was growing over the wall and rolled it down the grass towards the Prince. He picked it up and ate it but did not sit up in case the girl should see the snake behind his head. And the maiden laughed and tossed him down another plum. "Come on, come on, come walk with me and I shall take you to my mother's house," she said. But still the Prince was afeared to move, and he said "I came by boat across the loch and must go back." "Oh, please don't go," the maiden said "it is so lonesome here!" And seeing that the maiden cared for him he said "I'm like a wild beast! I have this thing behind my back – my stepmother cursed me with a shirt that grew into a snake!" And rolling to one side he showed the girl the great snake coiled up behind his back. "I'm not afraid of a thing like that!" she said! And she ran off to tell her mother.

' "There's a boy out there behind the wall" she said, "and I've never seen a better-looking boy than he – nor a man. Oh mother, please let me ask him up to the house!" And so the mother went with her daughter back to where the boy was lying by the spring – and she recognised the lad as the monster that *Am Maraiche Mairnealach* had brought across the loch that afternoon. He lay there tall and handsome, with his plaid covering his hump. "I came to get water but the old man tricked me and sailed without me" he said. And the anger that was in the old woman left her. "Come up to the house," she said.

'More and more the daughter fell in love with the boy and he began a new life on the island. Oh this girl really fell for the lad and she couldn't live if she didn't get him. She wanted to marry him. And one day her mother said "Would you lose an arm for him?"

"I would."

"Would you lose a leg for him?"

"I would."

"And would you lose a breast for him?"

"Oh yes" said the daughter, "he is the man I wish to marry."

"Well" said the old woman "we'll see about that when the morning comes."

'Now the husband of the old woman was long dead but she had four of a family – one daughter and three sons, and three strong lads they were – and she said to the eldest, "Run out now and catch me the fattest wether you can find and bring it into me."

'So next day before daybreak, the eldest boy set out with his two brothers for the hill, and high up in the hazelwood they found this big wether and they killed it and they skinned it and they brought it down and hung it up

Hamish and the Stewart family gathered round Ailidh Dall as he sings a short song in the afternoon sun, Sutherland, 1957. (HH, BB)

for their mother. She told the boys to salt the hide and nail it up outside the castle wall and then she got down a great big iron frying pan and put it on the kitchen fire. She asked the girl to put two knives and two plates on the table and sit down opposite the boy. Then she asked the boy to light the lamp and the two of them sat there facing each other. Then she got the girl to take out her breast, her right breast, and the boy looked at it.

'Of course, the meat was in the pan by this time and the old woman was turning the pieces. The fire was blazing and the fat was sizzling and the brute was hungry. The snake which was all coiled up like a shirt round his waist began to uncoil. And oooh there was a great smell coming off that meat – and suddenly the brute lunged forward right into the pan! Into the boiling fat it went – and out again! It burned itself! And instead of going back around the boy's neck it landed right on the girl's breast – and the old woman was ready for it! She had a big sharp knife of beaten steel – she slashed at the snake and with a single blow cut through its head and right through the young girl's breast and down they fell onto the floor. And bang! The old woman put a basin over the two of them and put one foot on top of the basin. Then she told the girl to hold very still and she stuck the knife in the flames of the fire and held it there. Then she turned the knife three times round, down the breast of the girl, and she sealed the wound where the young girl's breast had been. And the boy was just a lad again and straight as any lad should be. The snake and all the hump were gone and the Prince was handsome as ever he was!

'Then the old woman bent down and lifted the basin off the floor, and underneath lay the shirt, as beautiful as new! "There" she said, "is the present your stepmother gave!" And she lifted the shirt up with the point of her knife and threw it into the fire. Bang! It went off with a bang that took away half the fireplace and filled the kitchen full of smoke! That put an end to the feast for that night but now nothing stood between the two youngsters and their happiness so as soon as the girl's breast was healed, they got married. And a golden breast was made for the princess and she was a bride as beautiful as every bride that lives.

'Well it was a great wedding and all the folk on the island came and another old hen-wife and her son came in with the guests. Now this hen-wife used to come to the castle to do washing and cleaning, and she went into all the rooms of the castle so she knew everything about the young couple, both before and after they were wed and sometimes her son would go hunting with the Prince. Well, one day this hen-wife said to her son, "Son, if you were smart you could be in the place of the Prince!" "Och" said the lad, "how could I be that?"

' "Just say," says the old hen-wife "that you have knowledge of his wife!" Then he'll ask you "What knowledge have you got of my wife?" And you'll say "Well, the comb that she has for combing her hair is solid gold like the sun." And he'll laugh and say "Everybody knows a Princess has a golden comb for her hair!" Then you'll say "Ah yes but I have other knowledge of your wife!" "And what might that be?" the Prince will ask. Then you will say, "She has one breast of flesh – and one breast of gold! And when the Prince hears that he will be consumed with anger and jealousy and he'll leave the island just as sure as he came! And you will be free to claim the Princess for yourself!"

'So, one day when they were hunting, the lad said to the prince "Your wife is a beautiful woman." "Oh yes," said the Prince "I have a beautiful wife – and a good wife."

' "Yes" said the boy "but even though she's good and all that I've seen her – I've seen her combing her hair and I know what sort of comb she has!" "Och yes," says the prince "you might have seen her combing her hair . . ."

' "Yes" said the lad getting bold, "I've seen that and I've seen more! One of her nipples is soft mauve like the heather, the other one yellow as the gold of her ring!"

' "Oooh – you son of the Devil!" said he, and he struck down the son of the hen-wife with one blow from his hand, and he thought twice about killing the boy then and there on the hill! But he cringed like a coward—so the Prince raced back to the castle and told his wife what the lad said and he beat her and kicked her and called her a whore! Then he rent his clothes and went out of the castle. He took up his bundle and he went away as a beggar-man. He went away from the island and all alone he wandered from place to place.

'Years went by but one day he came to a wood. And he was following a path through the wood when he heard a cry coming out from the trees. He stopped and he listened and he heard the cry again and he went towards the spot from where the cries came and there he found a man lying on the ground – dead pale and very ill.

' "What's wrong?" asked the beggar-man as he put down his bundle. "I was heading for the spring, when this sickness came on. If only I could get a drink from the spring I'd be as well as ever." Now the beggar-man had heard of that spring in the woods and he said "You can't get a drink from that spring – it's guarded by wild animals so fierce that nobody . . ." "Oh yes," said the man, "that spring's guarded all right, but just now it's midday, all the animals are asleep. Go now – there's a lion there and the lion has a cup under his paw. If you could only get that cup from out beneath the lion's paw and bring a drink to me I would be cured – and you have command of all the world! He's sleeping now."

' "Well," said the lad, more like himself, "I'll see what I can do," and he crept forward through the wood towards where he could hear the water gurgling from the spring. And he came to a clearing with soft moss and grass, and lying in the sun he saw all kinds of wild animals – asleep. Foxes, wolves, leopards, deer and antelope, wild goats and birds of every feather and, at the end of the clearing, guarding the well, lay the lion with the cup underneath its paw. Silently, in bare feet, the lad crept towards the lion and when he was very very close he stopped – then, very slowly, he put his hand to the cup and stood up straight. Turning round, he saw the sleeping animals waken, and one by one they rose and disappeared into the forest. Then he turned to the lion, and without fear he ordered the lion to leave the spring and not return. And when the lion had gone, the boy dipped his cup into the cool spring and drank; and then he filled it to the brim and took it back to the sick man. And the man drank from the cup and he rose to his feet.

' "Oh," said the man "I'm very grateful to you. Once more I'm as well as ever I was," and he drank again from the cup and handed it back to the lad. "From this cup you shall drink any drink that you wish and any place in the world you wish to be in – you'll be there!"

'And the boy drank from the cup and without thinking he thought "I wish I was back on the island of Loch Leug" – and bang he was there at the gate of the castle! But his hair was long and his beard was rough and he was dressed in the same old rags. He was still a beggar-man and nobody recognised the young Prince. So he stood at the gate and began on his pipes.
'Oooh that island had been a sad, sad place since the Prince went away. His young wife had taken to her bed and not risen till that night when he came back with his music. Lying awake in her room she heard the notes coming up from the gate, and she raised herself up on one elbow and listened, and she knew it was he, and she rose from her bed and listened to her husband playing far below in the moonlight.

'Now her mother had died many years before so she went to speak with her brothers. First she went to the bedroom of her youngest brother and said "What would you do if my husband came back? What would you do if he came to the door?" "Break every bone in his body – that's what he deserves!"

'Then she went to the second brother and said the very same thing to him. "What would you do if my husband came back? What would you do if he came to the door?" "Put him" he said "in irons on the floor and starve him to death like a fiend!"

'Then she went to the room of her eldest brother, and she knocked, and as she came through the door he said "God save us my sister – the Lord God be praised!" And he asked her, "How did you get up? It's years

Hamish leads the Stewart yoke on the road from Sutherland into Caithness, 1957. (HH, BB)

since you last stood on two feet!" And he went to her. And she said, "Dear brother, I have come to ask you a question – if my husband was to come home, what would you do to him?" The brother paused, and she went on "Would you treat him badly?"

' "Oh no" said he. "He was deceived and lied to most treacherously! Lies led to wickedness and wickedness lies!" And when she heard this, she drew her brother across to the window and pointed to the beggar-man outside the gate. "That's him down there" she said, "I know him by the music that he plays." And then the brother said, "I remember when I brought the wether home when you were young. He who took the crooked road now stands upon the straight. He who made the wound hath healed the wound."

'And when morning came, the beggar-man was brought inside the castle and a great hunt mounted for the wicked hen-wife and her son and when they were found they were put, both, into a barrel of tar, and paraffin was poured over them and they were set alight with a match! And that's the end of the story. The young woman was soon in fine health and the beggar-man a Prince in his kingdom again.'

What a beautiful and many-layered story that is. It sums up so much about human hope and the Traveller life. It says so much about Sutherland and the Celtic world. From my early teens I had gravitated towards the west in my travels in Scotland – from a feeling, like that which many people have, that 'the west is where you go', but now I know 'the north is where you should go'! The mountains of the north west, have them both and it all.

Gordon Stewart

HORSEMAN AND TINSMITH

Going up the hill whip me not
Coming down the hill hurry me not
On the level spare me not
In the stable forget me not with clean water:
Strike me not if sick or cold
Chide me not with bit or rein
When you are angry, strike me not.

Our feet were tied to the road. When I was a boy, it was a horseman I
wanted to be. It was the horses took us out. If we were just a fortnight
late, the folk out in the west would be wondering what had happened. I've seen
the women out there standing waiting for us. Once March came round we'd
feel a wee bittie heat in the sun, like bees in a hive we'd be wanting out and the
horses would be stamping, chaffing the bit.

By the 15th March Allie MacLeod would have left half a cart of
hay for us at Dalmichie and a stack of peats at Dalnessie Bridge. Old Ewan
Donald, the shepherd up at Laid, on the west side of Loch Eriboll, he used to
keep watch on the Tongue road; and when he saw us coming down the brae,
that's three miles across the Loch, he'd set off to meet us at the camp at Mussel
Burn. Nine miles he'd walk to ceilidh with us: he couldn't wait, you see, he
couldn't wait for us to come up there to Laid in a day or two – he came down
to meet us, to ceilidh with us. A kind of before-hand revenge that was! He was
a very poor singer! But he'd get our people to sing and he'd get Ailidh Dall to
tell his stories and Michie, she was a very good singer, she'd sing for him. Ooh
we all liked Ewan Donald – I'm a very poor singer myself like! Then after a day
or two we'd follow him up and camp at Laid, in behind his house. What a view
you get there!

Life on the road was all work for me like. Holiday views we had
– Coldbackie sands, Bettyhill, Durness, Lochinver, moor, mist and mountain,
we had all that but, looking back, it was a hard old time we had. Very hard. But
I'll tell you this – we were good living folk and they loved us, the old crofters,
they loved us coming round. We'd never steal, we made things, we brought

Gordon Stewart, Bonar Bridge,
Sutherland, 1995. (TN)

A horse stands in the wind near the old Traveller campsite at Midtown, Melness, Sutherland. Beyond the Kyle of Tongue rises Ben Loyal. (TN)

things, we'd have good crack, and ceilidh most places twice a year. Our people would always go to the kirk when we were out on the road. Ailidh Dall would take communion at Scourie and Tongue, and so would the Williamsons. Old Katie she's the last of them — she's ninety-one. Very religious the Travellers were, just like the crofting folk. All that is the past now, for us like. I came off the road in 1958.

Five jobs I've had in all my days — plumbing, farming, fencing, coalman, and now I've got me Orange Trousers! I'm retired — I work for the County — diesel road-roller driver. Road-laying through the summer, road-gritting through the winter; a hundred hours a week, plus travel-time! It's just like being on the road, except I'm paid and go home at night. You sit up high in a road-roller, you go at the same speed as a yoke. I've got time to look around — you can't go fast on a road-roller. Sometimes I think it's just like the old days, driving out in the very early morning with the hill-mist rising: the curlews calling up the rain, the sun rising, the first snow on the tops, the light on the water, I've known myself to stop the car. Just stand there and look around, and I've felt the tears come up behind my eyes. Every mile of those roads knew Stewart feet: I still hear the carts, you don't get used to being without horses. Loch Assynt, Kylesku, Melness, Brae Tongue, that's the King of Campsites — for me like. I was tarring up there the other day.

Five years I've got. I'll take my leave at sixty, leave the County. Take things easy. They'll get by without me. I've paid plenty money in. I'll

Above. Gordon Stewart's mother, Joanne, outside her bow-tent at Tuiteam, Glen Oykel, 1957. (HH, BB)

Left. Joanne Stewart and her mother Anne Stewart, Tuiteam, 1957. (HH, BB)

retire at sixty, work for myself as handyman. Half this house I built myself: the other half'll keep me busy till one of us goes under! Work's a habit dies hard in me. And my wife, Frances, she's the same. Work six days and rest on Sunday, that's us.

A hundred hours a week I do all winter long – not many's the day I don't come home tired, but work today is nothing, nothing, to the work I did when I was young, out on the road. That was work. An ill-treated horse had it good compared to me! Eighteen year on the road I had. If you want to know about horses, tinsmithing, tents, I can give as good as you'll get – though the Traveller life was dying fast when I was out and it was no life for me like, not in the long term. The Traveller life in Sutherland was done. So, when I finished school, I served my time as apprentice plumber, down in Lairg, with Alfred Dravina. He was a Pole stayed on after the war; a man very fond of a dram. It was a quarter-bottle morning, lunchtime, afternoon. What Dravina drank at night I never saw. He got me to join him dram for dram, and me but fifteen years of age. It went on for a year! I was doing two thirds the work, thickening my liver, and taking only half my money home! It was mother put her foot down. She went to Willie MacKay, down on the farm, and asked if he had work. 'It's nae sae much the money,' she said 'but Dravina's going to kill the boy with drink!' 'I'll take the lad on for three months,' Willie said, 'Time of the lambing and the ploughing – I'll learn him.'

I liked the farm, I liked the animals, I liked old Willie and I stayed on fifteen years. I liked Willie MacKay very much, in fact, if his nephew hadn't come in to take over the farm, I'd still be up there now. That man was what I call a shit! So that was the end of that! Fifteen pounds one and six a month I got. I'd been getting two pounds a week from Dravina. He was dead inside two years. The Germans broke his heart but it was the drink that killed him.

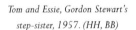

Tom and Essie, Gordon Stewart's step-sister, 1957. (HH, BB)

On the farm, each week I gave my wage, all but ten shillings, to my mother, Joanne, up at Remarstaig. She did some hawking but I was the wage earner. You could enjoy yourself on ten shillings in those days. With half a day on Saturday, you could go down to Lairg by bus, have a couple of pints, go to a hop, buy a sandwich and pie or a packet of chips, and still get home with three or four bob in your pocket. I lived at home then. There was us, Ailidh Dall and his family, and Peter Stewart and his family. We had three houses up there.

Essie Stewart was Blind Sandy's granddaughter. We were brought up like brother and sister. We were just like that! Snap! The two of us. One would never spill milk on the other. All our lives it was, where I went she went and where she went, I went. Then Eddie Davies came in and he broke it up. We were the only youngsters up at Remarstaig, so when she went away the joy of living, for me like, went out of it. I was working five and a half days down on the farm and a big extra burden came on my shoulders at home. All the work was there for me to do. There was no one else to do it. They were all getting on, or very old. I had to take Ailidh Dall out to the stable to the dry toilet, carry water for washing, bathing, drinking; do the peats, do the fire, feed the horses. Eddie Davies! He came in and did the dirty. That's what I thought and, deep down, I think it yet. So like Essie then I married out – married a cousin of Eddie Davies!

They were never well-suited – Essie and Eddie. I used to go out with them sometimes, and they were always bloody arguing: stuck at each other's throat twenty-four hours a day. She's a bit debauched now, but she was a really bonnie lassie in her young days. He was the first man came along. She should have had more patience. Eddie Davies – he'd cause trouble in a graveyard. If he got in one of his moods he'd just belt you – whoever you were! Essie had a hard life with him! Too much drink. He earned a lot of money at the pearls – but what came today, went today with no thought of tomorrow. That was Eddie Davies – this year, next year, sometime, never! But there we are – she made her nest with him and had her kids by him. And I married his cousin.

Essie's mother, Michie, was my mother's sister-in-law. She died in the Davies' house in Ardgay. And I'll tell you this, they weren't left empty-handed when she went. There were big times down there after Michie died, cars bought, meals taken, drink. Among the Travellers, the daughter that stayed to look after the parents would always get the house and most of the money. That was Michie, that was the way of it with the Stewarts. And it was the same with the Williamsons – unmarried – the money passed straight down at home. I've seen pockets thick with fivers! 'It's always best' old Jock Williamson used to say 'to keep your money in a box then you can aye count it! And I'm damned if you can do that in a bank!' But before he died he put a pound or two in the bank as well!

The crofters called us 'The Summer Walkers' but it was horses, more than us, that walked. Down in Argyll we heard of the Travellers pushing prams – but in Sutherland no Traveller would ever set out without horses, at least one good yoke. Some of us would be walking round about, sure enough, but the horse was king with us like.

Each cart had what we called 'the wee box', a kist about one foot high. And the wife would sit on it, when she was cooking and she'd have what we called 'the meat box' beside her. In the tent there'd always be the door, the stove, and herself at the centre, sitting there with 'the wee box'. For the money it was, and all the mother's personal things. Very precious it was and she sat on it. In the meat box was the food, with a section for cutlery. Mother would sit there at the stove and hand the food round, on a plate, or on a paper she laid down like a tablecloth. She'd cook with a pan on the stove, or a trenny on the fire, that's a three-legged cooking pot. A trenny holds its balance on rough ground, like a milking stool. It's having a third leg short that does the trick!

Everything was very well organised in a bow-tent: with us, a big bow-tent was a home from home. The sleeping would be at the two ends. The older folk would have a tartan curtain across and at the bigger end the youngsters would 'make do'! 'Love, fight, or die' we used to say. Rough and tumble there would be – like lion cubs! But most times I was on my own, no brothers, no sisters. We'd take dry straw out with us for bedding. If the site was wet, we'd lay down bracken or heather, then a blanket, or maybe a ground

Gordon Stewart leading his family's pony 'Meggie', with Black Anne riding, and Peter Stewart's family following behind, 1957. (HH, BB)

sheet. Sleeping was no bother for us like; it was gaye comfy, especially if there was a big blow. Rain was no problem, a good canvas was waterproof for years. Smoke would keep the midges out!

But camping for us was work – not holiday! Once I'd got the tent up and laid out the floor, I'd see mum and Black Anne in; then I'd go out to tend the horses, get sticks and peats, dig the drainage ditch, bring water in . . . it was a bitch. There I was, fifteen years of age, working like a man with three hands, and needing a bloody good crowbar that we never had! I've seen us tramping twenty miles a day. Cruel days. We'd have one stop, to give the horses drink and food. Twenty miles a day. That was my life. Big tarpaulins we had – fifteen by fifteen feet – the same size as the farmers used. We'd tie the boughs and drape the tarpaulins over, with the stove and the door in the middle. The chimney would come through the roof and we'd put a wee mesh of chicken wire down to stop sparks holing the canvas. The horse-harness, the tool box, the stake and all that would be put in behind the tartan with the old folk.

Sometimes our family would travel out alone, Black Anne, my mother and myself, but normally we'd travel with three yokes and the three families together. That's how we were when Hamish Henderson came up to see us. We met him first at Tuitem in Glen Oykel. He came not an hour too soon! The Traveller days were dying fast. He came to get old songs and stories – and he got plenty. The Stewarts were never short of things like that. Some days, Old Sandy could still walk behind the cart, he'd hold a chain at the back, but he was blind as the night and he only knew where he was by the sounds of the road – like a train-driver – he knew all the sounds and the gradients, the bridges and waterfalls, but at the camp there was nothing he could do but tell stories. He'd brush down the horses to keep himself warm! It was prayers, piping, stories and songs and that was it for Ailidh Dall! He was a good father to me like and sometimes he'd pass the peats to Black Anne, but that was it! It was Essie and I did the work.

It was no life for me – build a tent and travel on, build a tent and travel on. Camping at a place like Tongue or Melness you had three or four days, but sometimes we were moving every day, and I was the only young man there to work. And some places we'd be working tin, ten hours a day. Wind and rain two nights in three! Cars hooting. Horses bolting! Things never stopped for me like, and bad got worse – because the Stewarts stayed out on the road when the old folk weren't fit to hawk, not even fit to walk the road. Breaking camp – I'd have to hump them up into the cart – Black Anne and Ailidh Dall. Then sitting still, they'd get freezing cold, or the water would be collecting up around their arses. So we'd have to call a stop and get them down and warm them up with a fire and a cup of tea. They were hardy folk, they wouldn't complain – but after I started work, I was glad to call it a day on the road.

Without me, they all stayed at home. They couldn't go by themselves and there were no young ones coming on. We'd meet the Skye Stewarts on the road, they were all right, they had plenty young men. They could put up a tent in minutes between them – but me, I'd be struggling an hour by myself! One man with two fifteen-by-fifteen tarpaulins in a gale – that's Charlie Chaplin! A bow-tent is strong once it's up – but it's getting there! You can't zip it up like a modern tent. So it was all work at the camp and then out on the crofts cutting peats, carting peats, harvesting, clipping neeps – helping out the crofters who lived far out.

A lot of the crofts had just a widow woman on her own – with some it was the First World War, with some it was the Second and with some the menfolk would be working away from home. Oh they liked to see us come. They'd feed us well. A hard old life it was for them but they were very kind people. When I was a coalman I used to meet again the folk we knew when I was young, and they would mind the old days and speak about Old Suzie, Black Anne and my mother and, to tell the truth, a lump would come up into my throat. And I'd stop the lorry afterwards and think about the old days and I'd feel old Sandy's arm upon my shoulder and think of myself walking him round the camp, telling him what was going on and all that.

I wish I knew his stories better than I do – I'm no story-teller – Norman MacLean he's the man for stories! You need to hear them regular, or you forget. There's only four or five us speak Gaelic now. I see the television, but I can go a year without speaking to a soul. Though saying that, I used to use Gaelic on the coal – down at the coal-yard they said I was the best salesman as ever they had. The *ceard* was bred a salesman, you see. He had to be – a travelling salesman is what he was. Going round the houses, talk was half of everything we did. I had the Gaelic and speaking to the wifies, pleasing them was bred in us; the knowledge how to please was what we had. Taking round the coal, for me, was hawking near enough – a different face would come up every hour and a good halt be taken most places, out there in the west. But now all that is in the past – it's the Orange Trousers that I have and plenty overtime!

Six years I was a tinsmith on the road. It was my uncles, Brian Stewart and Peter Stewart who learned me the craft. But mainly it's a thing you learn by doing, and most of all you learn by your mistakes. The first things that I made were the cups the crofters would leave beside the well. And I used to make mugs for the children; from the Tate and Lyle syrup tins, green and gold, with the lion and the bees all round. I'd just turn the lip and fit a handle on. Going to a party, the children would take their own mugs, and syrup tins were just the thing. The mothers used to keep them for us, for when we came round, and old corned beef tins: we'd burn them down to get the solder out.

By the age of twelve, I was near enough as good as Brian and Peter, and the womenfolk started selling everything I made. One day the orders would come in, the next day the women would take the orders back. We made three different kinds of milking pails, we made big pails for water, small pails, skimmers, milk-basins, creaming bowls, steamers for cloutie dumplings, sieves, basins, baths for babies and for washing clothes. Those were the big things. Then we made jugs, cups, ladles, spatulas for the frying pans. I've known us at it from half-past seven in the morning till late into the evening, when a rush was on. Work like that was hard on the eyes.

The tools we had were the stake, a mallet, a compass, the ratch-stick – which was used instead of a rule – the hammer, a rising hammer, and the switcher, a piece of wood to beat the metal on, that was. And you needed solder sticks, a soldering bolt, and roset which is like a resin, used with the solder. Why the anvil was called a stake, I don't know, but it stands in the ground like a T-shaped cross – and sitting there maybe it looks like the Cross on which they crucified our Lord. The Jehovah's Witnesses call the Cross – the Stake. But I think it's called a stake because it's not a big anvil like a blacksmith's, a tin-working anvil is like a three-legged pick-axe and you just stake it in the ground to work on it. There was a murder down in Perthshire, when a Townsley stove in the head of a Stewart with a Traveller stake.

March was the new year for us like – we'd get fresh tin from Adam Munro, down in Lairg and hit the road. A box of eighty sheets of tin, three foot by two, would weigh about a hundredweight. We'd split the box between the two families – Peter's and Brian's. Whoever was the richest would buy the first box and the other would buy the second box around June. There was a profit to be made in tin in those days. We worked long days and we made money at the tin. We had to. It had to see us through the winter. The Williamsons used to get their tin from Inverness, or Wallace and Fraser, in Tain. Out in the west, if we ran low, we'd share things out, or we'd send a letter down to Greenock for tin and up it would come by train. And Simon Mackintosh, who was blacksmith up in Strath Gairloch, he used to keep tin after Alec John Williamson's father asked him.

The Williamsons were always on the lookout for lead. If they saw a pewter pot in somebody's window they'd ask them, 'How much do you want for that?' And maybe they'd buy it, and keep it for solder, or they'd sell it on. We all had to make do. But a thing like roset we had to buy – pine or fiddle resin was no use with the solder. Looking back, of course, that pewter and lead must have done a few brains and blood-vessels damage. I apologise on behalf of my ancestors! Hindsight is a wonderful thing.

Top. Typical utilitarian items made by Traveller tinsmiths – a small pail and small basin, made by Lindsay Williamson, 1950s; a spatula and a pea-strainer made by Willie MacPhee, 1976. (TN)

Below. Close-up of the punctured base of Willie MacPhee's pea-strainer. Note the six-petal, floral pattern: it is identical to that found on early medieval bowls in the find known as St Ninian's Treasure. (TN)

A speciality I had was making steam-pudding tins. Cloutie dumplings were a favourite with the crofter women and with us and what you needed was a pudding-tin about seven inches across with a lid, with a hole, and that would be put inside a tattie-pan or cauldron. And we made ovens – two round pails which fitted together. The first would be about a foot deep and the second would be about three inches deep, with a good rim. The cake, or chicken, would be put inside the big pail and the small pail fitted on top; then the whole oven put on the stove, or into a good peat fire, and hot ash would be put inside the rim of the top pail, so that the oven got good all round heat. We called them Dutch Ovens. You could get a good roast, or a good bake out of that. The tin we worked was normally about a sixteenth of an inch thick, too thin for a coal fire, but with sticks, or peats, or ash, our ovens would see a winter through, and pots would last one to three years. Rust was the problem.

When we came home at the back-end, all the smithing gear was polished, greased and put away for the spring. Tin was never a winter job – the damp would eat into the iron and rust off the tin. Everything we sold was newly made as orders came in on the road. You needed the warm weather to make a go of the tin.

I'd never speak against the Travellers in the pub or that, or back off at the time of the fists getting closed – but the Traveller days are finished. You need a car up here. A horse is just a luxury these days. I like my car – I've driven down from Bonar Bridge to Inverness in thirty-five minutes. That would have taken us three days by yoke!

My marriage broke up when I was away doing the fencing. Three children we had. Ten years I was a fencer, all over the Highlands and Islands. Out there in the west I could speak the Gaelic again – and the kind of money I

Left. Gordon Stewart's bungalow, Bonar Bridge, 1995. (TN)

Right. Gordon and his wife Frances Stewart, 1995. (TN)

could earn would turn a tinsmith green. Very fit I was in those days. You had to be. But then I came back here, and I married Frances MacNeill — settled Travellers they are, two generations back. Frances had a daughter of her own, grown up like my own children. We were too old to start a new family so we've tried to adopt.

Frances and I, we would give our left arms to have a child, both, but the Social Services say 'No'! 'Too old!' is what they say. We've been married now for fifteen years, we have a house, a car, I earn good money, we're just a stone's throw from the school — but 'no' they say 'no adoption!'. Foster yes, 'we will allow you foster children,' they say — but then it's me says 'no'! I cannot bear the thought of having a baby here for just a month or two, or even worse — a year! To have a bairn and give it back away would break my heart. We would give our child love. We could not have children here, would come and go, like business! We'll take a child for life — or not at all. That's what the adverts say about a dog! So why not us? We have the woods, the golf club here, nowhere could you find a finer place to bring children up. Yet they say 'No!' and there is nothing we can do — not nowadays.

You see, I was an adopted child myself. It was Essie and Lindsay Williamson got me adopted. They set things up — same as they did for Essie Stewart, my step-sister. The Williamsons lived up in the birchwood, above Edderton. They had five children born that died. They got to know about an unmarried lassie with a bairn she did not want, so they set it up for me. There was nothing official, no papers signed, no social-workers — nobody outside the families knew anything about it. I was taken up to Remarstaig, to my mother, Joanne Stewart. Joanne was not old, she was still young, but she was not married and she was looking for a child of her own. She was the daughter, had to stay at home, she had to look after Black Anne and fortune blessed her, some might say, with me! Joanne had a nice wee house she needed filled, and I'll never regret that I went up there to Remarstaig. She saved me from the dung-heap. She loved me well and I loved her. They were always short of money, but they would have given up their lives for me.

My real mother went away to New Zealand. She was a Morrison. She got the hell out of it, as they say. My father was, I think, a shepherd from up Loch Eriboll. Things were different then, it's not like today — with welfare benefits and no one minding what you do. My mother was herself — and paid the price. I never knew her face, or heard her voice. Water finds its level so they say, it is the lights on things that change.

Horses. If you've grown up with horses, worked horses — the thought of them, the smell of them, stays with you. Did you ever hear how the Traveller men would test if a mare was set with foal? 'Take a small quantity of water and pour it into an ear. If she's in young she'll shake her head, if not, she'll shake her whole body.' Easy. I've seen that! It was the horses, more than the tin, gave the Traveller men pleasure in their livelihood. I worked serious with horses from the time I was about ten. I'd lead them, groom them, harness, yoke them, break them. For four or five years I bought and sold. The Stewarts would sometimes break horses but it was the Williamsons who were the real horsemen. Great crack you'd get from Peter and Johnnie, about horses doing this and that and all they'd bought and sold and broken over fifty years.

The usual thing for the Stewarts was 'buy in the west, sell in the east'. I've seen us go out with one horse and come back with five or six. There was a big horse sale in Lairg, in October, and we'd bring them home for that. They might come back to carry deer, or be off to the knacker's yard. Whatever it was, we'd double our money first, or make a fiver – or try!

Almost every croft had a horse in the forties. The Ministry of Agriculture used to take a stallion round, and it was mostly us would buy and break the foals. We'd get a field and let them run free all summer. We wouldn't put a hand on them. Winter was the time to break the horses in. In the spring we'd sell, or take them back out to the west – maybe back to the very croft they came from if a crofter liked the line he had. All the Travellers aimed to set out in the spring with a grand young horse, then a crofter with an old horse would see the young horse and come down to the camp for a deal, or he'd offer us a few pounds for a swap. Age goes with age, that's what we found. An old crofter would rarely want a frisky yearling – he'd go for a well-tried mare in middle-age, whereas the younger men would take a filly, or a colt, fresh on the bit.

To make the deal, you'd barter – then the big spit on the hand, a shake of the hands and 'good luck' we'd say, or 'good luck to you – and the horse!' Then the money would be passed. Whatever the deal was – exchange, part change, or straight cash, whether I was selling, or you were selling – they'd always have to cross our hand with silver. It would be a half-crown then, a florin or a two shilling piece. And you know where the Travellers used to put that? The silver from the deal that moved a horse? They'd put it inside the lining of their bonnet, or their cap. 'The luck-penny' it was called and put straight away in the bonnet. It was always silver like. That closed the deal. That was what the Stewarts did.

After the handshake there was no comeback – that was the deal done, that was the guarantee. Though I've known us take horses back. If we came round a croft three months after a sale and the crofter said 'That horse you sold is a wicked brute!', or 'I cannae hauld him back!', we'd take the horse, give what we gave and then re-break the horse or work him with the other horses and bring him back to Lairg for auction.

We got a lot of horses from the Duchess of Westminster at Achfary. They had horses up on the hill just running wild. She'd send Alec Ross out to bring the horses down to a big fank where we'd take our luck with four or five – some young mares, but mostly stallions, young colts, because up on the hill, at eighteen months or two years, they'd be mounting the mares and serving them and the Duchess wanted rid of them – she didn't want inbreeding in her stock. She was a good woman to us like.

The Traveller men would go down to the fank and look them over. We'd lean over the wall and watch them round: then we'd lay nooses down, and whip them tight like a lasso – capture each horse by a front leg. Then we'd take them by the nose and put a bag over their heads; after that we'd get a halter and a rope on. 'A devil rope,' we used to call it, one man on either side. It would soon slip tight down round the nose, to close the nostrils. The horse would kick and rear but soon get winded. As it got weaker, we'd slacken the rope. That was it! After a few days they'd be calm enough to be tethered behind the carts and on we'd go.

We got those horses for pennies – to take them away – but they were big spunkie horses, many of them. The Travellers liked to break a big horse, they liked a difficult horse nobody else could handle. They liked a horse would make a story run for years! We took a kick or two, but the Sutherland Travellers never went in for horse racing like they do in Ireland. Horses were work and livelihood and that was that. The nearest thing that I ever saw to racing, was when we'd be going into Thurso for the horse fair and two or three yokes were on the road – then I've seen us canter up behind a yoke, for a joke, and we'd canter side by side, or over-take, pretend to race, enjoy ourselves! We'd do all that – but I never saw a Traveller let horses go, though I have seen good racing over there in Caithness.

We didn't cut horses ourselves. We'd bring them back to Lairg, to Alec Grey at Culvert Farm, out by Shinness. He specialised, he wasn't a vet, but he'd cut horses all his life. With a knife, he'd cut the balls clean out. Good big balls they'd often be! No anaesthetic, just cut, take, and cut again! He'd seal the wound with a red hot iron. 'Keep them,' he'd say, 'spotless – for a day or two,' the horses he meant – 'with clean bedding and good food, they'll be right as rain in a day or twa!'

You know the Travellers have the cant language? Well up here we had the *Beurla Reagaird* as well, so all the old Travellers had their secret words of command for horses. That was all right for them like – but when the horses were sold on to the crofters there could be problems. Out there in the west, in the old days, it was all Gaelic, but there was no system for the horses. It was just like a shepherd with his dog – every man had his own way of doing things.

My uncles used to run through the words that they used with a buyer but any horse finds three languages difficult! On the big farms in the east it was different, the horsemen had very strict rules for dealing with horses. Working on the farm at Lairg, I learned a bit about what they call the Horseman's Word; that was a big thing down the east coast but by the time I got it, the horseman's days were gone, just like the Travellers'. Hamish Henderson, he's a great man for the Horseman's Word. There was big ceremony with that in the old days in the stable, or out in the barns, or under the oak tree.

Now I'll tell you something about Hamish Henderson. He came up to see us and get the tapes of Ailidh Dall, but old Sandy – he didn't take to Hamish when he walked in first and that's the truth. Hamish was a heathen coming in – singing on a Sunday, recording on a Sunday. Asking Sandy to pipe on a Sunday! That's what he did – come in on a Sunday. That was not on with the Stewarts. Sunday was the Day of Rest. I'm not a religious man myself but even now I make that my day of rest, Sunday. Hamish really put his arse out when he came in that day. He reversed out saying 'I'm a heathen myself like' and Ailidh Dall said, 'If you come back Monday, Tuesday, Wednesday, I'll tell you your stories – but I'll not be telling stories the day.' And that was that. It was the same on the road and up at Remarstaig; my mother wouldn't let the grannies wash a plate on Sundays. On Saturdays, I'd have to cart two days' water from the well, and if the water ran out on a Sunday – thirsty we went! Four wooden casks filled to the brim I'd see into the house on a Saturday. Monday morn I'd start again and there'd be four hours of washing up for us to do. The Sutherland folk took religion very serious. No wireless was played. They were very very strict and so were we.

It was two years later the Big Fellow came back with his 'Big Box' to get his recordings! The second time he came was with Norman MacLean. That was at Altnaharra. He's famous now. It was Norman broke the ice. He played the pipes. And he'd play for Sandy and then Sandy'd play for him. I don't know what day it was that year, except it was not a Sunday! 'You know this tune?' Norman would say, and off he'd go – he was only a young loon at the time. I'll never forget Norman's face as he watched old Sandy tuning up – back and forth, eyes closed, feeling for the drones. I watched his eyes grow big, his face swell up, his fingers start – as though he was playing Sandy's pipes himself! Then Sandy gave it else – ooh he could play! Norman had been to the Mod, he was some piper, and he knew Sandy was good! I saw the smile break out on his face as the music came out – oooh Sandy was good that day. He was putting on a show for the young loon and for Hamish. Now, Norman's a good piper, like no other piper I ever heard, but sometimes when I hear him play, I hear the old man coming through – that's what I think. I hear old Sandy playing! Ooh they

Joanne Stewart by the stove and chimney of her bow-tent, Sutherland, 1957. (HH, BB)

got on very well, those two – and Norman had the Gaelic, you see, but Hamish, he was a learner. Well, Norman only stayed two or three nights but he broke the ice with his pipes and after that we all got on fine with Big Shamus, Shamus Mhor. That's what we called him. I'm just telling you – that's how it was, for us, like.

Ailidh Dall had a hole in the wall up at Remarstaig, by the fireplace, and in the hole he kept his chanter. Of an evening he'd sit listening to the wireless and if he heard a new tune he liked he'd switch off. Then he'd start humming, fingering – then he'd pull the chanter out from the hole and there he'd have the first six or seven notes of it . . . And the whole night he wouldn't talk to nobody till he had the whole thing right: back and forth he'd go, working his fingers across the chanter – blind he might have been but everything he heard went down into the computer, as you'd say today. He'd be learning or piping every night of his life.

Sandy also had the old stories and it was after that first hiccup that Hamish did the recording in the Tongue Hotel and in pubs and big houses on the road. We went into them, because Hamish needed electricity for the tape-recorder. Batteries were no good for Ailidh Dall, some of his stories would go on for three hours! The Stewart family didn't drink, not drink much in those days. The pubs would send out a bucket sometimes if a party of Travellers stopped – but we weren't welcome in the most of the drinking places then and we had little enough money for the booze. They weren't steeped in it like me today. Just a beer or two. So when Hamish took old Sandy down to the Hotel and handed round the drams, he opened up and talked and the Gaelic songs came out of him. I mind Ailidh Dall asking how tall Hamish was. 'Six foot four' I said. 'A strapping lad,' old Sandy said, 'a great tall bugger with a black box you are! But it's a grand fellow you have with you here . . .' Meaning Norman! He was sounding him out you see. Anyway after that, the stories and the music came out and they went away in the black box. We never heard them back.

Hamish didn't have a driving licence in those days, nor does he yet – but that summer he drove this van all over Sutherland! A40 it was. It was Bobby Botsford's van. That was 1957. Strictly legal it was, because with the Suez Crisis there was petrol rationing, and learner-drivers got permission to drive, like in the war. Suez was a great boost for Hamish Henderson! He told us so himself! Oooh he could drive that van – get petrol like nobody else! Never was Hamish short of a gallon or less than the full shilling, as you might say! We had a great time in the van – I was chief mechanic, that's what he said.

Sometimes Hamish would camp with us; he had this wee ridge-pole tent, and sometimes he'd go off on his own to stay in the hotels. I mind travelling back one night from Armadale to Melvich, after a long session at the Munros, recording songs, when the headlights failed! We only had sidelights! Those wee glow-worm lights A40's had, like nothing! It's a steep and windy road – there we were – rough-stone, single track, black mist, no white lines – but Hamish, he was happy as a tomcat with a stack of drams inside him! Sixty, seventy mile an hour – out of this world! Ailidh Dall was in the front and suddenly he saw, or thought he saw a bright light coming out of the darkness! 'Is that a car?' he shouted. 'No!' we all shouted back 'It's not a car! It's the Strathie Inn!' At that, of course, Hamish started breaking hard! 'No stopping, Hamish!' Sandy shouted, 'You've had enough! Drive on, drive on, Mr Henderson!' We made it like! Slack wiring was the cause of it!

You know the 'Old Horseman's Farewell to His Horse and Plough'?

Noo whorday is drawin near
An I mun sune leave ye
I worked ye baith for mony a year
Tae pairt wi ye does grieve me.

Admired by a' when in the yoke
Twa beauties side by side
There's nane I ken can equal you
In a' the kintry-side.

Wi' glossy skin and harness clean
And brasses like the stars
Not like some that I ha'e seen
Bespattered o'er wi' glore.

But now I'm weary doon the brae
My limbs are stiff and bent
I've got my leave, I've pu'd my day
But I ha'e naithin to repent!

That's a country piece, not a Traveller piece, but that was the way of it with Ailidh Dall; and one day, I like to think that'll be the way of it for me.

Part Two
The Pearl-fishers

Eddie Davies

SIXTY YEARS IN THE RIVER

*Britain excels for crops and trees and is will suited for feeding cattle and beasts of
burden. It is remarkable for plentiful springs and rivers abounding in fish—the salmon
and the eel are particularly common. Seals are very frequently taken, and dolphins and
even whales, besides various kinds of shellfish, such as mussels, in which are often found
excellent pearls of all colours: red, purple, blue and green, but mostly white.*

THE VENERABLE BEDE

In the fifties, the pearl-fishing still gave us a good living: my father, my
brothers, my uncles, we spent all summer on the rivers. The hawking, the
tinsmithing, the horse-dealing were dying then – the Traveller life, up here, was
done – but there was still money in the pearls. So when Essie Stewart and I got
married in 1959, she didn't give up the Traveller life, she came away with me
– pearl-fishing. Twenty-five years on the road we had. No horses for us, we
always had cars, or a van: the Pearl-fishers, the Davies, that's who we two were,
and the four children – they came in on the holidays. Good times, bad times,
but if I'd kept just a few of the best round pearls, each year, since I was young
– I'd be a wealthy man the day. A couple hundred thousand pounds! Not joking!
But we needed the money. Day in day out we needed the money – so here I sit
in a council house, with a Metro on the lawn waiting for its MOT, and nothing
but two disability pensions! One for my back, one from the RAF. I've got the
telly and a video. What more could I want? The Lottery! What do I get? A visit
from the Social Work to chat about my drinking. The expenses that man gets to
visit me!

But give and take, I'd have my life the same again. Good times we
had. Pearl-fishing's a thing gets in the blood – every river different, every
morning different, every mussel lifted promising a pearl. Bring me a little jar
stuffed full with cotton wool and tell me you've got pearls – and you'll see a
smile break my face. Pearls. My father's eyes would flash at the very mention
of the word. I see him now!

The river pearl – people don't know about them. Every river
breeds its own – colour – lustre – sheen – texture. Show me a pearl and I'll

*Eddie Davies, on the road,
Sutherland, 1995. (TN)*

Eddie Davies searching shallow water in the river Evelix for pearl-mussels, Sutherland, 1995. (TN)

name the river! I boast? Why should I not boast! Eddie Davies, the pearl-fisher! It's sixty years since I found my first pearl in the Naver! Aah it was a beauty. My father gave me thirty shillings for it. That'd be what – two hundred pounds the day? It was he who spent the money. No wonder I'm a man who likes his dram – but I'll tell you this, a lifetime in thigh-boots has given me a knowledge of the Highland rivers and the Scottish pearl that only Bill Abernethy can rival now, and he's no friend of mine.

It was Abernethy found the Big Pearl, down in the Tay. After that – goldrush. Murder. They were coming up in droves. People were leaving their jobs. Eleven thousand pounds it was valued at. They were going down in wet-suits. They slaughtered the rivers. They'd work the river like a factory – big gangs of them. They slaughtered the Tay, they came up to the Spey, they slaughtered it. They came up here to our rivers and they slaughtered them. It was greed – it was the new A9, it was the motorcar, you see, in the old days it was all walk, camp out, walk on – just two or three of us. Like farmers, here and there we'd pause and leave a bed undisturbed for future years. But these were cowboys! By nineteen eighty, the old-time pearl-fishers up here in Sutherland, we were picking at a carcass. It was the Buffalo all over again! Don't get me started on that, it breaks my heart – but I'll talk to you about the pearls.

Most of what I know, I learned myself, or picked it up from my father – but I'm not a man afeared of books, we had the Cairncross catalogue, and from the library we've got out books on the bivalve mollusc, on pearls, and jewellery. A pearl is a by-product of an eco-system. It depends on geology, on rainfall, the flow of rivers, on the life-cycle of the salmon and the sea-trout, on sunlight, on the river-mussel, and on time. A pearl, you see, is just a grain of sand, or aggro-parasite, that has got stuck against the side of a shell, or inside the flesh, of a mussel, and been rubbed and ground round and round for years. This body, this irritant, whatever it is to start with, soon picks up a lustrous coating from the mucus exuded by the mussel – to stop the itching! It's the same mucus with which the mussel makes its shell. The outside of a shell is always dark and rough but the inside is always smoothed by the flesh to mother-of-pearl. A mussel will try to get rid of a pearl but it can't, or if it does, the pearl gets lost. A pearl grows slowly bigger, or goes back to the sand. The pearl is an entirely natural creation, I've tried to culture pearls, put little grains of sand inside young shells and left them years but not once have I succeeded, as far as I know. Nature is a wonderful thing. In Japan they culture pearls round beads.

The river-mussel can live to a good age. Some people say forty years, some a hundred. They can grow well over six inches long, two inches deep, and four inches wide. I've seen mussels bigger than my hand; we call the big shells, braxie shells. They grow in great mussel-beds, in slack water but they're not 'pearl shells'. If I find a big braxie shell I just leave it, or throw it away. We leave the big beds. Age, not size, is the thing with the river mussel, though nothing is certain about finding a pearl. I've marked shells on and off all my life. To test how they grow – but the big gangs, they mark shells to show where they've been! The Oykel can produce a good pearl in five years; in the Spey it takes a good deal longer. I don't know why. I'd say it takes ten years for good pearls to grow in the Spey. It must be to do with the minerals in the water.

Eddie Davies the pearl-fisher, Grantown-on-Spey, 1976. (TN)

Essie Davies and Mary,
Grantown-on-Spey, 1976. (TN)

There are two main types of mussel-shell in the Scottish rivers – the more black and the more brown – the black shells are the best for pearls. On most rivers, like the Naver, the brown shells are down towards the sea, the black shells higher up.

In the old days, I've heard people would eat the river-mussel, and they must have found pearls. In Britain it was the Romans started it – down in England. You can get pearls down there, in the old rivers in the west and in the north. You used to be able to. But they got, what we're getting – years ago! Nothing! The Roman emperor heard about the river pearls and he ordered, 'Get the army at it!' Julius Caesar, I think, it was. Cleopatra, she used to drop a pearl into a goblet of wine and drink it down, but they would have been sea-pearls she drank, from the Persian Gulf or Aden. You remember Mad Mitch!

Acid will eat a pearl away to nothing, even the chlorine in tap-water can ruin a good pearl. I've lost a pearl or two but I've never destroyed one, never drunk one. It would be like sacrilege to me like. They come with a skin of slime from the flesh of the mussel. You can wipe it off with your fingers. You must use river water, or rainwater, to clean a freshwater pearl, not tap-water; then they should be worn, kept moist on the neck, or put away in cotton wool and wiped with baby oil now and again.

In the river, what you look for is an ugly shell. I know which shells will have a pearl as soon as they come out of the water. What I look for is a crooked shell, a deformed shell, bruised-up like on one side, a twisted shell. Alec John Williamson, he has one of the pearl-fisher songs:

I'm a poor humble rhymer from the parish of Kyle
I've travelled this country for many a long mile
I've been to Brig Orchy and Kingside as weel
And I've looked all around for this wonderful pearl.

One day out in Strathie I chanced for to meet
A keeper of rabbits coming hame aff his beat
Bent over the water at me he did yell
'Who gave you permission to fish here for shells?'

Just then in my glass I chanced for to look
And saw in the water a left-handed crook!
As I went for to land it he drew a bead on my heid
And it sank to the bottom — that wonderful pearl.

Next morning I rose and it started to snaw
I packed up my tent on the road for to go
Away to Drumbeg making baskets to sell
But all I could think of was that wonderful pearl.

So come all you pearl-fishers that now hear my song
I shan't say a bad thing about where you belong!
Farewell to Drumochter — it's there I did dwell
Farewell to the Black Mount and that wonderful pearl!

'A left-handed crook' — that's very good! Alec John's a very good singer. He makes up his own songs, but we don't know who made that one. The Black Mount, that's down in Perthshire. Old Willie MacPhee, Big Willie they call him, he was twice over the Black Mount as a boy, with the snow on the ground and himself in bare feet! He did some pearl-fishing and he used to pipe up here at the Falls of Shin. But he didn't fish up here, he only fished down there, in his own rivers.

A pearl-fisherman needs a 'rod' and a 'glass' and that's it. We always made our rods of hazel wood. One wood we never used was rowan, a rowan tree must be left to stand in the ground where it grew. The Travellers would never cut rowan boughs for a bow-tent; hazel or the ash, yes, but not for us the rowan tree. It's a superstition, goes way back. It's a beautiful tree.

My rod would be a hazel, maybe four, maybe six, maybe nine feet tall – an inch and a half to two inches thick. I like to have a slight bend two thirds along the shaft, a kink – for luck and for balance – for the pleasure of the hand. You slit the thick end with a knife, as though you were making a clothes peg. Then you bind the upper end of the cleft with binder-twine or string, to hold a spring in the 'claw' and stop any splitting of the shaft. Firm, with just a hint of give, the claw should be. I pare my claws to a beak shape, to grasp the mussel. They stand up, feeding in the sunlight, among the stones in the bed of the river, and they come away easy enough. There's a knack to it.

My 'glass' is just a wooden box, with a glass bottom; it cuts out the side-light and allows you to see deep in the water. My box leaks, so I keep casting water to one side. It's habit with me. It gives your arm a break. Some people use a big jug with a glass-bottom, like a foghorn; but I've always used a box. I make them myself; just three in all my days I've had, I'm very superstitious.

Waders, or bare legs, is what we'd wear. Good waders can be very expensive! Bare legs it was when we were young – and the stones could be very hard on the toes! It's shallow water that we mostly fish but sometimes in a river with deep pools we use a boat. It was on the Spey that I first tried a boat for deep water fishing. My father never used a boat. But I said, 'Why not a boat? Why not try the big pools from a boat with a nine foot rod?' I went to a sawmill and asked for a few bits of wood: five feet by eight inches was what I needed. I made a box-wood frame and stretched a canvas under it – just like a tent but upside down. Oooh the old fellow was all against it! 'It'll sink! You'll drown!' he was saying, but up to the big pool I went, six or seven feet of fast flowing water! Five o'clock. Beautiful summer morning, the sun rising. We always liked to work early before the salmon fishers would come on about ten o'clock.

We carried the boat and shoved it down the bank, onto the water. No oars, drifting down, hanging on to the branches. I tied the boat to a willow tree and swung round on the rope. I mind feeling the cool of the river come up on my face – and then I saw them! Even without my glass I could see them! 'They're sitting there like rows of crows!' I shouted. 'Don't worry about the bloody crows,' my father hissed out from the bank, 'get the buggers up before you sink!' Paradise. I've still got the rod upstairs here. It's nine foot six, and I've kept it all these years, for memories. I started work. Looking down through the glass, looking for the twisted ones, only lifting the crooked shells. Looking and lifting. Ooh what shells I got! The time goes quickly on the water. Suddenly, I heard my father shout, 'you're going to swamp!' The boat was sinking! Not

Top. The Davies family on a pearlfishing trip to Cookstown, Northern Ireland, 1959, (ED)

Middle. Edward Davies near the river Spey, Inverness-shire, with a family of Travelling pearl-fishers Jimmy and Katie Reid from Fife, c. 1970. (ED)

Bottom. Eddie Davies' sisters, Phammie and Violet, on the road by Loch Lomond, c. 1962. (ED)

with leaks but with the weight of shells! 'Pull me in, Da,' I said 'pull me in!'

It was like the draught of fishes on the sea of Galilee. He had a fire going and we sat down. 'You've pearls there.' He said. 'Keep your thieving hands aff my shells!' I said, even though I knew that every one of them would go to him! Aaah – I drank my cup of tea. Then I started opening. Before the salmon fishers came on, I'd filled my bonnet full of pearls, beautiful Spey pearls. But I was young! I didn't know about Cairncross, or the real value of the pearls. I said to my father, 'You want to buy my pearls?' 'Twenty-five pounds,' he said, 'the lot.' 'Good God,' I came back, 'there's a hundred pounds in here, or more!' But no – he would not budge. And that's what I got for what is still the best day of my life for pearls! Maybe that pool had never been fished, it was deep, far up, very dangerous water. The find of a lifetime, and I got twenty-five pounds! That was the way the Davies did it! My father liked the selling and he liked to keep it to himself. He liked to drive a good car! He'd save for a month – then blow the lot on a horse, or a car, or a roof for the house, or three nights of hard drinking. Died with nothing in his hand. I was with him.

Pearl-fishing, of course, is prohibited today, illegal by Act of Parliament. The river-mussel is a protected species. You see, we pearl-fishers had to open up the shells, and so the fish were killed. Now when the number of pearl-fishers was small, that was OK, but when they came up here like an army – that was it! We would know which shells to open but they would open every shell – wee shells, smooth shells – and that was that! They wiped the rivers clean. Something had to be done. Now you have to have an official permit. I have a permit. And you have to use a special tool, which opens the shell without killing the fish. If there's a pearl you have to turn the flesh out, but otherwise every shell must be kept alive and thrown back in the water. The law's right enough, difficult to enforce like, but right by me. Because what the cowboys did was kill the goose that laid the golden eggs! As a trade for local men, pearl-fishing up here is dead – but maybe, maybe in ten or twenty years the pearls will come again. My uncle Willie, he still goes out on his bike; he's eighty-four. I'll still be a young man!

I always used to open my shells, not with a knife, but with another shell. A big pearl you'd see there straight away, sitting proud in the flesh, in a membrane-like bag within the flesh-folds of the mussel. They don't fall out – mother-nature is a marvel! You see the big ones clear enough, like a pale cyst, but there may be small pearls, and for these you need to feel. I put my two thumbs right up through the flesh, you slide your thumbs up through the folds and the whole thing opens up. Like a woman. That's how you find the small pearls. When you were young, it got hold of you and when you're old it

Above. Eddie Davies with baby
Mary, Edward and Eileen, 1973.
(ED)

Left. The Davies children play by
the Naver; Sandra, Eileen and
Edward, 1973. (ED)

stays with you. There's the hunt, there's the find, and there's the beauty of the
pearls. 'Aaah here's a pearl,' I'd say, and Essie and the kids would gather round!
Out on the river, I'd put the best shells in my pocket and take them back to the
camp, or take them home, for Essie and the children. The delight of getting a
five pound pearl! The smiles there'd be, 'Ah Da,' they'd say, 'have you got a BIG
pearl?' Happy times. 'Look, look Ma,' they'd say, 'Da's got a beautiful pearl!',
worth the ache, the cold, the wet, the peeling feet, the midges – worth

everything. White like onions, I've seen my feet! Then we'd get in the car and go out for a run, buy chips or sweets, and Essie and I – we'd have a dram.

I was speaking of the rivers: from the Spey you get the grey pearls, gun-metal grey; sometimes they carry a bluish tinge. The Tay gives you the big white pearls, but they don't have the lustre we have on the rivers up here in Sutherland. The Oykel is a beautiful river, it's there you get the coloured pearls – salmon pink, rose-pink, beautiful, beautiful pearls in the Oykel – but they tend to the small. And you get the heather tinge, the soft red glow of the bell-heather, the soft blue sheen of the ling: old ladies remember the Oykel pearls. If I bring them a nice grey pearl, they'll say, 'Eddie, that's a nice pearl but when are you going back to the Oykel?' They love the colour of the Oykel pearls – pink, mauve, cream, the colour of a woman's breast, brought out to feed a child.

And the Evelix, it's a small river but a beautiful river; it runs past the playground where I went to school; it gives the salmon pinks and the mauves, small pearls like jewels. And then on to the Laxford. The Laxford was always a great river for me like. There's less colour in the Laxford, beautiful white pearls, satin-white, silver-grey, moon pearls I used to call them. From the Conon, a mix of colours used to come, way back that was; white, purple, pinks and greys, even shades of green I've seen from the Conon river. But the Hydro-electric, in the fifties, changed all that. You can still get pearls in the Conon, but with three big turbines going that's a very dangerous river, you might get an hour or two before the flood, but you need to keep your ear cocked or you could be washed away. My hearing's gone! That's why I got my second pension – service disability, RAF.

The Naver is a great river for pearls, the river 'of the great cleared Strath'. The colours there you get are white, the satin grey, and sometimes a soft pink/grey. And the Mallard, Borgie, Inverkirkaid, they all have their different sheens. Cairncross down in Perth, they always liked the golden pearls, but very rare they are. And, of course, you get the brown pearls, milk chocolate brown, dark chocolate brown, some almost black. You get the brown pearls everywhere; twenty, perhaps, to every precious pearl.

There's a market now for the brown pearls, and misshapen pearls, but they're worth little enough. The Japanese like them. The scientists grind them down and use them as a cure for stomach ulcers – and aphrodisiacs. That's what I've heard. Some people like to mix the brown pearls with the white. But it's the noble, pastel pearls – the round, or button-shaped, or teardrop-shaped – it's them that make a life worth living. An egg-shaped pearl, or a barrel-shaped pearl can be cut in half and made into a pair for ear-rings, or be balanced in a brooch. But the best are round or button-shaped.

Black pearls are not from here – they're ocean pearls, from the South Sea Islands. They come from the oyster, not from the river-mussel. It's the sea oyster that supplies the big international market; the oyster pearl is the most valuable pearl – large and white. They're found in the Indian Ocean. But you don't get the subtle shades we have, and in the world the river-pearl is much more rare. The Queen Mother, she collects Highland pearls. How many of hers are Davies pearls, you'll never know. I know my etiquette! Essie built up a big clientèle of special customers, in the big houses, but the Queen Mother – she'd not be allowed to trade direct with us. We dealt with Cairncross down in Perth, they controlled the market right across Scotland. Through Cairncross, a Davies pearl might adorn the brow of kings – but we would never know. They know their etiquette! Ours but to do and die!

When I was young, we mostly took our pearls to 'Willie the Watch', the jeweller down in Tain. Five pounds he'd give for a good pearl; a wee crooked man he was, Willie Ross. Of course, he knew very well we were just poor Tinker folk and he was putting all he bought, away down to London, to a Jew it was. Three times the price they'd be going for down there – or more! I mind during the war, when I was about ten years old, going in to see Willie the Watch, with my father. Sixteen pounds he got for a bottle full, at a time when he was working all week, in the wood, for two pounds! They weren't all his pearls, he'd buy pearls in from my uncles over on the Conon and sell them at the weekends, but even during the war there was a good price for pearls. I mind Willie putting up the glass to his eye and squinting and speaking with a voice that hardly squeezed up his throat. So thin and mean it was. 'Twenty-five pounds?' my father said. But Willie said 'Sixteen is the most I can do, Mr Davies, it's the war.' And that's what we got. But sixteen pounds was a lot of money in those days. We got on well with Willie the Watch.

Once the children got bigger, Essie and I used to go down each July to the Spey. It was our holiday – Grantown, Aviemore, Carrbridge – we had great times down there. Ice-cream, fish and chips, coca-cola, the Landmark Visitor Centre – the children loved it down there. They'd fish with us and they'd get their rewards. They all found good pearls in their time; wee Mary she was good, and Eileen found one of the best big pearls we ever found in the Shin. She's away over in France now, with a retired police inspector.

We weren't the only pearl-fishers on the Spey – it's a big river and it was always a popular river. The Reids used to come up from Fife, and Abernethy, and the Macmillans from Elgin used to fish the Spey, years back. Four brothers they were and very, very poor: pearl-fishers and pine cone-gatherers that's what they were; climb any tree, risk life and limb, the Macmillans. Four brothers they were. Old-time Tinker people, very shy. They'd earn a few pounds and drink it away. That was all they were after – supper, bed and breakfast – but they could climb trees!

The Macmillans wouldn't come near you, they were that shy, you could never get talking to them. If you came down the bank they'd fish the other side of the river. If they saw you coming up to the camp, they'd slink away into the woods. They lived all summer on the river, moved up and down. All they had was a poor bow-tent with blankets on, or plastic bin-bags: a week here, a week there, open fires blazing in the night – then on they'd go – just leaving great heaps of shells, like ant-hills, on the bank beneath the trees. The only two I got to know were Willie and Rabbie. I mind asking Rabbie if he knew any of the old songs and he said 'Me! No! Far too many convictions for that!' They're all dead now. Not one of them married. Rabbie was burned to death in his kitchen, both his brothers got killed on the road – knocked down on the same bend one year apart to the night! And the first one to go, got drowned, washed away, fishing – down below the Tormore Distillery.

Hard times they had. The Macmillans used to sell their pearls in Grantown-on-Spey, to a jeweller there, called Grant. He was known as 'The Duke'. Don't ask me why. He's long dead now but he used to rob them. They were simple folk you see. If they brought in a round pearl worth twenty pounds, he'd say, 'Oh that's a nice pearl – I can go as high as two pounds!' Or he'd give them a fiver for a big bunch of pearls. That would keep them going in food and a droppie wine for a week or more! That's all they wanted, they didn't have a car.

Genuine Scottish pearls found by Eddie Davies and Angus Williamson, 1994. The large mother-of-pearl button was carved by an Argyllshire Traveller over one hundred years ago: it was one of the objects Duncan Williamson found in his grandmother's purse in 1934 (see chapter 9). (TN)

They also used to go to a Mrs MacGregor in Elgin, and she was pretty fair. But the Macmillans, they didn't mind what prices they got, they didn't care – as long as they could buy food and drink that was that! A billy-can hanging over a big fire, a cup of tea and they sat happy as the forty thieves! They'd have a shaving mirror stuck in a tree, their shaving brushes laid out neat along a branch, soap and razors in a hole. Sunshine coming through the trees. A quart of cider sticking up beside their knees – what more could they want? Happy go lucky they were. Sell good pearls to Mrs MacGregor and they'd get drunk; singing, shouting, up in court. One day, after a big rowdy night in Elgin, fighting, just among themselves like, the police went round to Mrs MacGregor and they told her she was encouraging them. 'You're paying them too much money for the pearls'! That's what they said. Of course, she gave the Macmillans a good dressing down, she could do that – they were there like naughty boys, to her like! And they said they were sorry and after that she dropped her prices down! She was good to the Macmillans. But that was the way of it – there'd always be problems if the Macmillans found a nice pearl! We used to buy pearls off them ourselves.

One year when I was down on the Spey, I went to see the Duke with a fine round pearl to sell. I asked him what he'd give me for it, and he said, 'What do you ask?' So I said, 'Twenty pounds.'. 'Oh,' he said 'I can get pearls like that for two pounds, or less, from local people. Look here,' he said 'I've got a whole box full!' And he showed me a biscuit-tin, and it was half-full of pearls – worth a lot of money. Thousands and thousands of pounds! And they were all in there, dry, and a wee bitty dirty. So that night, back at the camp, I told Essie and we hatched a small plot.

Now Essie is a good-looking woman and she speaks very well – good Sutherland speech. So in a day or two, she got all dressed up, didn't look like no Traveller woman, or a pearl-fisher's wife – high-heels, lipstick, hair done-up – and we drove into Grantown. Thirty pounds she had in her hand. We parked the car down by the bridge. I walked well away with the kids and she went into the shop: she looked around at the jewellery, then asked the Duke if he had any of the Spey river pearls. 'Oh yes,' said the Duke and he showed her the biscuit-tin. Now Essie knows a good pearl when she sees one – and she saw plenty. So, casual as she could, she went through the box. It was the round ones she went for. And she made up a story that she was wanting pearls for a necklace she was planning for her daughter. And she bought a lot of good pearls for thirty pounds. They'd been out of the water for a long time, they had a scum of dust on them, he must have had them years. Well, when we got back to the tent – woow! We cleaned them up, we burnished them in the palms of our hands, got out the baby oil! They were lovely pearls. We brought them back to life.

Well, so far so good. Next day we went down to Grantown again and Essie went to People Woods, the small hotel, and she sold the lot. Oh she could sell! She wasn't like me, I was always very honest about my selling. If I used to say a pearl was worth twenty pounds, it was sold for twenty pounds, but Essie, she had no conscience about asking the best price she thought she could get! 'A hundred pounds' she'd say! She was a business woman, 'a bunwood sproggan', that's my big Essie! You know that song? Aaah she was good. You see the Traveller women were used to selling – not like the men. 'Fifty pounds' she'd say and often enough she'd get it. Anything is worth what you can get for it! That's what they say in business and that's what Essie went for. There we were, we caught the Duke at his own game!

I like Robert Louis Stevenson – Black Spot and all that. And 'Spot the Ball'!, Long John Silver, *Kidnapped*! Wee Sandra brings me books from the Migdale down: well, he wrote this poem and I speak it out loud – to myself like – here on my own.

> *I will make you brooches and toys for your delight*
> *Of birdsong at morning and starshine at night.*
> *I will make a palace fit for you and me*
> *Of green days in forests and blue days at sea.*
>
> *I will make my kitchen, and you shall keep your room,*
> *Where white flows the river and bright blows the broom,*
> *And you shall wash your linen and keep your body white*
> *In rainfall at morning and dewfall at night.*
>
> *And this shall be for music when no one else is near,*
> *The fine song for singing, the rare song to hear!*
> *That only I remember, that only you admire,*
> *Of the broad road that stretches and the roadside fire.*

You should learn that one. Well – that's what we did for a year or two down on Speyside, when the weather was bad, and we couldn't be fishing, we'd go down to Grant and Essie would buy a few pearls and trade them on. We did very well – but someone must have told the Duke, or maybe he saw Essie selling in the hotels, because one day when she went in, he said, 'That necklace must be getting pretty long by now!' He'd twigged you see and he said, 'You are Essie Davies the pearl-fisher's wife!' Just like she was the answer on Twenty Questions! Or she was Lobby Ludd and he would claim the *News Chronicle* prize! You remember that! Well that was the end of it for us, with

Grant like. He would not sell, or buy, another pearl from us after that – he knew he'd been had at his own game!

Grant was not a bad man. He lived with his sister, very quiet spoken, very proper: so dry, he was, we used to say he had woodworm! But his sister died and that was the end of the Duke. They had a lovely bungalow and everything he wanted – but on his own he couldn't cope. He was a good jeweller like, but when his sister died, he pined away and he died, and the shop got sold. Fate. The Macmillans dead, the Grants dead and Essie gone from me these twelve years. It was a terrible blow when she went away. I loved my wife, you see. I love her still – but she fell in love with a younger man and went away. It was not an easy life for her with me, I know that, out on the road, depending on the weather, the rivers being slaughtered, my back gone, four children crowded in a little house, drink being taken . . . But there we are – and many of the times were good times. It was the winters got us down – no work, no chance to get out – get the spondulicks! But come the spring we'd always be ready for the road again. First it was the Naver, up the Naver we'd go, just like the Stewarts in the old days, and we'd camp at Rhifail, north of Loch Naver, past Altnaharra. Ooh that's a grand, well-sheltered camping ground, trees all round and the river there runs clear, early in the year. It would be Easter time and the children would play on the grass and swing in the alders and chase round the birch trees – and when I came back from the river they'd run up shouting, 'Da, Da, did you get any pearls?' They loved to see me bring home a good pearl. Sandra, Edward, Eileen and wee Mary. Happy memories. Oh the happiness shining in their faces, 'Da, can we go to the shop, Da?' And we'd go out for a spin in the car, and Essie sell the first pearls in the Big Lodge – with the snow still there on Ben Klibreck. Crisps and a big Dundee cake we'd have in Bettyhill.

I mind one year we came down to Rhifail camp in the Austin Princess. It would be April, the light was going. We were all tired and there was a wind blowing and we had a job getting up the big bell-tent. Sandra was crying and crying and stamping and screaming. We were there between the road and the river. The ground was wet and the Naver in spate, so to get on fast with the tent, I tied Sandra with a tether to a tree. She kept on screaming but she was safe there crouched on a tree-stump, screaming, when suddenly a Landrover drew up, and a man got out and he shouted, 'Why is that child tied up to that tree? You cannot tie a child like that to a tree! Loose her at once or we'll call the police!' His wife was in beside him in the Landrover.

Well, Sandra, as you know, could be a wilful child! She was born deaf and a wee bittie disabled, and she could scream! She started to scream louder – as loud as she could – while Essie and I struggled in the wind. I said

'If you're wanting to help — give us a hand with the tent!' but he just stood there. I asked him what he'd do, with a river on one side and a road on the other. I didn't tell him the child was disabled. He said 'I'll stay on this spot till that girl is untied!' And Essie went across and picked Sandra up. At last he went but by then it was dark and the tent not up and the sleeping things had all got sodden on the ground. So we slept in the car, while he drove back to his lodge and his fire. It brings the tears to my eyes to think of it now. We always looked after Sandra. Today, she's the best daughter any man could ask for. She keeps house for me here and next year she's getting married. I have loved all my children — more than anything in the world.

But back to the pearls: the Davies like to fish, what we call flats, half-pools, with a run of water coming through. I like to see the weeds flowing, I like to be where the stones lie like cobbles in the bed of the river, and I like to see shells standing there like little black sentries! I've seen eels as thick as my arm. I don't mind them. I've seen them in good pearly water. I mind one day, years back, going up the Oykel and coming to a flat I'd not returned to for eighteen years and as I stood on the bank I gave a great shout! Ooooh I could see the shells in dozens — without a glass I could see them at twenty yards. My hair stood on end. I'm well up in what makes good pearly ground, and I stood there and I thought — this is it! I went over and I seen the weeds flowing, I seen a big eel moving, I seen the wee round stones and I seen the mussels! Just a wee bit scarce — not too many — that's the thing, you want a pearl-bed, not a mussel-bed. I knew it would be round pearls in a flat like that, and I came down that night with three beautiful round pearls in my pocket, two good buttons and a host of small pearls like barley-rice.

Eddie Davies at the well from which his family took water for nearly fifty years. Dornoch, 1955. (TN)

And I remember once, before the war, we were out in March, cold weather, snow on the ground – up at Applecross in Wester Ross. The whole family was there, going round the houses at Loch Carron, on roads we'd never travelled before. One Sunday morning we had no food, so dad sent us boys out to knock at a house or two. An old keeper and his wife gave us scones and milk and some oats to take back. Very friendly they were and we told the old chap we were pearl-fishers, and he told us about a river six miles away – never fished. 'A standing rock marks the spot,' he said.

So we set off – no rods, no glasses, no boots. We followed the river until we saw this strange rock and then we saw the flats – the weeds waving, the little stones, the rows of shells! We ran. No one for miles. Yells of delight! Into the water we went in our shoes. Untouched for years – maybe never fished – the shells were old, fine shells, 'Every fifth one twisted for a pearl!' I shouted out to Dickie. 'Every fourth one twisted over here!' he said, 'just keep at at!' We worked until we saw the darkness coming on and never felt the cold till we were half way home. What a day we had! Dickie said, 'We must tie knots in our pockets to make sure the weight of pearls doesnae break the cotton through.' That's what we did and we came home laidened heavy with pearls.

'Where've you been, you bastards?' father shouted as we came in the tent. 'We got some scones,' we said 'up at the keeper's house.' 'Your mother and the weans hae starved all day for youse!' he thundered – but he could see something was up! We stood there with our hands in our pockets, all raggety-tattered but feeling proud and we couldn't help but smile. I said in a quiet voice 'We found a lovely river with pearls,' and I seen his eyes change, 'button pearls, flat pearls, round pearls – but the shepherd, he came down and told us "Nae fishin on the Sabbath!" so we had to throw them back!' I was only about ten, but I was teasing him – and then we reached into our pockets and out we brought handfuls of pearls. 'Da, look at this! Look at this, Da!' we said. Oooh the breath came out of him. In forty years he'd hardly seen the like! 'Two hundred pounds or more,' he said. To hear 'two hundred pounds', in those days was the Football Pools! Next morning father got the train down to Tain to see Willie the Watch, and that's what he came back with – two hundred pounds! And new clothes and boxes of food, and a few days later we met some of the Skye Stewarts and we bought a yoke from them for thirty pounds. What a horse that was. Late-cut, wild as a bloody mule! See a mare and he was off! But it was a good cart and we sold him on when we got home – got a car.

I'm very superstitious. A pearl-fisher has to believe in luck. Like the time the one-eyed dog showed me the big pearl over there in Ireland. It was 1968 and we went to Donegal. Everything went wrong. My poor wife had the toothache, it was raining and the three bairns were there in the bell-tent fighting and squabbling. Mary hadn't come along then. Five pounds was all we had. We didn't know the river, we'd only heard about the river. The river Esk it was. The water was high and I wasn't finding pearls; there were plenty of shells but no pearls. Gangs of boys would come down to the river and shout at me, but I just kept at it. It was the year the Troubles got started.

Two days passed. Nothing. I told Essie 'one more day'. I'd gone further up the river and was working away when I heard voices. There was a wind blowing. I looked up and there was a big gang of youths shouting, 'English bastard, get out of our river! You fucking bastard!' All that kind of stuff. They'd seen our car you see – the number plate. They started throwing stones. I said 'I'm just looking for a few shells.' It was getting nasty so I said 'I'm not English, I'm a Scotsman. I come from the Highlands of Scotland, I'm a Sutherland Man!' And one of the girls said 'Listen to his voice – he's not English, he's a Scotsman!' And after a bit they stopped throwing stones and they drifted away. The girl said I should go further up the river away from the road, 'there's more likely pearls up there'.

So I went up and I found a deep sheltered spot away out of the wind but as soon as I started to work the pool I heard this pad – pad – pad – coming down through the trees. I looked up. First I saw nothing. Then I thought it was the boys coming back, so I picked up a big stone from the river and stood there in the water like a stag at bay! Then I saw this dog – pad – pad – pad it came down to the water on the other side of the pool, down a little sheep-path. And it stopped and stood there looking at me. It was the most peculiar looking dog I ever saw! Just one eye and a laughing face, all twisted up on one side. And it stood there and the wind was rustling in the leaves and I was half-afeared: then it made this little noise like a baby waking up and pointed its nose down at the water. A little laugh it made, then it backed away, right up the bank and turned and ran – and I flung the rock at it. And as soon as I'd done that, I felt sorry.

I waited, then went across to where the dog had pointed its nose and there in the water was a beautiful black mussel, a mussel with a fine twist in it and I took it up with my rod. I knew it was a good shell, so I sat on the bank with the shell in my hand wondering whether to open it or take it back to Essie when pad – pad – pad, and ha – ha – ha, and looking round I saw the dog right there behind me! Grinning like, baring its teeth. I shouted 'Get out of here you brute!' It stood its ground. Half black and half white in the face, showing its teeth, a bearded-collie type of dog with just one eye, like an old man – ha – ha – ha it went again, curling its lip and baring its teeth! 'Get away you brute!' I shouted and I almost threw the shell right there at the dog—but before I did, the dog started to wag its tail and it lay down in front of me, looking at me. And I opened the shell and inside was a beautiful rose-coloured pearl. I said out loud, 'You beauty!' And when I looked up, the dog was gone.

Well, I went back into the pool and got three more pearls — button pearls, good pastel shades. I'll never forget that dog — or whatever it was. Essie sent the pearl across to Wallace and Allan in Ayr, and we got twenty-six pounds for it. They wired the money back to us at the Post Office. That dog kept us going, you might say but 1968, that was the last time I was in Ireland. My son, Edward, he served there in the Marines — six years he did.

Three years, five months I was in the RAF, National Service. I'd always wanted to join the RAF. You see, I'd got to know the RAF boys in Dornoch during the war. I thought I'd go away into the RAF and come back with my wings. I was eighteen and went away down to England. We all did six weeks basic training, then I was selected as a batman/waiter! And got sent to Bridgnorth, Shropshire. I didn't like it! I got fed-up. I deserted. Came back up here and went away to Ireland, with my Uncle Dickie. 1948. We went down to Connaught and worked on a farm then we got a job in the sugarbeet factory.

Hard work it was sometimes — but I met beautiful girls in Ireland, Mary Tobin was one, Briget Cash was another, she was a Traveller. I was after them all right, but they said they'd have to tell their father, very Catholic they were — everything was different in those days. Nothing came of it. I sometimes think I'd like to go out there now and see how they are.

We stayed eighteen months in Ireland, then we came back. Dickie was all right, but I was picked up by the police, straight away. They were a wee bit rough with me up here but then I got sent down to England for a court martial and they said, 'If you wear the uniform you'll be all right and we'll just charge you with being "absent without leave".' So I wore the uniform and I got six months in Colchester. That was the jail, very tough it was in those days, still is, I believe!

The Commanding Officer asked me, 'Why did you do it?' 'Freedom' I said, 'I come from the Travelling people in the Highlands of Scotland.' 'I knew that!' he said, 'by your accent – I used to fish the Brora river.' 'That's my home river,' I said 'I'm a pearl-fisher, like my great-grandfather before me. You'll have seen us out on the water! All my people were in the Scottish Horse and the Seaforths – I should never have joined the RAF!' Well, we got on very well after that. He got me to tend his garden, look after the greenhouses. Six months in the garden – English Country Garden! Then I was sent up to Edinburgh to the Officer's Mess at Turnhouse. It's there I did my eighteen months! After that I got my commission! Back on the Brora river!

It was my doctor got me the Service Disability Pension, when my

Mary and Sandra Davies at the camp near Grantown-on-Spey. Summer, 1976. (TN)

hearing went. It was the planes taking off – the roar of the engines. I served my time – in the river! It's twenty pounds a week, but half of it I lose because I get seventy pounds Occupational Disablement, for my back. I can still walk like – on my hands! But sixty years in the river is hard on a long back like mine. It's bend, bend, and bend again if you want to be a pearl-fisher. I walk towards the mountain:

> *Sae dauntingly, sae wantonly*
> *Sae dauntingly gaed he*
> *He played a tune and he danced aroond*
> *Below the gallows tree . . .*

So here I am – the Old Wee Tinker man – left on his own. I take a dram, but I still don't drink when I drive the car. I need the car. I drive Sandra up to the Migdale, and she's in for the test, herself. I've got my grandsons coming on and I still get out a few days on the river but, truth to tell, when Essie left this house – it broke my heart. She went away to the house over there and she didn't come back for three days and three nights. And I was here with the bairnies waiting. They weren't young like, but it was hard for them. Old

Katie Williamson – for her it was the worst crime that ever happened! 'The two of them should have got a whipping,' that's what Johnnie said. 'Ailidh Dall spoiled that girl!', that's what Katie said. The Williamsons – they wouldn't speak to her! I was up for attempted murder – but I got off with two weeks, extenuating circumstances – but I won't get started on any of that.

Eddie Davies beneath the alder trees at Rhifail campsite, Strathnaver, 1995. (TN)

> *Under the wide and starry sky,*
> *Dig the grave and let me lie.*
> *Glad did I live and gladly die,*
> *And I laid me down with a will.*

That's the epitaph Robert Louis Stevenson wrote for himself and – in forty years it'll do for me. I'm a Jacobite.

Essie Stewart

THE PEARL-FISHER'S WIFE

Here's health, wealth, a' yer days
Plenty o' money an plenty o' claes
A horn-cup an a wooden spoon
An a grat big tattie when the first yins doon!

I married at seventeen. Looking back it was too young. We were poor. After leaving the road, my mother went out to do other peoples' washing, I had no father, my grandfather was blind, I was working in domestic service, it was the natural thing to get married. My people were all old — Eddie Davies had a car, he had brothers and sisters, he went around with young people, he enjoyed himself, he did what he pleased, he was handsome. I was proud to marry Eddie Davies, the pearl-fisher. He was just about the only eligible young Traveller alive in all of Sutherland or Ross — and he was twenty-nine!

Twenty-five years Eddie and I were married, then it broke apart. It was a harsh, hard break — no contact for years — but I met Eddie, just two weeks ago! At our youngest daughter Mary's wedding. He was looking very sharp — full morning suit, top hat! He phoned to ask me if he should wear the kilt. I told him his legs were far too skinny now for that! So there he was in morning suit giving his daughter away — just like a toff! We had a great day, all of us together, down in Linlithgow, near Edinburgh. All the family were there. Mary's husband, he's into computers and electronics — but ten years pearl-fishing wee Mary did with us, who'd believe that today — the miles she walked! I remember Mary, up on the Mallard, all day, at four years old, walking, fishing, Eddie carrying her back down. Seven miles up we used to go. Now she runs a nursery class. She's got two boys, Nicholas and wee Connor, he's just a bairn. They're a lovely family but my family came apart — there's not much more you can say. Eddie took after the MacAlister side, very tall, very slim, very dark hair — with a temper. He's got the wide cheek-bones of the MacAlisters. The Davies were always small, more neat, and difficult, and Eddie always had a bit of that

Essie Stewart with her collie, Gyp, Strathconon, 1995. (TN)

The wedding of Mary Davies and Alistair MacIntyre, Linlithgow, 1995. Eddie Davies stands with his grandson, Nicholas, Mary holds her son Connor, Essie stands beside her daughter Eileen. (ES)

in him! Eddie Davies can be full of charm but he's a wilful man, a law unto himself, very possessive, very jealous – just like his father with the pearls! Eddie was a man would not let go – whether that was the Gypsy side, or the Traveller side, it's hard to say.

Twenty-five years is a long time. After we were married first, we did farm work. We had a cottage there in Lairg, just an hour's walk from Remarstaig. The second winter we moved over to a caravan at Rogart, on the Dornoch side. There was always work on the big farms on the east coast. We worked as a pair, or we'd do contract work for Eddie's father – harvest, tatties, neeps, hedging, ditching, planting, sowing – old man Davies would supply a family team, of seven or eight workers, to any farmer needing labour. He'd be paid and he'd pay us. And Eddie was still mending riddles and making potato baskets. Things were good. Money in the hand we had in those days – we'd go out in the car, eat out, drink out, do all the things that I never did at home at Remarstaig. But I missed my mother and granpa very much. We'd been very, very close and we always spoke Gaelic amongst ourselves whereas the Davies only spoke English. That was difficult for me – but I took to the pearl-fishing like a duck to water. It was the selling I did.

Eddie and I would pack up in the spring and disappear off in the van. We had no set routes – so it was not like life on the road with the Stewarts. Eddie went where he wanted to go, on a whim – to the Borgie, to Skye, to the

Essie Stewart prospecting for mussel shells, the Conon river, 1995. (TN)

Spey. We'd camp out by the rivers all summer; coming back to Rogart, just for a weekend or a week in the caravan. We had a bell-tent and the van but the new life with Eddie was more rough and ready than the old life with horses and the big bow-tents. The Stewarts liked to do everything like they did the year before, like when they were young. But with Eddie it was follow your nose.

The first time I was on the Conon river, I remember Eddie going off fishing and asking me to boil a cup of tea. I made a fire between the roots of a big old pine tree and put the kettle on, and soon enough the trunk was ablaze! I didn't kill the tree – but it bears the scars to this day. I was up there last week. I was very innocent. I'd been on the road every year of my life but with the Stewarts everything was very set, very traditional, very well-organised, old-fashioned. About living with a man I knew next to nothing. The old folk always made time to cook a meal – now we'd be making do with s-andwiches and I learned to drink hard pretty fast.

I did a lot of fishing myself – I liked to go out in the river. It takes years to know the rivers – really know where to fish, know when to leave alone, but anyone can get the basics, and in those days there were still plenty of pearls to be found. Later on, when the children came, we all went out. A team of six we were. They'd come away with us and earn their pocket-money, for six weeks every summer.

Sandra was born four years after we were wed. We don't know

why she took so long to come. I'd been to see the doctor. He told Eddie, 'Just
relax, take it easy.' And when she did come I got the German measles. She was
born premature, one pound ten ounces she weighed. We thought she'd die. We
were in the hospital for months, down at Raigmore – but she came through and
she grew into a big strong girl. After Sandra, she was named after old Sandy,
we had Edward, Eileen and Mary.

Many's the pearl I found – but selling was my job and I enjoyed it.
Meeting the people, making the deal, building up a clientèle. I liked all that.
Eddie was happy to keep out of the way. He likes to talk, but underneath he's shy
with people. Of course, anyone can sell a pearl once they have it! It's the finding
that's difficult. There's something wonderful about finding a pearl, or seeing a
new pearl for the first time. You never lose that thrill. If Eddie brought home a
beautiful round pearl, the day would be transformed. Then we'd go out for a
drive, go out for a drink, enjoy ourselves – and then it was up to me, to sell!

So we had good times but often enough you could fish all
summer and count the good pearls on two hands. It was hard, hard work. Back
at the camp, we'd just fall asleep at eight or nine in the evening, exhausted;
miles of walking, hours of fishing, hours of opening shells, lighting a fire,
making supper. These things had to be done. Midges or no, we'd just fall asleep.
It's the unemployed who spend their time in bed! Exhaustion. Bread and jam!
Wet boots, wet socks in the morning. Eddie's back went and so did mine. But
there was nothing else for us but to go back to the rivers again . . . If the
weather was bad, if the rivers were high, if the car broke down – there was no
fishing, no pearls, no money. Many's the week we lived on the Family
Allowance. We had to keep a vehicle on the road and we had to buy petrol to
get to the rivers – sometimes we went hungry for that ... In 1972 we got a nice
wee house in Ardgay; a council house, close to the school – but as things
seemed to get better for everyone else, things seemed to get worse for us . . .

It was after Bill Abernethy found the Big Pearl down on the river
Tay, things began to go down. That was 1968. More and more people came up
here looking for a quick buck! And every buck they got was a buck less for us
– or another five miles' walking out into the wilds! Bill Abernethy himself, he
started coming up. He had a big Volvo Estate and slept in the back and he didn't
just bring himself, he brought a team of divers! He was Director of Operations!
They marched all over, like they owned the place. He was banned from the
Sutherland rivers by *interim interdict*! But the damage was done and he found
ways round it.

Bill Abernethy came to our house in Ardgay, but Bill Abernethy is
no friend of ours. He looked to himself and he damned us and the future. He
liked to carry five hundred pounds in his shirt pocket, like a cattle-dealer. He

lived the life of a reiver – for pearls! It sounds great – being a pearl-fisher – but even he made less than a fortune. I hear he lives a frugal life down there near Blair; his house has a chair and a television set! His family were all pearl-fishers. He should have known better! But in the end you can't blame him – it was the car that killed the pearl-fishing up here – access to the rivers was made too easy. People in the south could take up a hobby and wreak havoc in every river in the Highlands. Of course the Davies always had cars themselves but they were local men. Eddie got me to drive. I taught myself in the yard of an old sawmill, where we had parked the caravan. I drove round and round. It was like a bullring. If I got out of control I'd just rear up into the sawdust! That was the Davies way. Teach yourself! But then you don't necessarily know more than you did to begin with – just something different!

But Eddie had a great eye for the quality and value of pearls. No one can deny that. He'd judge them, grade them, price them – no glass, no scales – just there in his hand. We had our special customers and we had local jewellers, but the main dealer was Cairncross of Perth. They were dealers for the whole of Scotland. They set the price. Very nice people they were, Mr Alistair and Mr James in our day. They have the Abernethy pearl in the shop window. Huge, perfectly round and almost perfect in lustre – it's worth one hundred thousand pounds today, they say. Each evening when they put it in the safe they wipe it round to keep it mint – but Eddie says he thinks it's cracking up!

Mr Alistair was very business-like, very correct, very proper, very old-fashioned. Mr James was more approachable, but both were gentlemen in every way. Sometimes we would send pearls down by post and sometimes, if we were on Speyside, we'd drive down the A9. We'd even send to Cairncross from Ireland. They took everything – big and small, they took misshapen pearls they called 'baroque', they took the brown pearls: even pearls eaten in on one side I've known them take, to cut and set in rings and brooches. They treated us with great respect and they paid reasonable prices, fair prices. If you questioned a particular valuation, they'd justify their offer.

When I went into Cairncross, one of the two brothers would be called and I'd be taken into the backshop, sat down and talked to, and made a fuss of. They enjoyed looking at what you'd brought. They'd take out their eye-glasses, get out the scales, grade them, weigh them, make offers. When business was concluded, they'd escort you to the door and say 'Goodbye, Mrs Davies', as though I was the Queen Mother herself. It was by the gramme they weighed. The biggest pearl I ever took in was forty-eight and a half grammes. It was from a dead shell with decay eating in on the underside but it was huge, and I got a hundred and sixty five pounds.

The Cairncross brothers loved their pearls, just like we did. They asked us not to send them straight out of the water but to keep them a while and polish them – with a soft cloth and baby oil – so they could see them at their best. Judge them at their best and make a fair offer. Pearls come from the mussel with something like a membrane of slime over them. You have to wipe this away, but if the pearls are left too dry, or if you let them rattle about in a box, they build a skin of dry-scum and they might even crack or splinter. It was always cash, or with a cheque, the Cairncrosses paid, by return of post. Their account was at the Clydesdale Bank, and if I was in Perth, Mr James would phone across to say that I'd be coming in, and the Bank would pay me on the spot – no clearance needed. Many a good night we had coming back up the A9 from Perth. Many a good week we had back at home – but never in my life have I known a steady income, never did we build a back-up in the bank, never did we own more than our clothes, a car and television set.

Well, the Cairncrosses were good but most of our best pearls we'd keep for our special customers. We knew what they wanted, they liked us, and we liked them. The Laird of Strathconon was one, his name was Peter Combe. He was a man who liked women. He had quite a stream of girlfriends up there at the big lodge – before he got married. He even had a black girl once; that was unheard of in the Highlands when I was young. He was a film-producer. He'd buy any amount of good pearls.

Pearls look beautiful on a dark skin, and they look good on a very fair skin; but I think they look best of all on black velvet. I always took them up to Strathconon in a box, wrapped in chamois leather – with a piece of black velvet to show them on. It's no good having pearls rattling about and it's no good having them rolling off a table or down the back of a settee.

I always enjoyed going up Strathconon. That's where I burned the Caledonian pine and Mr Combe was as fine a gentleman as I ever met. In the end he married a French woman and she wasn't keen on me going up there, so after she came in I stopped going. I think she thought I was one of his floosies! He's dead today. His father was Colonel Combe. They owned all the top end of Strathconon. Whenever I went, I would be welcomed in. That man never gave me a drink out of an opened bottle! I'd go up there and he'd greet me – 'Ah,' he'd say, 'the bad penny's back! Come on and have a dram and show me what you've got.' He'd go over to his oak cabinet and open a new bottle of Antiquity – that's what it always was, Antiquity. And if I stayed on a while, or if he'd bought a pearl with which he was especially pleased, he'd offer me his special malt, and go across to a small wooden cask. There was a measure beside it. He'd then set out two drams and we'd drink them down together. There must be many Davies pearls in Strathconon yet.

Then there was the Right Honourable Eva Hone. She liked the

Essie Stewart by the Caledonian pine she set alight in 1959, 1995. (TN)

Spey pearls and what she collected was 'the gun-metal grey'. She was collecting them for her son, for his vest: she wanted four matching button pearls, and for herself she was collecting a necklace. She was a very nice woman. She only wanted the best and she was prepared to wait to get it. She waited years for the gun-metal buttons, but they were ready for the boy on his twenty-first birthday. Most of the pearls came from her own river, the Spey, but the last one, Eddie found in the Oykel. It had more blue than grey, but it was a beautiful flat-backed pearl of perfect size, so I sent it off to her by post. She sent a cheque by return! And thanked us for all the trouble we'd taken in completing the set, and asking us to call by, when next we came down to the Spey. She had two children, Joanna and Rupert, and when they were small they used to play with my two older ones, Sandra and Edward. And they had a very boisterous black labrador, and one day their Shetland pony was standing on the terraced bank of the garden – when the dog came bounding down and jumped up against the Shetland! It just tumbled over and over like a barrel of beer off a cart! How the children laughed.

I met Richard Burton at Gerald Laing's house at Kinkell Castle. Mr Laing's wife, in those days, was a Red Indian, very, very beautiful. And he was a sculptor, I believe, but he was one of the very few men who's made me feel inferior. Why I don't know! That's all I can say about him – but Richard Burton, he was small and he was very, very nice to me, and he looked through the pearls. Unfortunately Elizabeth Taylor was not there! He bought nothing. Perhaps my pearls weren't grand enough. But Richard Burton was the perfect gentleman and his voice was as fine a voice as I ever heard.

Another time I went up, on spec, to the lodge of Lord Reidhaven to try to sell some pearls. There was a party going on and I spoke to a girl who turned out to be American. She went into the house to look for Lord Reidhaven. She came back, asked me to wait and offered me a drink. 'What will you have?' she asked. 'I'll have what you're having' I said. 'It's gin and dry vermouth,' she replied with a smile, and went off to a half-timbered bar in the hall. I didn't know then what a gin and dry vermouth should look like, but she came back with a large cloudy drink and Lord Reidhaven beside her. I showed him some pearls and sipped at my drink. He said he didn't think he would take any for himself but he had a friend at Covent Garden was a jeweller, and he asked, 'May I take a few small ones down to London to show him?' I selected two small ones – and was ushered out fast enough. Not a penny was I offered, not a penny did I get. I don't know why I was lax, but as I got to the door, I felt my legs begin to go. I had to put my arm out against the front door to steady myself! Then I aimed for the middle of the drive and set off. I think I made the

Essie Davies with Sandra, 1963.
(ED)

bend in the road before I crashed into the bushes! I couldn't stand up and my head was slamming back and forth like a ferret in a cage!

I had gone into that house twenty minutes before stone cold sober! Now I was legless, after one drink! What it was, I don't know. How I got back to the car, I don't know! One drink! In those days I could drink most men under the table. Today it's different – one drink and I'm anybody's – but in those days! Somebody spiked that drink. I don't know whether it was pure alcohol, LSD, cocaine, or some cocktail of drugs – but I remember crawling up to the car on all fours! I couldn't stand. The kids were scared out of their wits! They couldn't understand what had happened. I told Eddie 'I had one drink!' and rolled over. He wouldn't believe me. Anyway, they managed to heave me up into the car and drive me back to the camp. I crawled about in the grass, vomiting like a dog! Then I passed out! If that American girl had two of what I had she'll be damned lucky to be alive! I'm convinced it was a Mickey Finn.

It wasn't the Burkers – but that was the kind of thing the Burkers did! Drug you and murder you! Or murder you in your sleep. My grandfather remembered a doctor trying it on up at Remarstaig. Travellers always had a great fear of the Burkers, of being murdered, of bad doctors, of their bodies being taken away for dissection in the medical schools! Eddie used to tell the children about the times when he was out camping as a boy and he'd see the eyes of the Burkers watching from the woods waiting to strike. He used to tell them – just to frighten them! To stop them wandering off – but many of the old stories were true stories. Many's the Traveller was murdered, or disappeared without trace. There was a very bad murder at Rosehall – where we spent our wedding night. A cairn of stones marks the spot where the killing took place. It was a pedlar man called Neil Hughes got murdered there. This is the story Eddie told me:

'Neil Hughes was a pedlar. He was a big man, very strong, six feet, late fifties. He sold quality goods of a kind the Traveller women could ill afford – so he was not a rival for the Travellers he was a complementary addition to the sales team! He travelled all over Sutherland and Ross-shire with a donkey well-laden with packs. He had money and it was rumoured he always carried a gun. It was 1911, when he got to Sutherland for the last time. He spent a day or two at Bonar and was then seen spending money in the Invershin hotel, it's still there today. He had a big wad of notes. One man who drank with him was the Cadger Mackenzie, a crofter's son from Rosehall in Glen Oykel.

'That evening Hughes set off for the west and he set up camp on the loch side beneath Rosehall. He tethered his donkey, lighted a small fire and went to sleep in his tent; a small ridge tent, like the army use. A week passed over and the beast started braying – he haw! he haw! he haw! Passers-by noticed that the donkey had eaten its circle of grass right down to the ground and was straining its tether for the trees. Thin like! At the end of its tether, as you say! And there was no sign of the donkey's owner, so someone went to investigate. In the tent, they found the body of a man, fly-blown and dead. It was Neil Hughes.

'Now it seems Hughes had been lying with his head against the canvas, and been killed by a single blow from a hammer, delivered by someone from outside the tent. His goods were all stacked up neat alongside the body, untouched. Beneath his pillow they found his gun, still loaded. But not a penny did they find – all his money had gone. People from the Invershin hotel confirmed that they thought he must have had about sixty pounds in notes, when he had bought his last round of drinks in the bar. It was a time of hot weather, so with the drink and long walk, it was concluded that Hughes had slept sound as a log and not woken. It was murder!

'The police got called and the chief suspect was the Cadger Mackenzie. He lived on the croft, with his mother and father, just a quarter of a mile above the place of the murder. He was a man in debt and a wee bitty unstable. He was the suspect. He got questioned. The croft was searched, not once, but three times – nothing was found. Of course, a week had gone by. Under question, the Cadger gave nothing away – not a sign nor a pound! The police tried to force a confession but to no avail. Then the local minister had an idea. He asked Cadger MacKenzie to dig the grave of the murdered man – and rocky ground they gave him – up in the graveyard at Rosehall. They thought that digging the grave would force him to confess the ugly deed they believed he had done! But he dug the grave and he stood at the funeral, not a sign did he give. He filled and turfed the grave. Not a word did the Cadger MacKenzie speak.

'Nothing further could be done. Time passed, the case was closed. They never found a next of kin. Neil Hughes had come and gone, a man unknown. But a headstone was soon placed there on his grave. You see the local people felt sorry for the man – the murder was a mark on the whole community. And that was not all – a cairn of stones also appeared on the spot where the murder took place. I've placed many a stone on that cairn myself.

'Well, in 1914, the war came and the Cadger Mackenzie joined up – just like the others – like my father, my grandfather and uncle Willie. Mackenzie went to France and there he was mortally wounded. But before he died he asked for a minister to be brought to him and he confessed that it was he that killed Neil Hughes, the pedlar "with a single blow" he said, "from outside the tent". He had needed money for his debts. He had not meant to kill the man, just stun him with a blow – but the blow had been too hard. He asked forgiveness and it's said his last words were "At last, the slate is clean!" '

Well, that's the story Eddie got from Willie Johnstone, a man who was a boy at the time and remembered the whole thing – but Alec John Williamson tells the same story and his ending's entirely different!

'Neil Hughes was a pedlar. There were two big pedlars in Sutherland in those days, Neil Hughes and another man, a blind man who had a dog whose name was Frank. He used to walk behind the dog saying "Straight Frank, straight Frank" and Frank would take him wherever he wanted to go. Some people say he was putting it on – the blindness – but my father said he was blind sure enough. Now the blind man – he's got nothing to do with the murder! But Neil Hughes, he was about sixty years of age, he travelled with a donkey and he was, they say, a very godly man – or at least he pretended to be. Whichever way it was it was he that got murdered.

'Now Neil Hughes was not a drinking man but he was taking a drink this night and his donkey and trap were out in the road, outside the pub, up at Shinbridge. And when he'd had a few drinks he started looking at some of the serving girls. Probably he fancied his chances with some of them. Very nice some of them were and he was showing the girls that he had a lot of money on him – and there were other eyes on that money! Now, I don't know what went on in the pub, nor what went on outside, afterwards, but that night Neil Hughes went on out to Rosehall and put up his tent and tethered the donkey. He must have gone to bed because, it seems, he was asleep when he was killed – the blow was struck from outside the tent. Many's the time I've heard my father and uncles speak about Neil Hughes. When he was found all his teeth were out on his chest. The thick head of the axe had gone right through the back of his skull and spread his teeth wide on his breast. Neil Hughes was a harmless man, but perhaps he fancied a girl that night, and that was his undoing. Or, it might have been the money, it was sixty pounds he had. Under his pillow the police found a loaded pistol. It proved no use to the man at all. No Traveller likes to carry a gun.

'Now the murder happened in 1907, I think it was. Straight away the chief suspect was a man with debts, called 'the Cadger'. But there was no evidence against him and the trail went cold. But some years later a circus came to Lairg, with a fortune-teller, a Gypsy woman, and somebody asked her about Neil Hughes. They asked her where the murderer stood that afternoon. She said "The man who murdered Neil Hughes is at this very moment walking down a street in Chicago a very wealthy man!" Well, the news went round and it struck a bell with the people at Rosehall because they knew that George MacKenzie, 'The Cadger', as he was called, had taken ship from Liverpool for America! And there he had made a great fortune. That's what the Gypsy woman

Looking north-west into Sutherland. The Struie, 1995. (TN)

said and she knew nothing, nothing about any of this.

'And it came to pass years and years later, when everything quietened down, that the Cadger MacKenzie came back to this country and lived to a ripe old age, not up here, but down there in the south somewhere. That's the story as I heard it – but Eddie Davies, he heard another version and maybe his version is the true version. And in telling my story, I hope I do no man's reputation harm – because on the War Memorial, up at Rosehall, the tribute to those who died in France includes the name George Cadger – and immediately beneath that is carved the name Donald MacKenzie! So what the truth of all this is we'll probably never know – things get confused with time – maybe the real murderer was someone else entirely . . .'

Well, that's just one of the stories I've heard many times about murder. Why the Travelling People should tell so many stories about pedlars and Burkers and murders, I don't know – but the best one I know is a poem. It's about a pedlar, whose murderer was arrested in Elgin. That's where my father came from. His name was James Gordon. My father's name was Gordon Bremner. And, of course, my step-brother's name is Gordon Stewart! That proves nothing but it always keeps me interested in the story, so to speak. The Travellers always like a song or a poem to tell a story. And in this poem the murderer is said to come from Connaught in Ireland – that's where Eddie went, when he deserted from his National Service! The poem's called 'The Pedlar Lad' and they say it was a shepherd wrote it. It happened about a hundred and fifty years ago, down near the border, not up here:

THE PEDLARS *by Alexander Glendinning*

In the fall of the year, the last year of the reign
Of good old king George, of that title the Third
(Attention to details makes the narrative plain
And this tale of the pedlar is true every word!)
Two travellers were seen passing through Es'dalemuir —
A middle-aged man and a lad in his teens:
The first was a Connaught Boy newly come o'er
A dealer in ballads and needles and pins.
He was little in stature and dark in each feature
A rather low type of corrupt human nature.
Pock-pecked was he and blind of an e'e
He had a sinister look with the yin that could see!
Moreover he stuttered every sentence he uttered
A more ken-speckled feller there couldnae well be.

His comrade, a lad from near Hexham-on-Tyne
Had fled a harsh stepmother — begging his bread
Till he now made a start in the merchantile line;
And little by little began to succeed!
He bore on his back, in a small pedlar's box,
Pencils, symbols and seals — this and other nicknacks,
But his business was still on a moderate scale
Thirty shillings would have bought all he carried for sale.
He was feeble of body and weak in the mind too
Such a one as the world is not often kind to.

Our travellers faired on from one house to another
Trudging and talking kindly, like brother and brother.
Till they reached Upper Cassock — where's that — if you ask —
'Tis the uppermost farm on the course of the Esk.
A kind little girl, there pitied the sinners
Took them in the kitchen and gave them their dinners.
'And this will make me strong for crossing to Ettrick
And this will make you strong for crossing to Ettrick'
Were the sage-like remarks of the son of St Patrick!

(Perhaps it were meat, I should here introduce
To the reader — the worthy good man of the hoose.
A man of strong sense and quick watchful eye,
He came in, took a look at his guests and passed by —
The sequel will show, that to every time-server
He's a dangerous neighbour, is an accurate observer!)

The dinner discussed! At a hint from the girl
His comrade drew near to his box to unlock it,
Gave the girl a picture — a print by de Still
And closing the box, put the key in his pocket.
A circumstance afterwards pressed by the coroner
'He who carries the key of a box is the owner!'

The reader, perhaps, has heard of the Steps
Of Glen Derg — which means literally one of the gaps —
In that high range of hills, high and misty indeed,
Which divides Ettrick Forest from Es'dalemuir heid.
For the Steps of Glen Derg then our travellers set out
'Tis a long dreary road — but they'll find it no doubt!

Now the time must be shifted twelve days after that
And the scene to the wilds we imagined of late:
It's a cold misty day in the month of November,
A shepherd was going his rounds
When he found such a scene (one is apt to remember!),
A dead body all covered with wounds!

It was stretched in full view with its face to the sky —
As if making appeal to the All-Seeing-Eye!
The right arm which failed on that last evil day
The assassin's rude hand to arrest
Was lifted above as if pointing a way
To the land where the weary shall rest:

The left lay across — on his vest.

The corpse to the nearest farmhouse was conveyed
The same as we spoke of a few stanzas back,
And the same little girl came forward and said
'That's the boy who passed here lately carrying his pack —
That gave me the picture!' These words lit a lamp
Threw light on the subject! It was he, without doubt!
And his travelling companion — the horrible scamp —
Had murdered his victim and robbed him to boot!
At this stage the good man of the house without further advisement
Sat down and wrote out the subjoined advertisement!

BE IT KNOWN TO ALL MEN, THAT IN A WILD GLEN
NEAR THE STEPS OF GLEN DERG AND ONE MILE FROM THE PENN
THERE WAS FOUND A DEAD BODY THIS DAY AND THE SAME
PROVES THAT OF A PEDLAR — JOHN ELLIOT BY NAME.
A LAD FROM NEAR HEXHAM: MOREOVER AND FURTHER
THE EVIDENCE POINTS TO A TERRIBLE MURDER!

THE PEDLAR LAY THERE AS COLD AS A STONE
BUT THE PURSE AND THE PACK OF THE PEDLAR WERE GONE.
WHEN LAST, THE SAID PEDLAR WAS SEEN ON THE TRAMP,
HE WAS TRAVELLING NORTHWARD FROM ESKDALE TO ETTRICK
ALONG WITH JAMES GORDON — AN ILL-LOOKING SCAMP —
FROM THE COUNTY OF MAYO AND THE LAND OF ST PATRICK.

SAID GORDON'S A MAN — FIVE FEET FIVE INCHES HIGH
MUCH MARKED WITH THE SMALLPOX AND BLIND OF AN EYE
AND STAMMERS IN SPEECH. HE WHO HAPPENS TO FIND HIM
WILL JUST HAVE THE GOODNESS TO CATCH HIM AND BIND HIM
AND SEND HIM DIRECT TO SOME JUSTICE OF PEACE
OR ANY YOUNG P.F. IN THE TOWN OF DUMFRIES.

Upper Cassock, November the thirtieth day
In the year eighteen twenty and signed A.G.

The writer remembers, he long will remember
A cold misty morning — it was the first of December.
He was raised long before day and hurried away
With a note to Lord Napier at Thirlstane House.
Every bush that he passed seemed the pedlar's ghost!
Till daylight returning reformed the abuse.

Bambellas were running in every direction —
Like beagles let loose on the trail of a fox;
The scent had grown cold, yet with careful collection
They managed to hunt up the following facts:
A man had been seen — answering well the description —
Coming down from the wilderness carrying a box:

Selling goods at half-price, without stint or restriction,
Singing songs to the lassies and cracking his jokes.
He passed Brodger Hill, stopped at Kirkup o'er night,
Took the road in the morning with laugh and guffaw
Got his dinner at Thirlstane, turned to the right
And crossed Ettrick Water above Trushie Law.

Up Rankleburn now sweeps the hunter's 'Halloo'
But the course stopped short in the Linn of Buccleuch.
At the foot of the rocks lay the pedlar's box
But after the box there was no further clue!

Some weeks had gone by when the news came one day
Of a man caught in Lanark and there lodged in thrall
But as matters turned out, it was proved beyond doubt
That the Lanark man was — not the fellow at all!

It has often been said, that blood cannae be led
That Providence points to the murderer's tracks!
Be that as it may 'tis our duty today
To state what appears a remarkable fact!

As a farmer, far North, in the county of Nairn
Was reading a handbill stuck-up on a wall,
There came to his elbow a shag-headed caird
Begging coppers and blessing his honour with all!

He read on the bill 'five feet five inches high
Much marked with the smallpox and blind of an eye
And stammers in speech'. He looked on the creature
And finding the picture drawn true in each feature
He popped him in jail — and so ended the matter!

There was no such thing as a telegraph wire!
Man had not yet the art of riding by fire!
No lightening express running past on the rail!
A coach and four carried his majesty's mail!

When the stage from the north reached the town of Dumfries
This message was brought to the Chief of Police —
A MAN IS ARRESTED, SUSPECTED OF MURDER
COMMITTED IN ESKDALE, SOMEWHERE IN THE BORDER.
HE IS LODGED IN NAIRN JAIL. AWAITING YOUR ORDER.

A respectable farmer —Will Graham o' the Cote —
(The house which the travellers had spent their last night in)
Was posted to Nairn to identify Pat!
And swore on the book, that that was the right one!
So Pat, with a guard who looked well to his prize,
Was sent down to Dumfries to await the Assize.

At the courthouse, the courthouse is full to the door!
The star-wiggy Lords on their benches sit down,
The lawyers are bustling below on the floor
The court is just opened in the name o' the crown.
And where is the prisoner — hush, hush he is there —
Just stand in the box!' How the multitude stare!

This affair has been marked by peculiar atrocity!
We look in that face for the lines of ferocity
And what is before us? No fierce man, hook or crook,
But a very small man — with a sinister look!
The usual question is put by the Board
'Are you Guilty or Not Guilty?' 'Not Guilty my Lord'.
And the plea of Not Guilty is placed on record . . .

It would tire the writer, as well as his readers
To question the witnesses, follow the pleaders
We will merely relate, with remarks interwoven,
A few of the principal facts that were proven
Or if you would rather, we'll here lay before you
The gist of the Judge's address to the Jury:

'Gentlemen of the Jury you see in the box
A man charged with murder and robbery — both!
'Tis your duty with care, to examine the facts
And returning a verdict, remember your oath.

'The man at the bar — it is clear as daylight —
Was seen with the traveller now dead!
That they stopped at a place called the Cote overnight
And started next morning for Es'dalemuirhead
That they reached Upper Cassock sometime about noon,
Got dinner together and when dinner was done
The lad who was there having taken a hint
From the man at the bar, gave the girl a print.
Said girl, saw the boy take the box and unlock it
And close it again — put the key in his pocket . . .

'The travellers then left. We can trace them no further
But we follow — in sense — to the scene of the murder!
For the Stalbash Edge and the Summers Cleuchheid
Bore witness that day to a terrible deed!

'The prisoner awhiles disappears from our sight
But we find him, the very same day, towards night
Coming down on the Selkirkshire side o' the height!
He's travelling alone with a box on his back
And he comes not at all by the regular track!
He comes from the Cauldrons, a wild mossy glen
Halfway tween the Steps o' Glen Derg and the Penn!

'Tis gloamin'! When all the men at Kirkup farmhouse
Hear a desperate noise. And the reason is plain
All the collies about like a kennel broke loose
Are attacking a man at the foot of the lane!
The collies are squashed and the traveller put right
Brought into the kitchen and housed for the night.

'Next day the "new" packman is checking his wares
Just now he is selling remarkably low!
He wishes "to live and let live" he declares

"The goods are bought cheap — lightly come, lightly go!"
A rather unlooked for result of his sales
The articles sold found their way into court!

'And have proved to be goods — several samples at least —
Which a stationer in London had sold the deceased.
And the box that was found in the Linn of Buccleuch
Was the traveller's own box! These facts put together
Do prove beyond doubt that the Indictment is true
But proven or not — is for you to say whether!'

At this stage the Jury withdrew.

The court is all silent — the prisoner looks blue —
The verdict is 'Guilty' — the charge is found true.
His Lordship resumed fitting on the Black Hood
Yet pitying at heart the foul shadow of blood.
'James Gordon, this court has established your guilt
And the Law claims your blood for the blood you have spilt.

'Can you show any cause in this hour of your need
Why the sentence of death should not fall on your head?'
'My Lord, please your Lordship — whosoever may doubt it —
This murder, Heaven knows, I know nothing about it!
Heaven now witness both the false and the true
Heaven's Law and not man's lays this sentence — on you!'

'Now I beseech thee thus nearing the goal
Of your earthly career seek the peace of your soul
And confess of your sin cry mercy from Heaven
Where alone by man's blood, can man's blood be forgiven.

'I now order you to be removed to the same
Long single cell from which this morning you came,
That you be there confined — fed on water and bread
Till the next sixth of June that's ensuing.
Thence brought to the gallows and hanged till you're dead
And may Heaven in its grace save your spirit from ruin.'

Tis the sixth day of June — all the folks about toun
All the folks from the country for miles aroun
The whole town o' Dumfries is in front o' the jail
Assembled to witness the prisoner's finale!

With the hour came the man — priest and prisoner are there
The priest having crossed himself mutters a prayer
To the Virgin, to help in this hour of despair!
Then Cauldcrack steps in and takes charge of affairs!
Fetch the rope! And before you could cry 'Paddy tak care'
Draws the bolt and the prisoner is dangling in air!

At that moment a crash and a loud peal of thunder
Strikes the hearts of the gazers with terror and wonder!
Another bright flash and another loud crash
The rain falls in torrents — the huge living mass
Is off helter skelter to the houses for shelter!
And the murderer is left, all alane in the helter!

What became of the body I never have heard:
The doctors would hack it to bits I suppose!
When brought into the house, it was stretched on a board
And a galvanic battery applied to its nause!
When it instantly started to kick and make faces!
Those doctors! Wiell, wiell — they're pretty hard cases!

Alexander Stewart (Ailidh Dall)
with his mother, old Suzie the
story-teller, Bettyhill, c. 1935. (ES)

Ailidh Dall, left, home on leave from France, 1916; his blindness was caused by cataracts and came gradually after 1925. The young man beside him is his cousin Charlie. (ES)

It was you see the shepherd boy who found the body, wrote the poem – years afterwards. It's a very good poem.

In the tent we told both the old stories and the new stories. Ailidh Dall and Michie told them in Gaelic, Eddie and I would tell them in English. Sometimes the story would have a moral and sometimes it would be told just to excite or frighten people. It's easy enough to frighten children in a tent out there in no man's land.

One of the stories Ailidh Dall would tell was about a man who lived at Tarvie, that's between Gorton and Garve. 'Once upon a time there was a crippled tailor. He lived by a ford in the river and at night he would guide travellers across the river because if he did not they'd be met by a billy-goat, a vicious and dangerous killer! From every traveller the crippled tailor asked a shilling. This had gone on as long as anyone could remember and it was understood that it was a very necessary job the tailor did. But one day a

Ailidh Dall enjoying the patriarchal pleasures of old age, Sutherland, 1957. (HH, BB)

missionary came to the village to preach and he visited all the houses and he was set to go on his way when the crippled tailor appeared at his side and said "Knowing you are a good man and true," he said "I will guide you across the river – for free." But the missionary answering said, "I do not want or need a guide to cross the ford at Tarvie!" "But what" said the tailor, "if you meet the billy-goat?" "Oh" said the missionary, "I have a *skean-dhu* for goats!" "But what if your *skean-dhu* won't clear wool?" said the tailor. "Well," said the missionary "I'll draw my dirk!" "But what if your dirk won't clear leather" said the tailor with a threat in his voice. "Then I'll show him my grand-aunt!" said the missionary and with that he set off for the river.

'But there sure enough was the buckgoat – rearing up on his back legs beside a rock on the far side of the ford, waiting for him. The missionary stepped boldly out into the river but the buckgoat tossed its horns and went for him. The missionary bent to draw his *skean-dhu* – it would not clear wool. He grabbed for his dirk but it would not clear leather so he moved his staff from his left hand into his right and with two hands he thrust it into the belly of the goat. This was his grand-aunt! And he thrust it again and again into the belly of the billy-goat till it collapsed on the bank of the river, half dead. And the missionary went on his way.

'Next day the tailor was nowhere to be seen. On the second day, one of the old ladies of the village went into his house and found the crippled tailor lying ill in his bed. On the third day it was announced that the tailor was dying and would not see the morning. So all the people gathered round the tailor's house to say their farewells and thank the man who'd guided them across the river so many times, when they suddenly heard a splashing coming up from the ford and they saw the missionary striding back towards them with his staff. "What is the trouble here?", he asked. "It's a very sad day for us" they replied, "the old tailor who guarded the ford all these years is dying, close to death."

'At this the missionary went into the house and with his staff he flung the blankets from the bed of the crippled tailor. "Look at these wounds!" he shouted, "These are the wounds of the staff I hold! This man is the buckgoat, who has terrified you these many years!" And he ordered the man to rise from his bed and go to the kist where he kept his money and he did not let him rest until he'd laid every penny on the table. Silver, gold, and copper coins covered it – twelve inches high! Then he said to the crippled tailor, "Leave this house and cross the river! Go from hence and never, never return!" Well the old tailor stumbled across the ford and was never seen again. "Evil can freeze iron, wool, leather and the hearts of men," said the missionary "but nothing stand against the good of my grand-aunt!" And he laughed and the people cheered. Then he too, went on his way and left the villagers to themselves.'

That's like a fairy story but, my grandfather used to say, was a true story, and whenever we went past the tailor's house he would point it out and say 'That is the house where the wicked tailor lived!' Even when he was blind he did that. But I've not been down there for twenty years. And I couldn't really tell my grandchildren that's 'the house where the wicked tailor lived!' I don't believe it. Things change.

My Traveller days are done. My pearl-fishing days are done. I met another man and went away. Who can ever say if I did right or wrong? I'm not divorced. I've taken back my Traveller name – I'm Essie Stewart. I'm fifty-four. There's always good and bad in life. Two of the nicest people I ever met were Willie and Bella MacPhee, from down in Perthshire. That's what I want, when I win the Lottery, money for the children and a wee farm down there in Perthshire, with my dogs, a horse, and one of those Vietnamese pot-bellied pigs – and a Ford Scorpio Convertible!'

Part Three
Traveller Life and Culture

Alec John Williamson

DEATH, CURES AND MEDICINE

Cut your nails on a Sunday
See your blood run out on Monday!

In the old days a Traveller would be buried with a hammer in the coffin, a silver sixpence and a candle. These were for the hereafter. 'Knock on the door with the hammer, pay the ferryman with the sixpence, and light your way with a candle.' The last time I heard about that was when my grandfather's brother died and his wife wanted this. She was an islander, and she wanted him buried in the old way but the minister stopped it. 'Superstition!' he said. 'None of that nonsense. No blasphemy here!' Death was taken very seriously by the Travelling People and our people are still superstitious. We're very superstitious about death – and about ministers!

The wake, with us, would be a sad affair – the open coffin, drink taken, stories, reminiscences told. No music with us. People would come, place a hand on the brow. Nobody was allowed to leave the body unattended. Two nights of a wake and then you were ready to bury the body. The minister would lead the funeral procession to the graveyard. The family and friends would carry the coffin, or if it was a very long way they'd put it on a horse and cart. My mother, as you know, went up into a bus. A crowd of us would dig the grave and after the coffin was lowered in, we'd cover it with earth. After that we'd go back, and, on the spot where the person died, we'd build a cairn of stones, so no one would camp on that spot again; where the person died.

Death and the family are the two most important things for the Travellers. Very old, some Travellers live to be, but more of us die young, I'm very sorry to say. Willie MacPhee had a grand-uncle, George, died at Faslane at the age of one hundred and fourteen years – but look at my brothers. Peter, he died up at Kinloch at the age of eight. Meningitis that was. My step-brother,

Previous page. The burial of Donald Reid at Dunkeld, Perthshire, c. 1910. The boy, in the centre, holding the pipes (by his knees) is Alexander Campbell. The big man to his left is Andrew Campbell and his wife Mary Stewart is on the right. (WMac)

Opposite. A family gathering of Reids, Johnstones and Camerons, Perthshire, c. 1953. Adults from the left, William Johnstone, Annie Reid, James Cameron and Alex Reid. A few months later, Annie Reid was killed by a sailor at Gairloch. (WMac)

Jimmy, he died down at Faversham in Kent at a very early age; and my brother Lindsay, he passed away three years ago, aged sixty-six. He was the best singer, best story-teller, best piper of all our family. He lived next door. We haven't got over it yet and I don't think we ever will. I'm the last of my generation and I'm sixty-three. Smoking, heavy drinking, alcoholism, childbirth, unemployment, accidents, murder, cars, all these things hit the Travellers – like everybody else but more frequently. In the old days it was TB, pneumonia, meningitis, whooping cough.

Tragedy stood at the corner with us – the Shadow of the Valley of Death was something we grew up with. There was a young Ross-shire man, called the Little Dancer. He was, they say, a beautiful dancer but he took a shot at the market up at Ardgay, sat on the bridge and went into the river. He was drunk. He was found six weeks later at Dornoch, he came in there, on the beach. His wife was mourning his death and when she heard his body was found she went up to Garve. That's where there is what's called 'The Roaring Bridge'. And there she slipped into the water and she drowned herself. Wilsons to name they were, and the two of them drowned. No children.

Now a week after that, the Little Dancer's father was across at Muir of Ord market, when whom should he meet but the father of the dead wife. He was James MacPhee to name. Well the two men shook hands, 'Let's have a drink,' Big Jimmy said 'what's good for me cannae be bad for you!' Well, you can take that which way you want. It's like a riddle. One man lost a daughter and the other man lost a son and that's what they said when they met. So they went into the pub, and when Big Jimmy raised his glass, the father of the Little Dancer said 'Well Jim, what's bad for me, cannae be good for you! Here's to the twa o' them – in Paradise!' The two men who might have fought said that, and I hear they laughed!

The MacPhees are a big Traveller family, all over Scotland and many was the hardship they've had. I told you about Big Willie MacPhee down in Perth and his wife, Bella, that's his first cousin. Well, he's eighty-five years old. He still travels. He was out in South Uist, this summer. He still plays the pipes. He's got the strength of three men! But the deaths in that family! He can remember the outbreak of the First World War.

'We were there at the Brig o' Turk and my father was busking for the tourists. And the day was very, very hot, so my mother went into the wee Post Office shop, it's a museum now, and she asked for some sugar. I was standing beside her. "O Mistress MacPhee," the postmistress said, "have you not heard the news? Great Britain is now at war with Germany. The price of everything is up!" And they talked about how terrible it was and she said, "I cannae give ye sugar the day – naebody knows what will happen with the war."

Willie MacPhee, aged 85, in his caravan at the Double Dykes park, Perth, 1995. Willie is a piper, singer, story-teller, and great-great-grandfather. Born in Dunbarton, he has lived most of his life in Perthshire, but still travels all over the Highlands and Islands, busking for the tourists. (TN)

So my mother went out to where the coaches stopped, big four-horse coaches with the tourists in, and she begged a penny or two and then she went back to the shop and got her pound of sugar. Then we lighted a fire and brewed a pot of tea and when father came back, he told us the war had started.

'Many were the men I saw go away – and many were the men did not return. And after the war, there was something that I'll remember till my dying day – the Spanish 'flu. We were out at Milngavie and we were going into Glasgow past a place called Lambhill, where there's a huge cemetery, when we seen the hearses nose to tail, nose to tail – hearses all down the road. There were that many people dying in Glasgow that they couldn't bury them! They were burning them and putting them in pits. I saw it with my own eyes. I was eight years old. That's the God's honest truth.

'The next year after that my wife's granny, Bella McPhee, and her aunty, Maggie, were killed on the railway, at Jameson, God rest them, three and a half miles out of Dumbarton, at the foot of Loch Lomond. Granny and Maggie were walking in the middle of the line. The line goes twisting down with big bankments on every side and the drivers used to shut off steam at the top of the hill and go silent down the brae. There's a big incline down. The two of them were coming up to see my father and mother. We were camped by the railway, working at the harvest. Now Aunt Maggie, she smoked a pipe, God rest her, and she wanted a smoke so she went up to get a light from a surface-man, who was working in his garden there above the railway.

'It was five o'clock in the afternoon, and Maggie went up with her wee boy and her wee girl, for to get a match for her pipe. She was stood with the man, talking, when she seen smoke coming in the distance from a train. And granny was standing in the middle of the railway, waiting for her to come down. And she was deaf! So Maggie ran down the bank to get her mother – and she ran right up against the train and all three of them were killed. My granny, aunt Maggie and her unborn bairn. And her two children were watching. They saw it all happen.

'And when this happened I was down in Dumbarton with Maggie's brother, Geordie, and we were riding the trams, because the men were drinking. We were hanging, swinging on the back of a tram when it came to the crossing of the railway and it stopped. We jumped off and we ran to where we seen a big crowd leaning over looking down and we asked what it was. "Two tinkie women got killed by a train!" they said. "Two tinkie women?" said Geordie. "Aye," said a man, "they just carried the bodies into that shed." So we went down onto the railway and we asked the station master what it was. And he asked us our names and he said, "Maybe you'll know these woman" and he took us into the shed. And I'll remember this till the day I go to my grave,

Bella MacPhee plays the Jew's harp. First cousin and wife to Willie MacPhee, Bella was born in a tent in Kintyre and has lived all her life on the road, 1995. (TN)

they were lying side by side; my granny over there, God rest her, and my aunty over here, face up, with the cinders from the railway sticking into her face. And Geordie and I ran back to camp and told the rest of them what happened. I was nine years old.

'A year after that my father died. He took a shock and died at thirty-nine years of age. I was ten years old. And the very next year after that Bella's aunty Mary, her mother's older sister, she was killed in the Caledonian Canal at Fort Augustus. She was up there with all her family. And they met in with Stewarts and they swapped their horse and they ended up with a skew horse. But they had to go on, they were going up to Inverness – and that horse backed off into the canal. The cart went right over on top of them. Six of them got killed, five living, and one unborn child. Three children they had. All six got drowned, and the horse. That was Mary McPhee and he was a Townsley. It's a very tragic family is the MacPhee.

'After all that I never went to school in all my days. My sisters did – they were taken into a home – but I was the bad one, I always escaped, lived out on the road here and there best I could. And things stay the same. Just two years back, Bella's sister, Cathy, she was killed in a car crash, down at Lochgilphead. She was married on a very evil man, he was a very evil man. He was in prison for a long, long time but he came out, Isaac Williamson. He's dead now, and one shouldn't speak ill of a man when he's dead, but that man was evil and he killed her. He said he'd kill her! We didn't think he would. She was driving the car and he just catched at the wheel and he fought the car straight into this big wood lorry, forestry lorry. Both of them got killed. They were flown away by air-ambulance to the Royal Infirmary in Glasgow, but she died that night and he died in the morning. Their daughter-in-law and a wee baby were there in the back of the car but they were all right. They told what happened.

'If you're a Traveller you expect a hard life; things are easy for us now, we've got our pensions and Double Dykes, Perth, is a very good campsite. We've got a caravan right in the centre now and we've got all conveniences. But in 1990 we were out at the back when the big flood came and we lost near enough everything we had – the caravan was smashed to pieces, the water was over the tops of the lorries! I was lucky to save my pipes – we had to start again at eighty.

'We went to see that film *Braveheart*. We didn't like it. I watched them making *Rob Roy* at Aberfoyle in the fifties with Richard Todd – that was a good film. And they did that in the right places, did the filming in the right places and the next year after that, I went down to Langbank by Port Glasgow, that's out in the Greenock direction, and I was looking for a caravan. And they

Alec John pauses for a smoke on the road west. Suilven is a landmark which has guided travellers for generations, 1995. (TN)

had a caravan with a dint in the back, and it was the caravan Richard Todd had used for his make-up, waiting for the fights and that. So I bought it. And we lived in that caravan for eighteen months until my wife, Mary Campbell, died – she died in that caravan, across the burn on the Knock farm. So then I gave it away. It was a heart-attack – and later on I married, Bella. She's a cousin and she's a MacPhee like myself.'

Death, accident and murder – the Travellers always had a hard time of it and many was the Traveller who just disappeared. When that happened, we'd usually say it was the Burkers who got them. My wife, Mary, she's got plenty of stories about the Burkers. All the Davies have stories about the Burkers. They used to murder the Travellers to use their bodies in the medical schools. Burke and Hare were the names of the men who began it. Serial killers they were in their day. They came from Edinburgh but they worked all over. They murdered for money so that the doctors and students would have bodies to dissect and they were, I believe, very well paid for their pains! They were the original 'body snatchers'.

The man who started all this was William Hare, he had a lodging house, and Burke was his accomplice. One of the lodgers died, nobody knew who the man was so they sold the body for cash! Robert Knox, an eminent surgeon, bought the corpse for seven pounds ten shillings! Everything went very well, so he wanted more bodies. Burke and Hare went into the business! At least fifteen men got murdered and carted off for dissection. But at last they were apprehended and tried. This man Hare turned King's evidence and was set free but Burke, he was the brains behind the whole thing – he was hanged. That was in 1829. I've got a paper-cutting tells the whole story:

'Precisely at eight o'clock the procession began to move towards the scaffold. Burke was supported by two Catholic priests. When he arrived at the head of Liberton's Wynd, his face had an expression of wildness and anxiety, as if he were uneasy and uncertain of his reception from the mob and he hurried on with his eyes half closed. We regret to state the population received him with a shout of ferocious exaltation, and though the magistrates, with great good feeling, endeavoured, by waving their hands, to repress these most indecent expressions of triumph over a wretched criminal about to pay the forfeit of his life for his crimes, "Heave him off", "Bring out Hare", "Hang Knox", "Out of the way", "Turn him round"! But the unruly mob disregarded all these signals as well as the hands of the Rev. T. Marshall, uplifted in the attitude of prayer, while the more respectable part of those assembled expressed their strong disapprobation of this unseemly clamour. When Burke rose from his kneeling posture he was observed to lift a silk handkerchief, on which he had knelt, and put it in his pocket. He then cast his eyes upwards towards the gallows, and at ten past eight took his place on the drop, the priest supporting him. While the executioner, who was behind him, was adjusting the rope, Burke said "the knots behind", which were the only words, not devotional, spoken by him on the scaffold. Here the populace raised another insulting shout mingled with cries of "Burke him and do the same for Hare!" In the meantime his spiritual instructors, regardless of the clamour around, proceeded with their duties, and said to him, "Now say your creed, and when you come to the words Lord Jesus Christ, give the signal and die with the blessed name in your mouth." This advice he seemed to follow, for he waited only a few seconds on the drop when he gave the signal – throwing away the handkerchief. The drop immediately fell, and with a short but severe struggle, he expired, the multitude again exulting by long and continuous shouts over the last agonies of the victim.'

Well that was that! That was Edinburgh. But the doctors still needed bodies and, they say, coaches were sent out into the countryside to get corpses. Some would be dead but others were less so! The Travellers were the ideal victims. Even their own families didn't know where they were half the year. Disappearance was way of life with the Travellers.

It's because of the Burkers that the Travellers got afeared of the doctors – but it's a fear that goes way back beyond then. You see the Travellers couldn't afford a doctor, so they had to do without them. We had our own ways, our own cures and medicines. Kill or cure it was! The Travellers kept clear of the doctors and the doctors kept clear of the Travellers. Physician heal thyself was what we thought of them! It's different now but in the old days we were full of cures and superstitions and some of them were very good!

I mind once, when I was a boy, I was up on a threshing mill, cutting sheaves, and the knife slipped and I cut myself deep in the leg. I was silly, fourteen or fifteen years of age, I worked on. All day I worked and when I came off the mill that night, down the ladder, I could hardly walk. My boot was full of blood, spilling over, it was lucky I had a bike or I wouldn't have got home! My father looked at the wound and he cleaned it, and next day he got a piece of roset, what we used for soldering, and he melted it down and mixed it up with butter – just like a poultice. 'You'll have to suffer it as hot's you can' he said, then he laid it on the wound and doubled round the cloth. Well, in a few days the swelling was down and all the poison was out and that was that. I washed out the boot and went back to work. I remember asking him what he called a mixture like that. 'There's no equivalent in English' he said, 'but in Gaelic we call it "*treage*".'

And a boil. Bloody aggravating it was. On the back of my neck. The size of an egg. So my great-aunt, Katie Williamson's mother, said 'Take a bar of soap and knead it soft with water; roll the soap in sugar, then tie it firm against the boil with a bandage.' I did that – and soon enough the boil burst and cured itself!

Then there was this girl taking fits, epileptic fits. Her mother took her to an old Traveller woman and told her about the fits. The old woman sent the mother away and she said to the girl, she'd be about twelve or thirteen, 'Stand here with your back to the fire and lift your skirt right up to your thighs, and let all the heat get onto your legs.' Then she said to the girl 'Turn round where you are.' And the old woman put a knife into each of the girl's legs. Then

Alec John Williamson, inspecting the old campsite at Ledbeg, with Meall Coire an Lochan in the background and Highland cattle about to put an end to the joke! 1995. (TN)

she took some blood out of her and ran it into a bowl. She said to the girl, 'Don't be frightened – put down your skirt and turn round where you are.' Then she gave the girl a pair of scissors and asked her to cut her fingernails and place the clippings in the bowl with the blood. After that the old woman cut a lock of her hair from the girl's forehead and dropped it on top of the blood and nails. Then – don't ask me what – she sang a chant and put the bowl away saying to the girl, 'We'll look at the blood again tomorrow.' Next day the girl came back, the bowl was clean, and the girl was cured. Hair, nails and blood from the thighs – that was the cure! My mother heard about that out on Skye.

Another thing I heard from Skye, was a man who felt an illness coming on. Before he took to his bed, he went down to the shore and shot a seal and he dragged it back home. Then he got his wife to rend it down and turn the blubber into oil and each day he was in bed, he drank a pint of the seal oil, till he got better. What he had, I don't know. Nor do I know whether he was a Traveller or not – though he probably needed to travel pretty fast after that!

And it wasn't just people we cured! If a horse took a colic or got constipated the remedy was a quarter of tea – a packet-full straight in the kettle and boiled up very strong. Then you'd put the horse's head over your shoulder and another man would feed it from a bottle. That would do the trick – get the horse moving, as we used to say! I used the same remedy on a dog once. A woman, here in Edderton, Marie Manson, had a dog, a Staffordshire bull-terrier. Ooh she thought the world of this dog. And she asked me to come down and look at him. 'He's in agony,' she said 'he can't pass, he's constipated!' He was looking kind of fat, so I said to Mrs Manson, 'Have you got tea?' 'Oh yes,'

Duncan Williamson, Argyllshire Traveller and renowned story-teller in the caravan of Willie MacPhee, Perth, 1995. (TN)

she said, 'do you want a cup?' 'Not just now' I replied 'it's for the dog!', and I asked her to brew up very strong. Then I got a screw-top bottle, put a piece of cloth around it, so he wouldn't cut himself, and poured it in! 'Mrs Manson' I said 'the shed or garden is now the place for him!' Well, my goodness, boy, next day she was round to say the job was done! 'You must know a thing or two about dogs!' she said, 'he filled a bucket and a half!' That was a horse cure on a dog.

We had to make do – kill or cure! I mind once up at Durness, two Travellers, George Williamson and William MacNeill, his brother-in-law, getting a call from a crofter. He came into the camp to say that his horse had couped the cart and got a shaft in her side and some of her intestines were out. He asked if anyone there, being horse-dealers, could help. So Willie shouted out, 'See George up there – he's a vet!' Now that was a joke! George was not a vet, but they all set off back to the croft and they picked up two more men on the way. In the stable the horse was tied up, with a blanket round its belly to keep the guts in. George purified his knife with fire and he got the four men to hold the horse at each quarter and they got the horse down on the ground. It was a Sheffield steel carving knife. First he cut the wound bigger and then he forced the intestines back inside. From somewhere he'd got a huge needle and string and he sewed up the wound and bandaged the belly of the horse right round. 'I cannae promise anything,' he said. But three days later that mare was well. The Travellers were good at things like that. They liked to turn their hand to this and that. My father was blacksmith, cobbler, harness-maker, cartwright! In the hot summers the metal rings on the cartwheels would slacken off – the wood shrink and the steel hoops come loose – I've seen them roll away. Well, he could turn his hand to every job like that and many was the time we helped the crofters out.

Now, I'd like to tell you about an Argyllshire man, a namesake of mine, Duncan Williamson – he's famous for his stories and songs, and he's got plenty cures and remedies. Some of them we have, others must be inventions of his own people – so I'll let him tell his own tale. Duncan Williamson:

'There were nine in my family and only one of us was born in a hospital – and the one born in the hospital was the only one that died! My mother was born in the cave at Muasdale. They were on their way down to Campbeltown when granny started her labour, so they went into the cave and that's where my mother was born. Tied the cord herself in there on the stones. It's a big cave, not far off the road, with a big double chimney for letting out the smoke from the fire. One of sixteen she was.

'That was my mother – none of her own family was born in a cave, we were all born in the Furnace wood, in the big galley, or out on the road, in a wee bow-tent. No doctor, no nurse. Just a visit from a doctor cost half a crown, or five shillings – where were we going to get that kind of money? We made use of nature, Old Mother Nature, and even the doctors are going back to maggots and leeches in the hospitals now! I watched a programme on the television about that. Our family never used maggots, we only used leeches. When I was a boy, if we had a boil, or a bad sore, or a wound that turned septic, my mother would put down a leech on it and the leech would suck all the pus and the poison out. We boys used to go down to the ponds and bring back the leeches in jam jars, with holes in the lid.

'If you have sixteen kids things are bound to go wrong, sometimes! So mother had cures. Handed down from my granny they were. For nappy rash it was burnt ash. We'd burn young ash branches on a clean fire till the sticks were snow-white in the embers. Then we'd let the fire die and crush the burnt sticks smooth with our palms and fingers and mother would spread it, like talcum powder, on the sores. Or sometimes she burned sheep's wool and old blankets – burnt them right down till the wool was a black powder, black like gunpowder, and she used that for wet rashes and sweat rashes. And the MacPhees, they used to use wild bramble leaves, burnt down to the ash.

Duncan Williamson and Willie MacPhee enjoying an impromptu ceilidh—singing, making music and playfully insulting each other, 1995. (TN)

'Whooping cough and diphtheria – they were killers when I was young. My brother Jimmy, he was seven years younger than me, he got bad whooping cough when he was less than one year old and he was cured by a trout in the mouth. Cough, cough, cough! For days the bairn was coughing and coughing and getting very weak and very bad. So mother finally said to me – "Duncan, go down to the stream and guddle a small trout; and bring it back as fast as you can." And she gave me a jimmy-jar. And under a stone, I soon guddled a wee fish and brought it back, and she was stood there, rocking the bairn in his shawl – very feeble, cough, cough, cough! And now I swear, on my mother's grave and that I'll never smoke this cigarette if I tell a lie, that my mother then took the trout from the jar and held it by its tail, just above wee Jimmy's mouth. He was nine months old, and the fish was gasping, and the bairn was coughing and gasping for breath. The fish was dying – but so was my brother and my mother was going to kill the fish for the sake of the boy. And she held it there right in the boy's mouth until the wee trout was dead. Then she said to me, "Take it back to the burn where you found it, and throw it in, and something will eat it." Next day I woke up and I heard no coughing. The coughing was gone, and wee Jimmy's alive to this day – he's sixty-one.

'For an ordinary cough, for soothing a throat, my mother used a turnip. In the autumn she'd get a nice big neep, like a Hallowe'en lantern, and she'd clean it out and make a soup – but she'd keep the shell, the skin of the

turnip, and half fill it up with brown sugar. Then with four strings she'd hang it up in the roof of the tent at the back. And she'd leave it there and the sugar would turn to syrup and ferment. After that, if someone had a cough or a sore throat that was the cure – a spoonful of syrup from the big hanging turnip! If my mother heard me cough she'd say, "Come on lad" and take me in the tent and go up to the turnip – and sometimes soot from the fire would be there in the melted sugar – and she'd give me a spoonful of "mother's neep treacle"! That turnip used to hang there till the skin wrinkled like an old woman's face, and all the syrup was gone.

'The McPhees they had a cure for bad throats. If they had a very, very sore throat, they'd urinate onto one of their stockings and put it round their neck, "That'll put it away," they said. A woollen sock, a piece of cloth it would be – anything that would hold the moisture. That's what they did – urinate and tie it round like a scarf! That's what Big Willie told me! And if someone had bad bronchitis, they'd get a ham-skin, or a pork-skin, and heat it till the grease was just melting, and put it across the chest of the sick man and keep it there. And sometimes they'd put brown paper on the chest, all smeared with tar, and the fumes would come up and give the man or the woman more breath.

'For an ordinary cold in the nose, it was oak bark. My father, if he had a headache, would ask me to go out and cut a piece of bark and place it on his head and tie it round with a handkerchief. And we would suck the bark of fresh willow – for the aspirin. I learned about the science of the aspirin when I was seventeen or eighteen, working up in Aberdeen. But long before that, when we were making baskets, we'd skin the wands and keep the bark, for chewing in the winter. It was the young willow bark, first year growth, when it was in full sap we took. The Travellers chewed willow like they chewed tobacco.

'Tobacco leaves were good for a wound. When my cousin, Willie McPhee, was a boy he got a notion to smoke and he borrowed his uncle's basket knife, and he was carving himself a pipe-bowl out a potato when he cut his hand, real bad. So his father took a big broad leaf of tobacco and he held it round and he put a bandage on to keep the poison away. And we would put salt, a lot of salt on a wound, to staunch bleeding. You had a moment of pain but then the salt got hold of the blood, salt would stop anything but a big artery bleeding. When I nearly severed my thumb, baiting the long-lines, fishing Loch Fyne, my mother put in salt and sewed the wound with strong cotton. There's a great gauge still and my thumb's not straight – but I've sparred with the middle-weight champion of Scotland, 1948, and I've thumped a few not so good out the ring!

'We had plenty of uses for tobacco. Tobacco was for snakebite, for poultices, and my father used to use tobacco when cutting his hair. He used to cut his own hair so he'd make an ugly job of it! Then he'd steep tobacco in water – to make his hair glow, like a modern rinse! He'd rub the juice into his hair and the tobacco would bring the colour back and get it growing again, so the jagged bits would equal out faster. "I'll not look long like a sheep," he'd say "a couple of days and you'll never know the difference!" It was him that told the joke about the man in the butchers. "Do youse have a sheep's heid?" the man asked. "No," said the butcher, "it's just the way I pairt my hair!" He stayed blond all his life, never went grey. And the MacKenzies up at Fortingall, they were very dark, but every year they liked to dye their hair peroxide white!

‘My family was lucky, we were very healthy. We lived in the wood up at Furnace for thirty-seven years. When the diphtheria came to Furnace the school was closed, several of the children died but for the Williamsons, up in the wood, it was holiday! No school – snaring, fishing, blaeberries, hazelnuts and down on the shore picking shellfish. We used to go up to Inverary to the steamers, and every three months the Duke of Argyll used to come down in his big car and drive up into the wood – wearing his kilt and a *skean-dhu*, his clothes all worn and big holes in his socks. He was very kind to the Travelling People. It was his ground we were on. He liked to hear the old stories and songs but the main reason he came was to get his toes done! My father was very good with a knife. The Duke of Argyll would come to have his toe-nails cut and pared and a wee bit crack with the Williamsons! Tobacco or cigarettes he'd leave us sometimes. My mother smoked an old clay pipe all her life and if the stem of a pipe broke my granny would take a pin to her finger and poke out the blood and use the blood to mend the pipe. I've seen her with a pipe with three breaks in it, all mended with blood. So there they'd sit round the fire talking – the Williamsons and the Duke of Argyll. It was fairy-tales, magic, tales of the supernatural he liked, and we had plenty of all that. He let us take out the firewood and keep the rabbits down.’

Now Duncan Williamson doesn't have Gaelic but I think they've got more of the Traveller life left down there in the south than we have up here in the north. They've got more people down there. And they're very interested in the supernatural down there but we've still got a few things up here – I've seen them myself – that I defy any man born of woman to explain. We've had reports of a ghost on the road to Tain! And reports of fairies in the west. How much of this is fact I cannot say, but our family used, years back, to know a man who had the second sight. Ian Chisholm was his name. Once he was working in his crofthouse when the door opened and a sea-otter came in. And it stood there girning, showing its teeth. He thought it was going to come for him so, very slowly, he put his hand behind him, to get a tool to defend himself – but as he did this he lost all the power in his arm. The otter was spitting and baring its teeth. He tried to shout at the otter, to frighten it, but he lost all power of speech. He sat frozen like a dead man, petrified with fear! Then the otter turned and left the house without a sound. But suddenly, before he could look away, there was a little girl before him in the doorway!

'Did you get a fright, Ian?' she said, and closed the door behind her. 'I did,' he said. 'And do you know who that otter was?' she asked. 'Of course I do – it was yourself!' And then he asked the girl where she got her tricks. 'It's my granny teaches me,' she said and she went to the window and looked out across the bay. 'Shall I tell you what's on board that ship?' she asked. 'It's meat' he said. 'Would you like it delivered to the shore or to the house?' she asked. 'I don't want it – nor do I want any more of your tricks!' said Ian, knowing now she was a witch.

But the girl took no notice of the man and went to the fire and took a bowl of water back to the windowsill. Then she drew a comb across the face of the water and on its surface she scattered a handful of peat. Ian Chisholm tried to speak, but no sound came out of his throat; he tried to raise himself up out of his chair but the power was out of him and not a muscle could he move. Then the girl blew upon the face of the water and slowly round and round with one finger, began to stir the glore and as she did this, Ian heard the wind begin to blow and the black clouds of a storm came over the sea . . .

Once more Ian Chisholm struggled to raise himself from his chair but he was paralysed, like a dead man; he just sat there helpless as he watched the ship begin to spin and the sea was whipped into a fury of spindrift, spray and spume. He struggled to cry out. He thought his last breath had come when suddenly the door was flung open with a bang and the girl's mother stood there, panting. When she saw what was going on she rushed to the window, grabbed the basin of water and flung it on the fire. 'Enough of these games and wickedness!' she said, 'go home to bed at once!'

Well, the girl stood there silent – then she smiled and looked at Ian, and she went to the door, where she turned and did a little curtsey, before running home. After that the storm abated and the strength gradually came back into the man. But I've heard that Ian Chisholm walked like a cripple for three days after that, for that girl had witchcraft sure enough!

Now, Ian Chisholm was not a Traveller, and I don't think the girl was either. But that happened out on the islands and it's a story all the Travellers had. Oooh there was plenty of that out there. And I'll tell you this – when our people first came to the mainland it was thrown at them by the other Travellers that they were wizards and witches and all that kind of thing. Living out in the open, cooking on the trenny, that's a cauldron with three legs, people would think we had witchcraft, that we were just like the crones in *MacBeth*, on the blasted heath.

But I also have a story from this side, from the east, about something that happened not far from here. There was a big dance. Don't ask me where. Don't ask me when. But it was a big dance and suddenly this girl got up and stood in the middle of the floor and said she'd dance 'any fuckin' man aff his feet!' Her name was Mary Finlayson. 'I'd even dance the fuckin' de'il himself aff his pegs the nicht!' she said, shouting it out to everyone there. Well, the band struck up and she started dancing all by herself in the middle of the hall! When, bang, in through the door stepped a handsome young man, dark-haired, tall, well-dressed — and well-educated too, very likely. 'You' he said 'you are the woman I've been looking for! Come here and dance with me!' and there in the middle of the floor the two of them danced together. Other dancers came in around them but this pair never stopped! On and on they danced till two or three in the morning — until there was nobody left in the hall except that woman and that man! The band had gone but he now made his own music — mouth music — and this was the tune he played . . .

It's real dance music — it's what the Travellers call the Devil's music! It went on and on — mouth music — with no words but every now and then in among the sounds you'd hear a word or phrase 'Mary Finlayson — will this do you? Mary Finlayson — will that do you? Mary Finlayson — you can dance all night but there'll still be another measure in this reel!' He never stopped. 'Dance all night, dance back to back, dance with no face, Mary Finlayson and still I'll measure out another reel, Miss Finlayson — another reel, Miss Finlayson! Will this do you? Will that do you? I've got you now Miss Finlayson! Will you take my will, Miss Finlayson?' That kind of thing!

Well, the tune he played, Travellers call 'The Devil's Tune'! Others call it *Bog An Lochan* but whatever it was, next morning they found the girl — lying cold, spreadeagled on the floor of the hall. She was not dead — she came round when they got her home, but she was never the same woman again. They say the light-hearted woman who went to the dance that night was not the woman came home next day! She never married — I've heard it said —

nor did they ever find out who the dark stranger was. But it was the Devil himself, sure enough!

There's another tune like *Bog An Lochan* for dancing to and its called *Calum Mac A Bhi Torrach* which being interpreted means 'The Mating Dance of Calum MacPhee'! It's also known as 'Tail Toddle' and it goes like this.

You see sex and the Devil got put together up here and that's one reason why the Travellers were very quiet about sex. You'd get a touch of sex in Ailidh Dall's 'Ossian' — but Ailidh Dall was very proper, I never heard him sing the bawdy songs we have down here in Edderton! I'm a reprobate! Like Robbie Burns! Do you know that song 'The Maid and the Miller'? It goes very fast — has to go very fast — I got it from my father, but I've heard tell it is a very old song — that Boswell sang it to Dr Johnson! Now there was a very proper man — drank tea!

Bella MacPhee walking behind the family cart. Kintyre, 1930. (W Mac)

THE MAID AND THE MILLER

As the maid and the miller
Sat beside the fire
He put his hand upon her toe
What is this my deario?

It's my toe — trip and go
Let me down — safe and sound
Said the maid to the miller hi ho!

As the maid and the miller
Sat beside the fire
He put his hand upon her knee
What is this my deario?

It's my knee — nic nac
It's my toe — trip and go
Let me down — safe and sound
Said the maid to the miller hi ho!

As the maid and the miller
Sat beside the fire
He put his hand upon her thigh
What is this my deario?

It's my thigh — sic sac
It's my knee — nic nac
It's my toe — trip and go
Let me down — safe and sound
Said the maid to the miller hi ho!

As the maid and the miller
Sat beside the fire
He put his hand upon her tummy
What is this my deario?

It's my rumble, belly, guts!
It's my thigh — sic sac
It's my knee — nic nac
It's my toe — trip and go
Let me down — safe and sound
Said the maid to the miller hi ho!

As the maid and the miller
Sat beside the fire
He put his hand upon her mouth
What is this my deario?

It's my mouth — for to eat
It's my rumble, belly, guts!
It's my thigh — sic sac
It's my knee — nic nac
It's my toe — trip and go
Let me down — safe and sound
Said the maid to the miller hi ho!

As the maid and the miller
Sat beside the fire
He put his hand upon her nose
What is this my deario?

It's my nose — for to breathe
It's my mouth — for to eat
It's my rumble, belly, guts
It's my thigh — sic sac
It's my knee — nic nac
It's my toe — trip and go
Let me down — safe and sound
Said the maid to the miller hi ho!

Willie MacPhee plays 'the moothie', 1995. (TN)

As the maid and the miller
Sat beside the fire
He put his hand upon her tits
What are these my deario?

It's my tits — for to suck!
It's my nose — for to breathe
It's my mouth — for to eat
It's my rumble, belly, guts!
It's my thigh — sic sac
It's my knee—nic nac
It's my toe — trip and go
Let me down — safe and sound
Said the maid to the miller hi ho!

As the maid and the miller
Sat beside the fire
He put his hand upon her c. . .
What is this my deario?

It's my c. . . — for you to f . . . !
It's my tits — for to suck
It's my nose — for to breathe
It's my mouth — for to eat
It's my rumble, belly, guts
It's my thigh — sic sac
It's my knee — nic nac
It's my toe — trip and go
Let me down safe and sound
Said the maid to the miller hi ho!

Now I don't think anybody would say that is proper song! But it gives you a thirst for a dram! Afore ye go I'd like to give you two more poems. We don't know who wrote the first — it's anonymous:

One murky night, with wind and rain
My steps were getting weary
A shepherd's house stood on the plain
On the lonely strath of Dheiry.

When I came knocking at his door
His light was shining clearly
Be bade me sleep upon the floor
Deep in the hay of Dheiry.

I left my blessings on his ewes
And on his croft sae eerie —
'My sorrows never on your brow
Nor them that dwell in Dheiry.'

That's called 'The Lonely Strath of Dheiry'. It's down Ullapool way. This last one's called 'The River', I wrote it myself, and I've dedicated it to my three daughters Violet, Christine and Dawn.

THE RIVER

Here's to the river,
That ancient life-giver
And to the salmon that frolic its length.

There's riches in store
For them follows its roar
And there's something divine in its strength.

O God of mankind
Who made land, bread and wine
And the sights of delight here before me.

Immortal your hand,
Cups the sea and the sand
When the Shin river dances in glory.

Ailidh Dall, the
Sutherland / Caithness border,
1957. (HH, BB)

Contemporary Ancestors and the Transmission of Song

Hear the voice of the Bard!
Who present, past, and future sees
Whose ears have heard,
The Holy Word,
That walk'd among the ancient trees.
WILLIAM BLAKE

The phrase 'It's my rumble, belly guts' provides a wonderful fulcrum to Alec John Williamson's song 'The Maid and the Miller'. The word 'guts' gives dramatic surprise and contemporary punch to a very old song – but the most remarkable thing about Alec John's singing of 'The Maid', is his delivery. The song is sung so fast, that the words conjoin to become abstract, staccatoed mouth-music – out of which the ear isolates occasional, 'erotic soundbites'. All Travellers like their songs to have strong narrative thrust: but this song is essentially rhythm. It is presented as a conscious exercise in verbal dexterity, a demonstration of skill, as a tongue-twister. With its repetitive use of ever-longer 'rounds', the song is also a superb example of a methodology, by which oral memory can be developed and exercised. A similar 'educational' structure lies at the core of 'Old Macdonald had a Farm'; and just as that universal, Scots children's song is used to develop memory, participation, rhythm and a sense of melody in children so 'The Maid' is adult entertainment.

Although usually sung by Alec John alone, 'The Maid and the Miller' invites the participation of two people, a man and a woman, and exemplifies the dynamics of an oral culture in which the old unities of poetry and song are not differentiated. In addition the 'performance' as a whole is a living example of the group choral activity believed to underlie the origins of European drama. The artistry is didactic: it explores and hones the relationship of master and pupil, a presenter and chorus. 'The Maid and the Miller', which on the surface seems to be a simple, bawdy song, is in fact a contemporary continuance of traditional practices that have preserved oral literature in non-literate societies over millennia.

Robert Stewart, 'Polly', pipes in full military regalia outside an enlarged bow-tent (a galley), Aberdeenshire, 1930s. (JS)

All traditions evolve but the stronger the core, the greater the continuity and the more vital the tradition. Alec John Williamson's performance might excite an Ann Summers house-party but, more importantly, it illustrates the precise mechanism by which the kind of ancient epics, declaimed by his grand-uncle, Ailidh Dall, come down across centuries very minimally modified; *Am Maraiche Mairnealach*, *Am Bron Binn* and *Ossian* being classic examples. For the Travellers, such stories and songs were camp-fire entertainment, but they link living tradition in the Highlands with very early Celtic literary precedents and practices: they embody the historical continuum, the felt kinship, which is so important in all Scottish culture and which connects the late twentieth century with the pre-Christian *Gaidhealtachd*.

The transmission of culture is just as important as the culture itself. Modern institutional education tends to divorce the 'literary' transmission of culture from the living reality of that culture. Huge bureaucracies have grown up around almost self-contained educational establishments – at the expense of the lived culture, the real culture carriers and poetic force that culture should embody. In more traditional and less institutionalised communities, the process of transmission is an integral part of the lived culture. Nowhere is this more true than in the Travelling community. The lifestyle is the culture, the culture is the lifestyle.

Great stories like *Am Maraiche Mairnealach* are genuinely worth literary analysis and interpretation: so is the process by which such works are handed across the centuries. The story proceeds via a sequence of surreal surprises, distributed along the narrative with masterly measure but however fantastical events and insights are, most relate to direct Traveller experience. The story is brilliantly cinematic and highly sexual, the narrative line is strong and the moral perception wonderful – for example when the bedridden princess rises at the end of the story to tell her three brothers of her husband's home-coming. Ailidh Dall's 'tinker romance' has the simplicity and reverberation of an Old Testament story but it reveals deeply Christian truths via a profoundly Celtic imagination. The history of *Am Maraiche Mairnealach* as a story, transmitted over time, is of equal fascination. Hamish Henderson relates 'When I first heard it, from Ailidh Dall in 1957, it was not the first I knew of it. I remember, around 1938, seeing mention of it in J. F. Campbell's *Popular Tales of the West Highlands*, which he got from 'Old Macdonald, travelling tinker'. It begins as follows.

' "There was a king and a knight, as there was and will be, and as grows the fir tree, some of it crooked and some of it straight, and he was a king in Eirinn." What a start that is! Campbell then goes on to relate the story much as the Stewarts have it in Sutherland. The wicked Queen persuades her stepson

"Sheen Billy" to put on a shirt and the shirt turns into a *beithir*, a great snake round his neck . . . Old Macdonald told of the freeing of his hero from the snake, and the making of a golden breast for the lady but the end of the story seems to have been, for some reason, lost – and there's a twist: Campbell relates how 'the old Tinker's son vainly tried to repeat [the rest] in August 1860, for he is far behind his father in the telling of old Highland tales'. Thus Campbell's version is of great interest but incomplete. Would he be surprised to learn that grand versions of Macdonald's story are still being told by Gaelic-speaking Travellers one hundred and thirty years later? I think he would!

'*Am Maraiche Mairnealach* is a pan-Celtic story. It seems certain to have originated in Brittany. It is close to 'King Lindorm' and other stories discussed by Gwennole Le Menn in his study of the Breton Analogues *La Femme au Sein d'Or*. Story-tellers from Brittany are known to have been made welcome at the court of David I, who became King of Scots in 1124. Presumably they told their tales in French and from there the stories went out into Gaeldom to be treasured by the Travellers. The story these Bretons told was also the source of a fine Scots ballad 'The Queen of Scotland'. It describes how a wicked Queen revenges herself on a young man, Troy Muir, who has rejected her advances. She gets the young man to lift a stone in her garden; a serpent lies under the stone, it wraps itself round Troy Muir's body. A young girl offers her breast to the serpent to save the young man, and at the end her breast is restored to her by Heaven.

> *As Heaven was pleased, in a short time*
> *To ease her first sad pain.*
> *Sae was it pleased, when she'd a son,*
> *To hae her pap again.'*

Even after the collapse of the Roman Empire, there was a basic cultural unity across Celtic Western Europe but direct connections between Scotland and Brittany were few and far between. The age of migrations and the solidification of the Q Celtic – P Celtic linguistic divisions, had created clearly separate political and cultural zones but even today we can see continuing linkage through Highland Traveller culture. *Am Maraiche Mairnealach* establishes a literary connection, *Am Bron Binn*, Ailidh Dall's song about 'Arthur, King of Britain', establishes a historical connection, and the ancient 'educational' methodologies of the Stewarts and Williamsons, suggest a third connection between old Brittany and Scotland.

Brittany retains the largest Celtic-speaking population of all the Celtic countries. And, despite historical pressures from centralist French

Jane Stewart, Traveller singer and organist from Mintlaw, Aberdeenshire, c. 1960. Jane was crippled as a young girl, but left at home to look after all her younger brothers and sisters while her parents hawked the roads of Aberdeenshire. A CD of her songs has recently been published. (JS)

governments, Brittany has preserved, in its fishing villages and deep-wooded hill-country, an intellectual tradition which might, romantically, be described as Druidic. One very ancient song, still sung in Brittany, is called 'The Druid and his Disciple'. It is usually sung by an individual singer but is based on unaccompanied presentation and response of just the kind apparent in Alec John Williamson's 'The Maid and the Miller'. Like *Am Maraiche Mairnealach*, 'The Druid and his Disciple' paints a dramatic word picture of the beliefs and values in the old Celtic world. And even more than 'The Maid and the Miller', 'The Druid' can be seen to be an exquisitely structured teaching tool, an educational exercise designed to stretch, extend and reinforce aural skills and oral memory. Like Victorian headmasters, Druid teachers instilled the habit of exactitude:

DRUID: *Handsome boy, beautiful Druid's son*
           Tell me my handsome one —
           What do you want me to sing to you?

DISC: *Sing me the series of number one*
           So that I can learn it.

DRUID: *There is no series of number one:*
            There is single necessity;
            There is Sin — father of sorrow —
            Nothing before, nothing after.
            Handsome boy, beautiful Druid's son
            Tell me my handsome one
            What do you want me to sing to you?

DISC: *Sing me the series of number two,*
            So that I can learn it today.

DRUID: *Two oxen harnessed to a shell:*
            They're pulling it — they breathe, they die.
            There's a marvel for you.
            There is no series of number one:
            There is single necessity;
            There is Sin — father of sorrow —
            Nothing before, nothing after.
            Handsome boy . . . etc.

DISC: *Sing me the series of number three*
            So that I may learn it today.

DRUID: *There are three parts of the world:*
            Three beginnings and three ends
            — of man as for the oak.
            Three kingdoms of Merlin
            Full of golden fruit, bright flowers
            Little children laughing.
            Two oxen harnessed to a shell:
            They're pulling it — they breathe, they die.
            There's a marvel for you.
            There is no series of number one . . . etc.

DISC: *Sing me the series of number four*
            So that I may learn it today. [Repeat as appropriate till last verse of poem]

DRUID: *Four stones to sharpen,*
            Stones to be sharpened by Merlin
            Who sharpens the swords of the valiant.
            There are three parts of the world . . . etc.

DRUID: *Five terrestrial zones,*
            Five ages in the duration of time —
            Five rocks on our dead sister . . .

DRUID: *Six little children of wax,*
            Given life by the light of the moon.
            If you don't know — I do!
            Six healing herbs in the cauldron!
            A little dwarf stirring up the brew
            One pinkie finger in his mouth.

DRUID: *Seven suns and seven moons,*
            Seven planets — the hen included!
            Seven elements rise in the stour of the air.

DRUID: *Eight winds which blow eight fires high*
            Eight fires with the Great Fire lit
            In the month of May on the mountain of the earth.
            Eight young calves white as the foam
            Eating the grass of the deep green isle;
            The eight white calves of the lady.

DRUID: *Nine little white hands on the threshing floor,*
            By the tower of Lezarmeur
            And nine mothers grieving bitterly.
            Nine sacred virgins who dance
            With flowers in their hair
            In robes of white linen
            Round the fountain they dance
            In the light of the moon.
            Nine piglets with a great sow,
            The size of a mountain
            At the door of their sty
            Stand snorting and snuffling:
            Little one, little one, little one
            Run to the apple tree
            The old boar will teach you a lesson!

DRUID: *Ten enemy vessels seen coming from Nantes.*
            Bad luck to you, bad luck to you!
            You men of Vannes!

DRUID: *Eleven armed priests coming from Vannes*
         With broken swords and bloody robes they come
         On crutches and three hundred more than these eleven!

DRUID: *Twelve months and twelve signs! The penultimate!*
         Saggitarius is lifting up his bow with arrow ready!
         The twelve signs now are all at war:
         A beautiful cow, the black cow
         With a white star on her forehead comes
         From the forest deep she comes
         Deep in her breast an arrowhead.
         Her blood is flowing like a flood
         She slumps forward down, her head comes up!
         The trumpet sounds! Fire and thunder!
         Rain and wind! Fire and thunder!
         Nothing! Nothing more!
         Nothing! No more of a series of numbers . . .

Alec MacPhee, piper and
basket-maker, Perthshire, 1946.
(WMac)

Sung or chanted in its completeness that marvellous 'round' poem lasts about fifty minutes. It was collected in the early nineteenth century by the Breton folklorist and poet La Villemarque (translated here by Hamish Henderson). He entitled his song 'The Series – The Druid and his Disciple'. It illumines a world within which memory was fundamental to knowledge and to art. Today, rote learning is out of fashion; few university students can repeat more than a few lines of poetry, few professors know more. Almost all contemporary poets have to 'read' their poetry – whereas the Druidic poets of Old Gaul are known, after long apprenticeship, to have been able to speak tens of thousands of lines by heart – aphorisms, riddles, poems, songs and stories.

The accumulation of huge reservoirs of knowledge in 'oral' form raises important questions about how, and to whom, such knowledge, such art, should be passed. There is no doubt that some people have aural and oral capacities much above the average, that some social structures are better adapted to nurturing oral tradition than others, that certain educational processes are more efficient than others. This being so, all tradition-bearers need to address a crucial question, how and to whom do I pass what I have?

'The Druid and his Disciple' was collected by Vicomte La Villemarque in the early nineteenth century. He knew he had found something ancient and fine and, as a poet, he seems to have modified what he heard – but published his song as a major 'folk' poem. In doing this the Vicomte behaved a little like James MacPherson when he published his famous, bogus *Ossian* in the eighteenth century. But whereas MacPherson's work remains much less interesting than the genuine folk traditions on which he based his work La Villemarque's work has been brilliantly vindicated by recent scholarship. It exists at one with the tradition from which it came.

In 1959, Claudine Mazeas, a young Breton folklorist, working entirely on her own, recorded a living, 'contemporary' version of 'The Druid and his Disciple', almost identical to La Villemarque's. She got it from an old horseman named Denis le Guen, and which he had learned from a very old man about sixty years before. Almost certainly she was tapping (and taping) the same, original seam that La Villemarque had found more than a century earlier. The story she tells of how le Guen received his song is a hair-raising and archetypal example of the 'oral tradition' in action. It can be paralleled by similar 'transmission' stories in Scotland.

Denis le Guen grew up on a small farm at Villemarche on the north Brittany coast. He was seventy-eight when Claudine Mazeas recorded him singing his magnificent version of 'The Druid and his Disciple'. He told her how he came to learn it.

'I was about ten or twelve years old. At harvest-time itinerant,

Willie MacPhee, 1965, with his son Andrew and his grandson John, relaxing after busking for tourists at Aberfoyle. (WMac)

agricultural workers used to come to our farm. Among them was an old man called Gwilliam Diegirer. He was a native of Villemarche but worked in various villages round about. He could not read or write, but he had many songs and on winter evenings he would come to our kitchen, drink his bowl of cider and sing for us. And by hearing the songs I found I could remember them just by the repetition. His big song was 'The Druid and his Disciple' . . . He never told me where he learned it or when he learned it, or how he learned it – but it must have been about 1820 or 1830.

'One day after he'd sung the song, I told him that I'd learned it and knew every word. He got angry. He didn't believe me, he called me a "snotty nose" and a "dirty little flea", and he asked "How could you know a great long song like that! No man or boy has ever learned that song off me!" And to show him I had the song I sang it back to him! The whole song, no mistakes, right through—and back to the beginning! And when I'd finished he couldn't understand how I'd done it! He became livid. He stormed out of the house and, as far as I know, he never sang that song again.

'He couldn't believe it. It was extraordinary. He'd sung that song

many times, no one had gathered even a verse or two. It required a very good memory, all the different parts – and then having to sing the whole song backwards so you ended at the beginning is very difficult. Maybe it seemed supernatural to him that a boy could have this gift! I had a gift, I heard the song, I liked the song and it stuck in my memory. I thought he would be pleased! He was devastated. I felt guilty – but I never forgot the song nor the man who gave it to me.'

Recognition, jealousy, pride, despair! The old man's mortality was made manifest in the transmission of 'his' song! Youth and age ranged with and against each other. Who but a worthy successor could so brilliantly take up his song? What force but life itself could so devastatingly triumph over age!

The importance of that incident lies not just in the dramatic collision of two lives around a fire and a cider-bowl but in the strong light it casts on the whole process of cultural transmission and the psychology of men. The story echoes various, archetypal master-pupil relationships – Saul and David, John the Baptist and Christ, Verrochio and Leonardo da Vinci, Salieri and Mozart.

In the arts, genius is often associated with irresponsibility but usually it is actually highly responsible, at least to itself. In traditional cultures a conscious sense of artistic responsibility is necessary, because individual genius has to link with the follower – here and now – or not at all. The modern idea of the neglected genius nurturing future generations, when public recognition has followed death is not possible within a genuinely oral tradition. Until the invention of the gramophone and tape-recorder, oral transmission had to be live and the experience lived. The extent to which recorded sound, film and television will change this in the future is as yet unknown. But it will, necessarily be something other than the visceral subversion experienced by Diegirer.

In Scotland, various Traveller stories affirm the archetypal nature of the le Guen experience. The Argyllshire Traveller, Duncan Williamson, has become one of the great story-tellers in twentieth-century Scotland. His account of the crucial event in his own development as a teller of stories is this: 'Granny was a great story-teller, and when she was going to tell us a story she'd look into her pocket to find the one she chose. The Traveller women didn't carry a purse but they all had a pocket tied round their waist, on a string, or a thin rope. It was like a sporran, but on the side, and it carried all their private things and money, like a handbag. I never saw my granny without her purse tied to her side. I have it in my bedroom yet – it's over a hundred years old today – all made by hand and there's a great story attached to it. It never came off, day or night, it was round her waist and we never knew what was in it, besides the stories she told. If we ran down to the shop for her baccy – when we got back

John MacDonald and his granddaughter Annie, piping for the tourists in Glencoe, Argyll, 1950s. (WMac)

she'd say "Now I'll tell you a story – from granny's pocket," and she'd open it up and peep inside and pick out a story, never letting us see where they came from, or what else was in the bag.

'One day my little sister Jeannie and I came back from school and we went into granny's tent and she was sleeping and the pocket was folded up and lying by her side. That was the first time in my life that I saw granny with her pocket off. And Jeannie said "Let's take granny's pocket!" and very, very carefully we lifted the pocket and we took it behind a tree and we peeped in. Amazement. There were things of all descriptions in that pocket – bangles, thimbles, needles, pins, big buttons of pearl, shirt-buttons, brooches, ear-rings, threepenny pieces with the acorns on, a pipe-cleaner, tobacco, pieces of pipe – but we couldn't find one single story! So we took the purse back. We crept into the tent and wrapped the string around and put it back just where it was, and granny was still asleep. She was lying there fast asleep – little old lady, old big buttony boots, lacey-boots, she had to lace them with a howkey pen and a pin and beside her there was a billycan of tea, cold black tea, and we ran off to play.

'It must have been about five o'clock when we came back to the camp and granny was up – with the pocket back around her waist. So we shouted to her, "Granny dae youse want any tobacco?" "No, weans" she said, "nae baccy the day" and she looket up and she poked at the fire. Then we said, "Granny, Granny tell us a story". "Sit down weans and I'll tell ye a story," she said and we went into the tent and sat down as she bent down to peek in her pocket. "Well weans – let me see what I can find in here the day," and then she stopped, and she looked very hard at me, then she looked very hard at Jeannie, then she looked at me and she said, "Well weans – I'm nae gain' tae tell ye a story the nicht." "Why Granny, why no story the nicht?" we asked. And she looket straight at me and she said, "Duncan, somebody's been in my pocket! Whilst I was asleep somebody's come in and my stories hae gone – every one." And though my Granny lived till I was seventeen year old she never told another story. She's buried in Elderslie, by Paisley, where William Wallace was born.'

Duncan Williamson's account, however embroidered, has the clear stamp of truth on it. Perhaps the old lady knew her powers were failing. Perhaps she was getting stubborn and bad-tempered. Maybe she'd felt she'd gone through her repertoire of stories enough! Whether her actions were selfish, benign, conscious or unconscious, there can be no doubt that that old lady placed a sudden, memorable burden on her grandson's shoulders. She must have known he had a talent, which she suddenly forced him to develop and carry on his own. Her ploy dramatised her own importance, and the mysterious secrecy implicit in story-telling; she thrust the guilt of responsibility on her grandson, her chosen one! Duncan Williamson still feels guilty about what happened (like Denis le Guen). Expiation of guilt is a powerful force in the creative arts – as in love. Today, Duncan Williamson says he knows three thousand stories.

Another example of the 'testing' nature of the transmission of oral culture comes from the Perthshire Traveller, Belle Stewart. It concerns her father, a man who died very young, shortly before the First World War. He was a very good singer, and up in Glen Isla he got to know a ploughman with wonderful versions of 'The Road and the Miles to Dundee' and 'Queen amang the Heather'. This ploughman didn't sing in public, nor did he want, it seems, to pass his song on to a young Traveller who had recently changed his name to MacGregor! But he loved to sing, he sang at the plough and he sang in the bothy, and Belle tells of how 'to find out the richt words o' the sangs, my faither sat for a hale week, every nicht, ootside the door o' the bothy, till he learned every word o' they twa songs! Of course, if he had coaxed that plooman outside-in, or upside-doon, or roond-aboot, he would ne'er hae sung – but there by hisself in the bothy, he sang every nicht. Sae my faither sat there every nicht a' week – and that plooman never knew my faither learnt they twa sangs aff him.'

That act of transmission is very similar to le Guen's experience. It was an act of musical piracy! The story also reinforces the importance of 'quality selection' at work in the folk process, and it shows how precious the best songs, sun by the best singers, are. There is a profound critical intelligence working within the many-headed-body of the folk tradition. It's quite possible that the young ploughman was seriously keen not to give 'his songs' to an itinerant, semi-professional singer, but it seems, more likely than not, that he was aware that the MacGregor was after his songs and that he made things difficult, but not impossible, for the young Traveller! Faint heart never won a fair lady!

All these 'oral' exchanges have the memorable permanence of initiation ceremonies. They are as affirming, as glorious, as life-permeating as first-love, first-killings, last-rites and forgiveness. Today, no singer in Scotland carries the two songs of the Glen Isla ploughman better than Sheila Stewart, the granddaughter of the man who risked a beating, to gather the songs as he knew them best sung. Presumably this unknown ploughman in Glen Isla had that special gift, that 'keening passion', that Sheila calls the *caoineadh*, that edge the Spaniards call the *duende*, that ancient 'pibroch note' that she continues.

In the media age traditional singers are well aware of the electronic and technical advances now so important to the whole world of song,

Jeannie Robertson, the great Traveller singer from Aberdeen, with Carolyn Paton, c. 1960. (HH)

music and story but, as always, the questions of choice and quality remain. It is a fact of great interest that when Claudine Mazeas first recorded Madame Bertrand (the greatest traditional Breton singer of recent times) she began with 'Skolven', her oldest song: and that when Hamish Henderson recorded Ailidh Dall, he began with *Am Bron Binn*, his oldest song. They wanted to begin, as it were, at the beginning and pay respect to the deepest layers from which their gifts had come up to them. Both songs are about fifteen hundred years old. And when Henderson first met Jeannie Robertson he began, he states, 'by singing the old ballad "The Battle of Harlaw": immediately she asked me inside, saying, "she'd show me the richt way o' it!" Now "The Battle of Harlaw" is only about six hundred years old! But it did the trick and confirms the conscious sense of value and responsibility these great singers and story-tellers feel.

'And the ancientness of Jeannie Robertson's repertoire was not just Scots, or narrowly Celtic – she was heir to strands of quality she had come across from all over:

> *From the hag and hungry goblin*
> *That into rags would rend you*
> *By the spirit that stands*
> *By the naked man in the book of moons defend you,*
> *That of your five sound senses*
> *You never be forsaken,*
> *Nor wander from your wits with Tom*
> *Abroad to seek your bacon.*
>
> *While I do sing "Any food, any feeding,*
> *Feeding, drink, or clothing."*
> *Come dame or maid, be not afraid,*
> *Poor Tom will injure nothing . . .*

'Little things like that can cast huge light. It comes from "The Hag and Hungry Goblin" and is a verse of Tom o' Bedlam's song. Jeannie had such things and enjoyed them as did Shakespeare. There are bits of Jeannie's "Hag" in *King Lear*! It's very old. It was old when Shakespeare used it and evergreen in Jeannie's hands, like his. The art the Travellers carry is, at best, truly great and is so because it has been tested by time, because it grows directly out of their own lived experience, and because they feel it.

> *Ding dong the Catholic bells*
> *Fare you well my mother*
> *Bury me in the old churchyard*
> *Beside my oldest brother;*
>
> *My coffin shall be black*
> *Four little angels at my back side*
> *Two to preach and two to pray*
> *And two to carry my soul away.*

'That marvellous little bedtime song is a version of "The White Paternoster" mentioned in Chaucer. Jeannie's mother, Maria, would sing this to her bairnies and say, "Good night, sound sleep, and a surprise awaukenin!" Meaning if you die during the night you'll be all right . . . And her daughter

Willie and Bella MacPhee play a duet on the Jew's harp and the 'moothie', Perth, 1995. (TN)

Lizzie became another great ballad singer with a strange and marvellous bagpipe inflection, which she got from her father, old Isaac Higgins. It was, of course, the tragedy of Jeannie's life, that her only son was to die as a boy.

'Jeannie Robertson was a Catholic – whereas up in Sutherland you have grand, puritanical Calvinism in all its rectitude. She is part of the great Episcopalian/Catholic and Jacobite tradition in north Scotland, but the Travelling People of the far north west took the cloak of the Free Presbyterian Kirk. There is a Sunday School morality implicit in much of Ailidh Dall's repertoire. He was an Old Testament moralist and a Gaelic bard, he was a man as affected by parade ground sermons as the sound of a cart on an unmetalled road. He got most of his best songs and stories from his mother – Old Suzie. I am proud that he felt able to give them to me – by doing that I have been able to give them back to the Scotland they came from – and beyond. In recording the tradition, I became part of the tradition.

'Christianity has been profoundly important to the Travellers but much more ancient and more local currents keep, like tides, returning. In Wedeck's *Dictionary of Gipsy Life and Lore*, there is a report of a dance at a Scots Traveller wedding at Lochgelly, Fife, in which Charles Stewart "conducts" a group of female dancers. "In the midst of the circle he danced and capered in the most antic and ludicrous manner, sweeping his cudgel around his body in all directions, and moving with much grace and agility. Sometimes he danced around the outside of the circle. The females danced and curtseyed to him as he faced about and bowed to them. When they happened to go wrong, he put them to rights by a movement of his cudgel. For it was by the cudgel that all the turns and figures of the dance were regulated. A twirl dismissed the females, a cut recalled them, a cut made them squat on the ground. A twist again called them up, in an instant, to dance . . ." This "Lord of the Dance", whoever, or whatever else he was, is undoubtedly an embodiment of continuing pagan forces endemic in Scottish life, and of a kind that Christianity has been accommodating, subverting, and developing for almost two thousand years. The continuity and democratic vitality in Scottish life is one of its great virtues. The wildness, shyness and evasion found among the Travelling People are part of a magic residue of former times. I think of the words of Bishop Leslie, "In the mountains of Aargyl, and Rosse likewyse and sinerie utheris places ar fed ky, nocht tame, as in utheris parts, but like wild hartes, wandering out of ardour and quhilkes, throuch a certain wildness of nature, flie the company or syght of men."

'The Travellers through their history, their cultural heritage, their unpropertied lifestyle have crafted themselves to become, as it were, the unframed mirror within which Scotland can view and be herself – backwards and forwards in time.'

Hamish Henderson and Essie Stewart, Sutherland, 1957.
(HH, BB)

Foreign Voices and the Written Word

'Before the night ends you will meet the music — there is a singer, a piper and a drummer — I have picked them up here and there about the street but I shall teach them, if I live, the music of the beggerman — Homer's music.'

W. B. YEATS

Since the sixteenth century, the Gypsies make recurrent and dramatic appearances in European literature. References to the Scottish Travellers are largely confined to British literature but where they do appear they create a clearly defined historical and psychological presence. The earliest images of Scots Tinkers are probably the woodcuts of bagpipers, by Albrecht Dürer, but the strangest image is *Dulle Greit* or 'Mad Meg', by the great Netherlandish painter, Píeter Brueghel. It comes from the period of the Thirty Years War and shows a huge middle-aged Scots Tinker-woman striding through a hellish landscape of burning cities, freaks and monsters. She is a very recognisable Brueghel-type but was almost certainly based on a real 'Traveller' Brueghel had seen. She is half-armoured, wears a saucepan on her head, and single-mindedly loots nick-nacks amidst the detritus of war. The painting is a symbolic representation of the Seven Deadly Sins. It is a surreal masterpiece, but it also provides insight into external perception of the Scots Traveller in the semi-chaos of late-medieval Europe. If they were still integrated members of Celtic society in Scotland, abroad they were clearly outside the pale. Shakespeare's vision is similar:

> *When shall we three meet again*
> *In thunder lightning or in rain?*
>
> *When the hurlyburly's done,*
> *When the battle's lost and won . . .*

Martha MacKenzie, by her tent near the mouth of Glen Lyon, Perthshire, 1976. (TN)

It is difficult not to see the witches in Shakespeare's 'Scotch Play' as being Scots Tinkers, or Scottish versions of 'Welsh crones' he'd met in the Welsh marches. He uses them as a dramatic device but they are integral to the whole ethos of the play – pagan intermediaries between nature and the supernatural, between past and present, between driven individuals and their destiny: they provide the 'primal soup' out of which Shakespeare creates his great Scots tragedy. (*Hurly* is the Gaelic cant word for a cart in the Gaelic Travellers' secret language, the *Beurla Reagaird*.)

Fillet of a fenny snake,
In the cauldron boil and bake;
Eye of newt, and toe of frog,
Wool of bat, and tongue of dog,
Adder's fork and blind-worm's sting,
Lizard's leg and owlet's wing,
For a charm of powerful trouble,
Like a hell-broth boil and bubble.

Double, double toil and trouble
Fire burn and cauldron bubble.

Scale of dragon, tooth of wolf,
Witches' mummy; maw and gulf,
Of the ravin'd salt-sea shark;
Root of hemlock digged i' the dark
Liver of blaspheming Jew,
Gall of goat, and slips of yew,
Silver'd in the moon's eclipse;
Nose of Turk and Tartar's lips;
Finger of birth-strangled babe,
Ditch-delivered by a drab,
Make the gruel thick and slab:
Add thereto a tiger's chaudron,
For the ingredients of our cauldron.

In Scotland itself, Henry Adamson wrote a long poem, in 1638, in which pearl-fishing on the Tay is described: because this is, historically, such a predominantly Traveller occupation, an extract is worth quoting. There is mention of the evil eye and witchery, and that the pearl-mussels excel in both 'taste' and 'touch'. Thus, while freshwater mussels must once have been eaten but no longer are, the eroticism associated with the finding and wearing of pearls continues:

Now let us go, the precious pearles a fishing,
The occasion serves us well, while here we stay
To catch these muscles, you call toytes, of Tay:
Its possible if no ill eye bewitch us
We jewels find, for all our days t'enrich us . . .

Content said Gall; then off our shoes we drew
And hose, and from us we our doublets threw,
Our shirt-sleaves wreathing up, without more speches,
And high above our knees we pulling our breeches,
In waters go, then straight mine arms I reach
Unto the ground, whence cleverly I fetch
Some of these living pearled shells, which do
Excell in touching and in tasting to —
As all who search, do by experience try,
And we oftimes; therewith I loudly cry
Good master Gall, behold I've found a pearle,
A jewel I assure you for an Earle!
Be silent, said good Gall, or speak at leisure,
For men will cut your throat to get your treasure!

Argyllshire MacPhees on the road,
c. 1890. The man on the left is
Alex MacPhee, Bella MacPhee's
grandfather's brother, the boy with
the sticks for the bow-tent is
George MacPhee. The woman in the
centre is Margaret MacPhee
(Clarke), Alex's wife, with her son
John MacPhee. The woman on the
right is Margaret Cameron with
her baby, Ellen, who was to become
the mother of Willie MacPhee. The
girl and boy are older children of
Alex and Margaret MacPhee.
(WMac)

In the early eighteenth century, Birt's *Letters from the North of Scotland* paint a valuable but uncomplimentary picture of itinerant carters in the Inverness region. 'You see a man dragging along a half-starved horse little bigger than an ass, in a cart, about the size of a wheelbarrow. One part of his plaid is wrapped around his body, and the rest is thrown over his left shoulder; and every now and then he turns about, either to adjust his mantle, when blown off by the wind or fallen by his stooping, or to thump the poor little horse with a great stick. The load in his cart, if compact, might be carried under his arm; but he must not bear any burden to himself, though his wife has, perhaps, at the same time, a greater burden on her loins than he has in his cart. I say on her loins, for the women carry fish and other heavy burdens, in the same manner as the Scots pedlars carry their packs in England . . .

'Some of these carts are lead by women, who are generally barefoot with a blanket for the cover of their bodies, and in cold or wet weather they bring it quite over them . . . Instead of ropes for halters and harness, they generally make use of sticks of birch twisted and knotted together; these are called "woodies"; but some few have ropes made of the manes and tails of their horses which are shorn in the spring for that purpose . . . The horse-collar and crupper are made of straw-bands; and to save the horse's back, they put under the cart saddle, a parcel of old rags . . . The wheels, when new, are about a foot and a half high, but are soon worn very small: they are made of three pieces of plank, pinned together at the edges like the head of a butter-firkin, and the axletree goes round with the wheel. These carters, for the most part, live in huts dispersed in the adjacent countryside . . .

'It is a common thing for the poorest sort hereabouts to lead their horses out in summer, when they have done their work, and attend them while they graze by the sides of the road and edges of the cornfields, where there is any little grass to be had without trespass; and generally they hold them all the time by the halter, for they are certainly punished if it be known they encroached ever so little upon a field, of which none are enclosed.'

Throughout the Jacobite period the 'royal' Travellers generally attached themselves to the Stuart cause, and many of the great Jacobite songs have been marked by Traveller contributions, but in the late eighteenth century Robert Burns found rich inspiration in the music of the Travelling People themselves. On the night he was born, January 25th, 1759, a great storm drove an old Tinker-woman to seek shelter in the Burns' cottage in Alloway. She prophesied the genius of the new born babe, and the youthful Burns was soon to enjoy many a rowdy night with 'the Tinklers' – observing, carousing, and collecting. In 'The Jolly Beggars' he delights in the anarchic, irresponsible hedonism of the Ayrshire Travellers. He does not call them Gypsies, he calls them 'cairds' and 'Tinklers'.

Poor Merry-Andrew in the neuk
    Sat guzzling wi' a Tinkler-hizzie;
They mind't na wha the chorus teul,
    Between themselves they were sae busy.
    At length, with drink an courting dizzy,
He stoiter'd up an' made a face;
    Then turn'd an' laid a smack on Grizzie,
Syne tun'd his pipes wi' grave grimace:

     *   *   *

The caird prevail'd: the' unblushing fair
    In his embraces sunk,
Partly wi' love o'ercome sae sair,
    An' partly she was drunk.
Sir Violino, with an air
    That show'd a man o' spunk,
Wished uniso betwen the pair,
    An' made the bottle clunk
      To their health that night.

But hurchin Cupid shot a shaft,
    That played a dame a shavie:
The fiddler rak'd her fore and aft
    Behint the chicken cavie;
Her lord, a wight of Homer's craft,
    Tho' limpin' wi' the spavie,
He hirpl'd up, and lap like daft,
    An' shor'd them 'Dainty Davie'
      O' boot that night.

     *   *   *

My bonie lass, I work in brass,
    A tinkler is my station;
I've travelled round all Christian ground
    In this my occupation;
I've taen the gold, an' been enrolled
    In many a noble squadron;
But vain they search'd when off I march'd
    To go an clout the cauldron.

'The Jolly Beggars' is a ribald drinking song but within it, Burns intuitively grasps crucial factors at the heart of Traveller life – sponataneity, pleasure, drink, music, sex, violence, craft metal-work, military service and desertion. The last point applies directly to the life of Eddie Davies and to the Stewarts of Remarstaig. Both Alexander Stewart (Ailidh Dall) and his elder brother, Jamie, did notable army service during the First World War but another brother, Donald, took to the hills. Alec John Williamson tells the story:

'Donald got married young, before the First War broke. No children came, so one year when he was down at the big horse fair at Ackey Brae in Aberdeenshire, he adopted a little boy and brought him back up here to Sutherland. When the war came he joined up, or got conscripted, and went away just like his brothers. He did his basic training down at Dundee, but Donald, he could not stand army life so he deserted. It was not the trenches, it was not the Germans! It was Dundee! He was never out of Scotland – he just skedaddled home. And he went away, away out into the wilds and he lived for eight years on the hill.

I heard his favourite place was the wood at Scourie, across the loch, north east of the township of Scourie, Glenbrae we call it – little stunted trees, scrub oak, bracken and pink rhododendrons. He went in there, like the SAS. In among the roots, he built a shelter. His wife would go out for food sometimes, come back the wrong way round. He was out of sight eight years! They were out in Barra, and in Uist. He grew a big beard, huge beard, to disguise himself. He was like the Red Fox. I've heard it said the Lairg police knew where he was but they left the sleeping dog to lie – they knew his brothers were over there in France, that his cousin Peter had been killed and all that, so he was never hunted down or taken into prison. Gradually he got back on the road, but to me, as a boy like, he was an outlaw – no boots sometimes, sitting by the stove, telling the big stories, black in the face! He lived all his life in bow-tents, 'never feel comfortable under a roof' he'd say. Donald died in his tent at Tierryside in 1942. I was nine years of age.

Most living Highland Travellers have spent some time in Ireland. This, it seems, is the continuance of very ancient practice. The Highlands, Western Isles and Ireland form one cultural and geographical zone within which they travel. Some have spent time in Central Scotland, but the Borders and England are foreign territory – however, the Highland Stewarts, the Williamsons, the Davies, the MacPhees all feel a natural, super-national bond with Ireland, and Ireland is integral to many of their oldest stories like *Am Maraiche Mairnealach*.

In one of his letters to George Thomson, Robert Burns makes an important 'middle period' assertion about this continuing, historical relation-

Unknown Travellers camped by the roadside, c. 1920s. (JS)

ship between Scottish and Irish culture.

'By the way, I have met with a musical Highlander, in Breadalbane's fencibles, which are quartered here, who assures me that he well remembers his mother singing Gaelic songs to both 'Robin Adair' and *Gramachree*. They certainly have more the Scotch than the Irish taste in them.

'This man comes from the vicinity of Inverness; so it could not be any intercourse with Ireland that could bring them, except, what I shrewdly suspect to be the case, the wandering minstrels, harpers and pipers, used to go frequently errant through the wilds both of Scotland and Ireland, and so favourite airs might be common to both. A case in point – they have lately, in Ireland, published an Irish air, as they say, called *Caun du delish*. The fact is, in a publication of Corri's, a great while ago, you will find the same air, called a Highland one, with a Gaelic song set to it. Its name there, I think, is *Oran Gaoil*, and a fine air it is.'

Seven years later William Wordsworth and his sister, Dorothy, met several Scots Travellers in Cumbria in the spring and autumn of 1800. These wanderers provided powerful inspiration to Wordsworth, at a moment when his powers were at their height. Dorothy writes in her Grasmere Journal:

'On Tuesday, May 27th, a very tall woman, tall much beyond the measure of tall women, called at the door. She had on a very long brown coat, and a very white cap without a bonnet – her face was excessively brown, but it had plainly once been fair. She led a little barefooted child about two years old by the hand and said her husband, who was a tinker, was gone before with the other children. I gave her a piece of bread. Afterwards on my road to Ambleside, beside the bridge at Ryedale, I saw her husband sitting by the roadside, his two asses feeding beside him and two young children at play upon the grass. The man did not beg – I passed on and about quarter of a mile further I saw two boys before me, one about ten the other about eight years old at play chasing a butterfly. They were wild figures, not very ragged, but without shoes and stockings, the hat of the elder was wreathed round with yellow flowers, the younger whose hat was only a rimless crown, had stuck it round with laurel leaves. They continued at play till I drew near and then they addressed me with the begging cant and whining voice of sorrow – I said I served your mother this morning (the boys were so like the woman who had called at the door that I could not be mistaken). Oh, says the elder, you could not serve my mother for she is dead, and my father's on at the next town – he's a potter. I persisted in my assertion and that I would give them nothing. Says the elder "Come let's awa' " and away they flew like lightning . . . On my return through Ambleside I met in the street the mother driving her asses; in the two panniers of one of which were the two little children whom she was chiding and threatening with a wand which she used to drive on her asses, while the two hung in wanton-ness over the pannier edge. The woman had told me in the morning that she was from Scotland, which her accent fully proved . . .'

These incidents led to Wordsworth's poem 'The Beggars': but a more important meeting happened on Friday, 3rd October 1800, when Dorothy noted William's meeting with the man who was to be a central character in one of the greatest poems in the English language 'Resolution and Independence', better known as the 'The Leech-gatherer':

'When Wm and I returned from accompanying Jones we met an old man almost double, he had a coat thrown over his shoulders, above his waistcoat and coat. Under this he carried a bundle and had an apron on and a night cap. His face was interesting. He had dark eyes and a long nose – John afterwards meeting him at Wythburn took him for a Jew. He was of Scotch parents but he had been born in the army. He had had a wife "and a good woman and it pleased God to bless us with ten children" – all were dead but one, of whom he had not heard for many years, a sailor. His trade was to gather leeches but now leeches are scarce and he had not strength for it – he lived by begging and was making his way to Carlisle where he should buy a few godly books to sell. He said leeches were very scarce partly owing to this dry season, but many years they have been scarce, he supposed it owing to their being much sought after, that they did not breed fast and were of slow growth. Leeches were formerly 2/6 100, they are now 30/-. He had been hurt driving a cart, his leg broke, his body driven over, his skull fractured – he felt no pain till he recovered from his first insensibility. It was late in the evening when the light was fast fading away.'

The man Wordsworth met combined qualities and characteristics still evident in many twentieth-century Travellers: his leech-gatherer might be a composite of blind Sandy Stewart, the pearl-fisher Eddie Davies, and Duncan Williamson who, himself, gathered leeches as a boy in Argyll:

> *Now whether it were by peculiar grace,*
> *A leading from above, a something given,*
> *Yet it befell that, in this lonely place,*
> *When I with these untoward thoughts had striven,*
> *Beside a pool bare to the eye of heaven*
> *I saw a Man before me unawares:*
> *The oldest man he seemed that ever wore grey hairs.*

*   *   *

> *At length, himself unsettling, he the pond*
> *Stirred with his staff, and fixedly did look*
> *Upon the muddy water, which he conned,*
> *As if he had been reading in a book:*
> *And now a stranger's privilege I took;*
> *And, drawing to his side, to him did say,*
> *'This morning gives promise of a glorious day.'*

> *A gentle answer did the old Man make,*
> *In courteous speech which forth he slowly drew:*
> *And him with further words I thus bespake,*
> *'What occupation do you there pursue?*
> *This is a lonesome place for one like you.'*
> *Ere he replied, a flash of mild surprise*
> *Broke from the sable orbs of his yet-vivid eyes.*

His words came feebly from a feeble chest,
But each in solemn order followed each,
With something of a lofty utterance drest —
Choice word and measured phrase, above the reach
Of ordinary men; a stately speech;
Such as grave livers do in Scotland use,
Religious men, who give to God and man their dues.

He told, that to these waters he had come
To gather leeches, being old and poor:
Employment hazardous and wearisome!
And he had many hardships to endure:
From pond to pond he roamed, from moor to moor;
Housing with God's help, by choice or chance;
And in this way he gained an honest maintenance.

The old Man still stood talking by my side;
But now his voice was like a stream
Scarce heard; nor word from word could I divide;
And the whole body of the Man did seem
Like one whom I had met with in a dream;
Or like a man from some far region sent,
To give me human strength, by apt admonishment

My former thoughts returned: the fear that kills;
And hope that is unwilling to be fed;
Cold, pain, and labour, and all fleshly ills;
And mighty poets in their misery dead.
— Perplexed, and longing to be comforted,
My question eagerly did I renew,
'How is it that you live, and what is it you do?'

He with a smile did then his words repeat;
And said that, gathering leeches far and wide
He travelled; stirring thus about his feet
The waters of the pools where they abide.
'Once I could meet with them on every side;
But they have dwindled long by slow decay;
Yet still I persevere, and find them where I may . . .'

'   The Leech-gatherer' is a favourite poem of Stanley Robertson, fish-filleter, story-teller and settled Traveller from Aberdeen. He knows it by heart. A nephew of Jeannie Robertson, he and his family are Mormons, he leads a strictly righteous life and speaks with a measured eloquence which has made him famous in folk-circles all over Scotland. The continuing high quality of so much Traveller talk affirms the poetic framework that Wordsworth set for himself as a young man in his *Preface to the Lyrical Ballads*. Qualities he found vital in eighteenth-century Cumbria are alive in the north Highlands today, and they provide good reasons why speech, poetry and song among the Travellers retains such vigour and simple grandeur:

'Humble and rustic life was generally chosen, because in that condition the essential passions of the human heart find a better soil in which they can attain their maturity, are less under restraint, and speak a plainer and more emphatic language; because in that condition of life our elementary feelings coexist in a state of greater simplicity, and consequently may be more accurately contemplated and more forcibly communicated; because the manners of rural life germinated from those elementary feelings, and from the necessary character of rural occupations, are more easily comprehended, and are more durable; and, lastly, because in that condition the passions of men are incorporated with the beautiful and permanent forms of nature. The language, too, of these men has been adopted (purified indeed from what appear to be its real defects, from all lasting and rational causes of dislike or disgust) because such men hourly communicate with the best objects from which the best part of language is originally derived; and because, from their rank in society and the narrow circle of their intercourse, being less under the influence of social vanity, they convey their feelings and notions in simple and unelaborated expressions. Accordingly, such a language, arising out of repeated experience and regular feelings, is a more permanent and far more philosophical language . . .'

John Ruskin, the art critic and social reformer, held very similar philosophical ideas to Wordsworth and two generations later, walking near Matlock in the Derbyshire Pennines, Ruskin came upon a watercress-gatherer and got into conversation with a man who turned out to be another Scots Traveller. 'I was a sailor for eleven years and ten months of my life – I lived for ten years after my wife's death by picking up rags and bones – I lives hard and honest, and I haven't got long to live. She had rheumatism and fever very bad; and her second rib grow'd over her henchbone. A' was a very clever woman, but a' growed to be a very little one. Eighteen years after her first lad she was in the family way again, and they had doctors up from Lunnon about it. They wanted to rip her open, and take the child out of her side. But I never would

give my consent. She died twenty-six hours and ten minutes after it. I never cared much what come of me since; but I know I shall soon reach her; that's a knowledge I wouldna gie for the king's croon.'

'You are a Scotchman, are you not?' Ruskin asked. 'I'm from the Isle of Skye, sir; I'm a M'Gregor – you'll know I was born in the church of Scotland, and I love it as I love my own soul; but I think thae Wesleyan Methodists ha' got salvation among them too.'

This short speech provides another remarkable resumé of continuing Traveller mores and lifestyle – martial service, a surprising range of knowledge, the vividness of speech (at once factual, concrete and poetical), the superstition, the fear of doctors, the strongly religious sensibility, the ability to charm and flatter listeners, and the complicit 'superiority' – evident here in the old man's recognition of the merits of Wesleyan Methodism. Such characteristics might be described as Scottish but they are definitely recurrent characteristics among many Highland Travellers. Duncan Williamson, in 1995, brings the narratives begun by Wordsworth and Ruskin up to date:

Bottom. Duncan MacGregor, camped outside Lochgilphead, Argyllshire, 1995. Relatives of the Argyllshire Williamsons, Duncan's family is one of the last Traveller families still on the road in Scotland. They work as scrap-metal dealers.

Top. A wider view of the MacGregor camp. It is May 1995, the broom and the bluebells are out but there are still no leaves on the trees. In the background is Loch Fyne and in the very far distance, the snow-covered mountains of Arran.

'My grandmothers's mother was dumb – born dumb and she married a MacDonald. His family came from Appin but he joined the Perthshire Militia. He was a piper and when he'd finished his service he started walking home from Perth. He went out along Loch Tay towards Oban. He was still a young man – his name was Roderick. He wasn't a Traveller – he had a brother and a sister on a croft up in Appin – but as he was passing beneath Ben Lawers he came to a quarry, where my great-grandmother's family was camped. Night was coming on, the fire was blazing and there was a big group of Travellers there – all singing! He was hungry and he was tired, so he walked into the camp. He was a young man, pipes under his arm! They gave him a cup of tea, a bowl of soup and they passed the whisky bottle round and he played for them all night long!

'And by the morning, he'd fallen in love with my granny's mother. Now as I said, she was dumb but she was not deaf – she heard the pipes! She was sixteen years of age and she was a most beautiful young Traveller woman and she fell in love with the piper, and Roderick never went back to his brother and his sister in Appin. Never. He stayed with the Travellers – the two of them jumped over the broomstick! They got married. And he became a good tinsmith and lived all his life with the Travelling People. They went down to Kintyre and they had nine children and not one of them was dumb. My granny was the youngest, and she ran away from home when she was sixteen and married John Townsley, that was my grandfather. I don't remember John Townsley because he died the day I was born, but I was the seventh son and he was the seventh son and he was pleased to know that I was born before he died

– because my father was also the seventh son.

'Now it was up at Tangy Glen that my mother and father had got married. That was the place where all the Kintyre Travellers used to go. It was a Gretna Green for Travellers. By the burn in Tangy Glen stood an old mill, and from there you can see across to Ireland and all the lands of MacDonald and the MacAlisters, and it was looked after by two old brothers and the eldest one was blind. It was where the Townsleys went to stay the night when they got married. Away you went to Tangy Glen and that was that! The old men had a pantry outside the house and they used to leave food in it for the Travellers, hams, cheese, bread, a bucket of water, all that kind of thing. You see, they liked the young Travellers coming in for the night. It was like a Youth Hostel up there! In the barn they would always leave a corner with fresh straw. They were MacDonalds, they were cousins of MacDonald-of-the-Rock up at Muasdale. The old men loved it – knowing their mill was the place where the young Travellers would come to get themselves married. They were bachelors, with no children of their own and they must have liked to know that life was going on. Well that was it, one night up Tangy Glen and you were wed. And if he left her, or she left him, you were in big, big trouble. My mother and father ran away up Tangy Glen, and they had sixty-five years together. Nine children my mother bore, and I was their seventh son. Johnnie and Maggie Townsley, they made up a song about Tangy Glen:

James Stewart far right),
Aberdeenshire Traveller, in the
British army during the Boer War.
Note the wristwatches – most
unusual at this early date,
c. 1900. (JS)

> *O my wee Maggie's a humpin-a-prookin*
> *A bun-wood sproggan – that's my wee Maggie*
>
> *O Maggie got a man, they cried him the nigger*
> *His face wasnae bigger than a penny figure*
> *A humpin-a-prookin a bun-wood sproggan*
> *That's my wee Maggie . . .*
>
> *O Johnnie got his bundle and Maggie got her can*
> *Up the glen to the auld blin man*
> *Up the glen to the auld blin man*
> *For to bide all nicht in the morning.*
>
> *So Johnnie says to Maggie, come into the shed*
> *I'll shake the straw if you'll mak the bed*
> *For this is the place where your mother she was made*
> *And we'll gang doon the glen in the morning.*

O my wee Maggie's a humpin-a-prookin
A bun-wood sproggan — that's my wee Maggie.

O Johnnie with his bundle and Maggie with her can
Up the glen to the auld blin man
Up the glen to the auld blin man
For to tak their tea in the morning.

So Johnnie says to Maggie now we been wed
We'll stay all nicht in a bonnie stray bed
And we'll gang doon the glen in the morning . . .'

A hundred years before that song was composed by the two young Townsleys, John Keats wrote a letter to his less obliging girlfriend, Franny Brawne. He had begun a tour in Scotland, was reading Walter Scott and was obviously fascinated by the Scots Travellers he was meeting. In the letter he enclosed a quickly flung together poem which draws a picture very different to but just as vivid as that painted by Brueghel:

Old Meg she was a gypsy,
She lived upon the moors;
Her bed it was the brown heath turf,
Her home was out of doors.

Her apples were swart blackberries,
Her currants pods o' broom;
Her wine was dew of the wild white rose,
Her book a churchyard tomb.

Her brothers were the craggy hills,
Her sisters larchen trees
Alone with her great family
She lived as she did please.

No breakfast had she many a morn,
No dinner many a noon,
And 'stead of supper she would stare
Full hard against the moon.

But every morn of woodbine fresh
She made her garlanding,
And every night the dark glen yew
She wove and she would sing . . .

Oh Meg was brave as Margaret Queen
And tall as Amazon:
An old red blanket cloak she wore;
A chip hat she had on . . .

A century later, Rudyard Kipling wrote 'Gypsy Vans'. It is a poem about the Gypsies, not Highland Travellers – but because it provides a critical picture of both 'traveller life' and 'respectable life' it articulates something fundamental about settled society's perception of nomadic existence:

Unless you come of the gipsy stock
 That steals by night and day,
Lock your heart with a double lock
 And throw the key away.
Bury it under the blackest stone
 Beneath your father's hearth,
And keep your eyes on your lawful own
 And your feet to the proper path.
THEN YOU CAN STAND AT YOUR DOOR AND MOCK
 WHEN THE GIPSY-VANS COME THROUGH . . .
FOR IT ISN'T RIGHT THAT THE GORGIO STOCK
 SHOULD LIVE AS THE ROMANY DO.

Unless you come of the gipsy blood
 That takes and never spares,
Bide content with your given good
 And follow your own affairs.
Plough and harrow and roll your land,
 And sow what ought to be sowed;
But never let loose your heart from your hand,
 Nor flitter it down the road!
THEN YOU CAN THRIVE ON YOUR BOUGHTEN FOOD
 AS THE GIPSY-VANS COME THROUGH . . .
FOR IT ISN'T NATURE THE GORGIO BLOOD
 SHOULD LOVE AS THE ROMANY DO.

Unless you carry the gipsy eyes
  That see but seldom weep,
Keep your head from the naked skies
  Or the star'll trouble your sleep.
Watch your moon through the window-pane
  And take what weather she brews;
But don't run out in the midnight rain
  Nor home in the morning dews.
THEN YOU CAN HUDDLE AND SHUT YOUR EYES
  AS THE GIPSY-VANS COME THROUGH . . .
FOR IT ISN'T FITTING THE GORGIO RYES
  SHOULD WALK AS THE ROMANY DO.

Unless you come of the gipsy race
  That counts all time the same,
Be you careful of Time and Place
  And Judgement and Good Name:
Lose your life for to live your life
  The way that you ought to do;
And when you are finished, your God and your wife
  And the Gipsies'll laugh at you!
THEN YOU CAN ROT IN YOUR BURYING-PLACE
  AS THE GIPSY-VANS COME THROUGH . . .
FOR IT ISN'T REASON THE GORGIO RACE
  SHOULD DIE AS THE ROMANY DO.

Field-Marshall Viscount A. O. Wavell used this poem in his anthology *Other Men's Flowers* and noted 'The gypsy in real life is usually both dirty and dull. So is war. Yet both gypsy life and war have a supposed glamour and are the subject of much poetry. This is due I suppose, to the persistence in man's memory of his old past as nomad and warrior. Just so, the house dog turns round several times on the carpet before composing himself to sleep, as if he were still making a couch for himself in the grass; or the stabled horse shies at a ditch because in them wild animals used to lurk and ambush his ancestors.'

In the broad spread of Celtic culture, a poetic connection can be made between the Traveller role in settled society and that of Lugh among the gods. Arriving late at the gates of the High King of Ireland, Lugh was told, there was no work, no role for him – all the specialist jobs had long been taken. But Lugh, like a true Traveller, claimed to be a Jack-of-all-trades and to specialise

Horses graze at the summit of 'The Rest And Be Thankful' pass – the road out of Argyll to Glasgow and England. As a boy, Duncan Williamson sat here in 1933 and watched Peter Pindar's German Circus struggle up towards the summit on its way to Inverary. 'There were horses, ponies and great traction engines with solid rubber wheels pulling trucks. It was a great scene, like Hannibal crossing the Alps, but just before reaching the top, the traction engine ran out of steam and blocked the road! So Peter Pindar had an idea. He opened up one of the trucks, and out stepped an elephant with a coolie in pyjamas, and the elephant pushed the traction engine up over the summit. Then it had a rest and then it pushed all the other stalled trucks and carts, one by one up to the top! There were three clowns, tigers in cages, jugglers, performing dogs, and a horse called Jennifer. I used to creep into the tent and watch the show. The clowns would pretend that Jennifer had said 'If you don't give me a kiss, I think I'll die!' And she'd roll over and lie there, just as if she were dead! And then one of the clowns would give her a kiss and up she'd leap! That horse could do two dozen tricks. Mr Pindar's wife was not an old woman but she died that year in Inverary and they buried her, here in Scotland at Kilmartin, and when my mother died, her grave was dug next to Peter Pindar's wife and that's where they lie, close side by side to this day.' (TN)

in everything! 'Warrior, craftsman, cup-bearer, singer, bear-tamer, sorcerer, he!' and after some haggling he won admittance to the great palace of Tara. This strange combination of skills and values was honoured and used by the Yeats brothers to make the greatest Irish art of this century. In one of his finest but little known poems W.B. links the values and life of Major Robert Gregory, to both Lugh and, perhaps, metaphorically, to the Travelling People:

> What other could have so well counselled us
> In all lovely intricacies of a house
> As he who practised, or who understood
> All work in metal, or in wood
> In moulded plaster, or in carved stone:
> Soldier, scholar, horseman he –
> And all he did, done perfectly
> As though he had but that one trade alone.

The art critic John Berger states in his book *Another Way of Telling* that, 'among the Ancient Greeks, memory was the mother of all the Muses, and was perhaps most closely associated with the practice of poetry. Poetry at that time, as well as being a form of story-telling, was also an inventory of the visible world; metaphor after metaphor was given to poetry by way of visual correspondences.' Celtic poetry and song continue that tradition today – as do the Travellers – in their naming of dogs, their naming of people, their love of language itself are very much part of that tradition.

Teenie Stewart at Ackey Brae, the site of the great Aberdeenshire horsefair, giving a young traveller a shot on her horse, c. 1955. (JS)

Loyal, Coinach, Cruachan, Ben
Mountain dogs for Traveller men,
Luath, Akie, Stack and Ledi —
Gyp and Fly tak doon the Gadgie.

In 1981 after a visit to the Scottish Highlands and meetings with various Travellers, Berger wrote a letter: 'The living can crowd out the dead. And where the density of the living population is high, the dead often cede. By contrast there are other areas, very thinly populated, where the dead assemble. 'Frequently these areas are arid or poor and it is for this reason they cannot support the living. Deserts and polar regions are the most extreme examples. Perhaps those who know the dead best are Bedouins and Eskimos.

'Many poor regions are nomadic. They are areas prompting or insisting on a nomadic way of life. And the reasons for this are simple and material. The land is poor and quickly, if temporarily, exhausted: one has to move on. But sometimes these areas are nomadic in another sense. Shepherds and hunters will describe how in certain regions the paths themselves come towards you. The habit of moving on is then a complicity between land and traveller.

'The Highlands are like this. The crofters' cottages crouch like animals sheltering on the ground for the night. There are encampments but no permanent assemblies. Everything moves on, the larches, the bracken, the

Bella Cameron and her granddaughter with Bella MacPhee at the Dunoon Highland Games, 1990. Nancy MacPhee is in the wheelchair. She died later the same year. (WMac)

Caledonian pines, the heather, the juniper bushes, the swamp grass. And then moving into the land – water: the rivers running to the sea, the sea with its tides entering the lochs. And across both land and water the wind. And over all the north west wind. The honking of the wild geese in the sky is like a fleeting measure, a counting in another algebra, of all this movement.

'There are castles, there are lines which could be and have been defended, but there are no final barriers. This is why herring can be fished from water surrounded by brackened hills. This is why the sky can appear to have more flesh on it, to be more hospitable than the land.

'Nobody really counted time until there were settlements and clerks. Here between the land and sky is a shore that smells of mountains and uncounted time.'

Finally, 'Salathiel's Song', a poem by the Scottish poet, Sean Rafferty, first published in 1994, shows how Traveller experience continues to speak to Scotland, and to writers, across time and across generations:

> . . .*A lumbering waggon*
> *on country roads rocking the linnets' cages*
> *cradled my cradle.*
> *I was suckled on milk and clouds*
> *I was weened on wormwood.*

Flood damage to a photograph of
piper Alex MacKenzie and his
family, Glen Lyon, c. 1920, creates
an image like an ancient fresco.
(WMac)

The colour of smoke
the sounds of water
the smell of tarpaulin
the taste of sorrel:
four simple lessons still unlearned.

That ribbon of smoke
across the valley
is a road we climb.

That plod of hooves
when loads are heavy
is water clopping into a pail.

The whisper of water
this side of silence
is green fire lighted
under a pot.

In a field by a stream.
When the mares were watered
the shadows of elms
came down to drink.

An hour before sunset
the fire was lighted
is embers now.
The cauldron scoured.

A day has closed
like a shut accordion.
The lanterns doused.

A watchdog howls
across the valley.
An owl asks why.

On a crooked road
from there to the next place
the travellers sleeping
their lurchers sleeping.

Children asleep.
But one child watches
the embers die.

Dark elm
far owl
faint star
my mother
my mother dark as the night.

Traveller family on the road at
St John's Well, Fyvie, 1926. (AS)

Appendix 1

NOTES ON GYPSY HISTORY AND TRAVELLER ORIGINS

*T*he *Oxford Dictionary* defines a Gypsy as 'a member of a wandering race (by themselves called Romany), of Hindu origin, which first appeared in Britain about the beginning of the sixteenth century and was believed to have come from Egypt. They make a living by basket-making, horse-dealing, fortune-telling, etc. And have usually been objects of suspicion for their nomadic life and habits. Their language (like themselves called Romany) is a greatly corrupted dialect of Hindi, with a large admixture of words from various European languages'.

The Highland Traveller People are not Gypsies. There is Gypsy blood in some of them, as in the Davies family, but by ethnic origin, by history, by culture Scotland's 'Tinkers' are not Gypsies. As nomadic peoples the two groups share affinities; as pressurised minorities they share the problems of their itinerant lifestyle – but they are separate peoples who established their separate identities many thousands of miles apart, many years ago. The Gypsies feel themselves a caste above 'the Travellers', and the Highland Travelling People identify themselves, not with the European Gypsies, but with the Highland clans.

About a century ago, Professor Eugene Pittard, after systematic, eugenic study of the Gypsies in central Europe, defined their physical form as slightly taller than the average European with legs long in proportion to the torso and their heads as most definitely long and narrow. Hair was black, ears small, eyes dark with the irises often heavily pigmented in a speckled fashion. Noses tended to be long, narrow and straight. Pittard gave them 'a highly honourable place in human aesthetics. Very fine men and beautiful women are often found among them. Their swarthy complexion, jet black hair, straight well-formed nose, white teeth, dark brown wide-open eyes, whether languid or lively in expression, the general suppleness of their deportment, and the harmony of their movements, place them high above many European peoples as regards physical beauty'.

Pittard's historical Gypsy 'physiognomy' can be contrasted with that of most Highland Travellers, in particular the Travellers tend to be broad-headed and high-cheeked. A fair proportion are tall but genetic and historic links are more likely to be found with the Scandinavian Lapps, the northern Siberians and the Canadian Eskimos than with Hindus from the Indian sub-continent. The fact that the Oriental Gypsies are the most conspicuous and widespread nomadic people in Europe, does not make all European nomads Gypsies.

Scholars today are almost united in believing that the Gypsies are an Indo-European group which originated in India whereas the Scottish Travellers are a people indigenous to the British Isles and probably, by group-origin, partially non-Indo-European. 'Tynklers' are documented in the city records of Perth long before the migration of Gypsies into Europe began but it is an interesting fact that the first official account of Gypsies in Britain is to be found, not in the south, where one might expect, but among the accounts of the Lord High Treasurer of Scotland, in 1505. They record seven pounds being paid to the 'Egiptianis' by King James IV at Stirling. The thirty-two year old king of Scots is known to have enjoyed music, song and dance and he seems to have paid for the novel and 'royal' entertainment these exotic strangers brought with royal generosity. In 1506, King James commended Anthonius Gawino, 'Erle of Little Egypt' to the King of Denmark in a letter. The early experience of the Gypsies in Scotland appears to have been good.

A generation later, in May 1529, royal accounts document that 'the Egiptianis that dansit before the King at Halyrudhous', received payment of forty shillings. The Gypsies' market value had fallen! – but they were still in business, and in February 1540, James V granted John Faa 'lord and erle of Little Egipt' special privileges and freedoms so that he could better control and discipline, criminal and rebellious members of the Gypsy community. For a short while, the Faws, the

Duncan Williamson inside his winter 'galley', with his wife Linda, and Tommy and Betsy, Lochgilphead, 1980. (GH)

dominant Gypsy family in Scotland were given control of something like 'a kingdom' within a kingdom. In June 1541 these dangerous privileges were suddenly withdrawn by an Order in Council revoking 'all letters of protection and other privileges' given to the Gypsies and banishing 'all Gipsies from the kingdom within 30 days, on pain of death'.

Over the years, Gypsies had become responsible for an increasing amount of common theft and social disorder in Scotland. In May 1527 the Council Register for Aberdeen records 'Egyptians convicted of stealing two silver spoons from Thomas Watson's house'. In 1539 two Gypsy women 'Barbara Dya Baptista and Helen Andree, thair complices to the number of ten personis, friends, and servants to Erle George, callit of Egipt', were charged with theft of 'twenty-four marks money of the realme'. They were discharged and given expenses against their accuser but banished from the town. They were represented at their trial by their 'capitane and forspeiker' George Faw – but on January 28th 1540, 'the said George Faw and Johnne Faw, Egiptianis, were convict be the sworn assys a boune wrytime for the blud drawing of Sande Barrow . . .' Law and order was not the strong suite of the Gypsy people, and this George Faw is almost certainly the same George Faw, who in 1539, was in court with Michael Miche, at Stafford in England; where he produced letters from the King of Scots and the Abbot of Holyrood asserting their joint good characters! The national border was consciously being used by the Gypsies as it suited law-breakers and law-makers on both sides of the march.

The Gypsies were outsiders – without land, without crops, without food animals. In the harshly seasonal north of Europe nomadic life was always a struggle. Some Gypsies were good craftsmen but they were not manufacturers, they might be entertainers but there was little security in entertainment. Circumstances forced the Gypsies to live by their wits, continually on the move and often too close to the law. Such a life cultivated sharp practice, quickened sensibilities sharpened passions and brought them into conflict with the host communities. The early enthusiasm for the Gypsies, as Godly pilgrims and exotic strangers, was gradually replaced by antipathy and legal repression across most of Europe. Remarkably similar patterns of acceptance, followed by popular anger and statutory rejection, can be traced in both Scotland and England.

Scotland's anti-Gypsy orders, imposed in 1541, were not, however, very rigorously enforced: over the following twenty years there are continuing reports of Gypsy life in Scotland and records of recurrent expulsions of Gypsies to Norway and Denmark (proof of their continuing residence), but power had now clearly been taken back into the hands of the King of Scots – and all Gypsies lived in his realm on sufferance. Some Gypsies married into Scottish families. Some integrated with the local 'Traveller' population. Perhaps some Faws became MacPhees at this time?

The particular issues and problems facing Gypsies in Scotland, was part of a wider historical phenomenon. The Protestant Reformation had, between 1505 and 1541, changed the face of Europe. In the fifteenth century, Gypsies coming into western Europe from the east had come as Catholic Christians and very consciously used 'pilgrimage' to justify and locate their existence. Pilgrims created markets and turned begging into 'alms giving'. By the middle of the sixteenth century, however, the old Catholic hegemony had been fundamentally fractured by the Protestant Reformation: Franciscan-style poverty and wandering were out of fashion; hard work, independence and servitude were order of the day. Parishes might look after their own poor but there was little sympathy for wandering strangers of suspect allegiance.

In addition, the exotic lifestyle of the Gypsies stimulated sexual desires, fantasies and popular jealousy. For five hundred years, in song, story, painting and music the Gypsies have been presented in European Art as dark, romantic, scheming, sexually ambitious people – with a particular sexual power. They are aware of this themselves. Shakespeare's Caliban was a creation of the imagination but he arose directly from contemporary English folklore: the Romany word for dark is *caliban*. An escape into the 'free world' of the Gypsies was a dream, more personal but not less strong than the dream of a 'New World'.

> What care I for a goose-feather bed,
> With the sheet turned down so bravely, O!
> For tonight I shall sleep in a cold open field,
> Along with the raggle taggle gypsies, O!

In the visual arts also, the image of the Gypsy was primarily sexual. A tapestry, dated c.1500, from Tournai in France shows a Gypsy woman dancing, with a length of inner leg bare to the upper thigh presented for erotic delectation. Another, from the same period, in the Currier Gallery of Art, New Hampshire, USA, is entitled 'The Visit of the Gypsy'. It shows a middle-aged Gypsy man with an obviously gentile woman. It is not clear whether he is telling her fortune, or about to begin some kind of medical examination, his right hand holds her right hand, both their left hands are visible – but there is also a very large, and 'inexplicable' fifth hand in the drawing. It is below the four natural hands and, magically, comes from 'nowhere'. It rests in the folds of the woman's dress, which sensually hides and yet suggests her sexual parts. This Gypsy is a magician, a fortune-teller, a doctor and seducer – 'A Jack-of-all-demony'! Such art expresses deep biological, psychic and social instincts, and served a market that knew what it wanted and where it stood. Brueghel's 'John the Baptist' shows a similar image of Gypsies as tricksters.

After 1541 the Gypsies became semi-outlaws in Britain for about three hundred years. They were not alone in being, or feeling, persecuted during this period. The number of itinerants increased as land enclosure and clearance moved north. Significant numbers of people lived 'on the road' – beggars, pedlars, tramps, old soldiers, sailors, families dispossessed or broken by economic change and arbitrary power – as well as travelling craftsmen and braziers, the Tinkers and the Gypsies.

The toughest legislation dealt with 'vagabonds'. In 1547 Edward VI signed an English parliamentary decree legislating that all 'able-bodied vagabonds be branded on their breast with a V and made slaves for two years to a master who might put them to use by beating, chaining, or otherwise, in such work and labour (how vile so ever it be) as he saw fit'. This savage statute was repealed after only two years, but it, like the absolute proscription of Gypsies, showed a green light to those empowered to control 'Travellers'. In 1665 the Scottish government affirmed the transportation of 'strong and idle beggars, Gypsies and criminals to Jamaica'. In the early eighteenth century the Scots Traveller James MacPherson was hanged at Banff as sheep stealer and Traveller chieftain. To what extent MacPherson was a Gypsy, a Scots Traveller, or just a rebel is not clear – but his bragaddocio, his musicianship, his defiance on the gallows, have made him a Traveller hero honoured in one of the great rebel songs of Scotland, 'MacPherson's Rant!'.

An early theory about the origins of the Gypsies was published in Italy in 1841 by Francesco Predari. It was entitled *Origine e vicende dei Zingari con documenti alle proprieta asiche e morali* and suggested that the Gypsies were descended from a prehistoric people forced by geological or political catastrophe to become or remain, wanderers. Predari's theory is out of date today but it does raise a point of real interest in any search for the origins of Travelling People to their pre-'historic' period. All individuals have direct genetic kinship with prehistoric ancestors. This must also be true of all social, cultural and national groups – but, whereas most modern cultures have very few cultural contacts with the original societies from which they emerged, certain isolated groups have retained extremely conservative social and cultural forms – the Stone Age tribes of New Guinea, for example.

Genetic links are naturally maintained more or less indefinitely and may be reinforced by sexual and social selection but cultural continuity can be almost totally severed and once that has happened restoration is impossible. 'Celtic' Scotland, for various geographical, racial, occupational, historical and cultural reasons has maintained a strong social continuity over thousands of years. Sea, mountain, martial prowess, protective webs of kinship, cultural conservatism, a particular sensibility and strength of character have nurtured a remarkable historical stability in Highland society. And what is true of Highland society is particularly true, in miniature, of Traveller society. Here is a group whose social forms have direct links with the pre-historic period and, perhaps, the Palaeolithic period.

Today, Scotland's Travelling People, housed largely on municipal campsites and in corporation housing schemes, might seem poor and appear to live an aimless group life but they are very definitely not the flotsam of recent times, not some collective 'Drop-outs Anonymous'. They are a distinct social group, they live in close-knit families, and they retain a recognisable culture. Their history is much older than the Highland Clearances which were, essentially, a nineteenth-century phenomenon. They are an adaptive group which has, for centuries, lived in a practical and recognisably symbiotic relationship with the majority, settled population of the Highlands. Despite prohibitions on both sides, there has been some continual mixing between the Travellers and settled Highlanders but the travellers have retained their separate lifestyle, a separate group psychology, and a partially separate, many-layered culture. Such separateness, against the wind of history, once more suggests the ancientness of the group's social origins.

What is the origin of the Highland Travellers – the *Ceardannan*? Personal stories are told about royal decent, Jacobite proscription, Rob Roy, Robert the Bruce etc. Although Scotland is full of noble families and royal blood quickly moves up and down within a small population, most of these stories are clearly fanciful. They are linked to the widespread phenomenon known by psychoanalysts as 'family romance', in which myths of exotic or noble ancestry are embellishments, or selections – as arbitrary as the tumbling of lottery numbers – but they cannot be dismissed entirely because the inbreeding traditional to the group does reinforce ancestral connectedness. Thus most Travellers have a strong sense of their family's origin and an equally solid sense of their group origin. To outsiders, two, possibly linked, group-origins suggest themselves.

1. They are descendants of the Palaeolithic hunter-gatherers pushed into northern Europe as Neolithic agriculturalists developed land uses and new social patterns in southern Europe.

2. They are the heirs of a caste of Bronze Age metal-workers who established a long-term role for themselves

as craftsmen/culture carriers among the largely Celtic warrior/farmers who have dominated north western Britain for most of the last two and a half thousand years.

In geographical and physiological terms some association between the Scottish Travellers and the hunting peoples of northern Europe seems probable. There is a continuing ethnic and cultural unity among the hunting peoples of the northern hemisphere from Norway to Canada. Why should that link not extend to Scotland? The physical, oriental features of these far-flung peoples are remarkably uniform and culture, lifestyle, psychological habits and perceptions all retain unifying connections. The only animals the Travellers have traditionally kept have been man's oldest friends the dog and the horse. Like all hunting peoples they share an almost pathological aversion, not to hard work, but to habitual labour and the discipline of the clock. They certainly display a pre-industrial, a pre-agricultural, sense of leisure. Despite economic and political subordination they retain a pride, a sense of style, an aristocratic nobility of temperament which seems to be a prerogative of hunting peoples. The values and satisfactions of the farmer are not theirs. Their sense of surplus is highly undeveloped. Work and play are scarcely differentiated. Acute awareness of the past is not balanced by organised plans for the future. The readiness is all.

Contemporary standards of Traveller craftsman-ship are not high. Their sheet-tin craftsmanship was utilitarian, cheap, skilful but make-do. For at least a century their role as Highland Jacks-of all-trades has restricted any real aesthetic development but in the eighteenth century they did produce fine work and one must presume there was some link between such workers and the really skilled craftsman of the medieval period. What cannot be denied is that the musical abilities of the Highland Travellers are exceptional and it is not possible to imagine that these skills were once much greater. Singers don't come better than Jeannie Robertson. Such singing will have been in demand, at all levels of society for hundreds, perhaps thousands of years. In addition to the musical and literary skills of the Travellers, the *Beurla Reagaird* (as described by Dr MacInnes) suggests another link between the Travellers and the accepted cultural framework of early Celtic society.

Today, the decline of the traditional Travelling way of life in Sutherland and Ross-shire is an irreversible fact. Most families stopped travelling in the fifties. The Davies continued travelling as a family until 1981, but only Eddie Davies is still 'irregularly' out on the road. Metalworking skills have been adapted to the scrapmetal business, horse-dealers have moved into road haulage. The fundamental cause of the decline was that the lifestyle had become an anachronism, and a combination

of circumstances destroyed the remnants of a population too small to sustain itself.

Despite the recent elevation of 'the Clearances' to the centre of Scotland's historical consciousness – it is a fact of history that the population of the Highlands doubled during the prime century of the Clearances (1760 – 1860). It was during the next hundred years of voluntary emigration, war, and rising social expectation that the Highland population was halved back to the size it was at the time of the Forty-five. It was this twentieth-century fall in the population that so deeply harmed the crofting community and sealed the fate of 'The Summer Walkers'. The clientèle of the north Highland Travellers was small and relatively impoverished at the best of times but, as living standards rose in the wake of the Second World War, the traditional market of the Travellers evaporated. Incomers, like those to the industrial/nuclear developments at Dounreay, found no use for Tinker goods and had no interest in Traveller chat. The Gaelic language, that the Travellers had helped keep alive, was disappearing across all of mainland Scotland and their nomadism became an anachronism in an age of tourism and catalogue sales.

Pensions and state welfare were anathema to the older Travellers, but the various monies available began, slowly, to be claimed. This too, had an effect on the old way of life. The demand for fixed addresses and the process of regular social security payments discouraged Travellers from long periods of wandering the roads. Younger Travellers settled full-time into schools; with more and more access to the televised pleasures of an Americanised lifestyle, they began to question the whole mode, the quality, and the future of their existence as Travellers. A life, to which generations had felt mechani-cally impelled, was now a question of choice – a choice with few prospects. But above all there was the fundamental problem of numbers. The reasons for the collapse of the Traveller population in the north west, can be listed:

1. Like the crofters, a significant proportion of Travellers were emigrating or marrying out of the area. The Williamson clan had family and horse-trading connections with America, the Stewarts with Canada. Others were settling in Lowland Scotland, in England, Australia and New Zealand.

2. The World Wars had a significant impact on the Traveller population. Some were killed, some married away as a result of their military service, others lost marriage opportunities.

3. New occupations were taken up, and many families settled into good Council and other accommodation. To travel out was frowned upon.

4. A strange residue of Victorian propriety seems to have prevented these 'most disciplined' north Highland

Travellers, particularly the women, from getting in 'the family way' as the timeless alternative to a planned marriage. It had remained 'understood' that Travellers married Travellers: marriage into, or out of, tinkerdom was a hurdle that only the boldest were able to overcome. Thus many of the Travellers, like numerous educated and religious members of the crofting community began to 'behave themselves out of existence'.

This all-embracing sense of propriety was the noble side of a self-destructive impulse that is widespread among the Travellers. Its converse can be seen in violence and drunkenness and conscious social irresponsibility – a suicidal challenging of the changing world. The most obvious example of this is the huge number of Travellers killed on the road. To stroll down the middle of a road is a pleasure and an act of archetypal defiance, an invitation to progress and the modern motorist to knock you down! The Macmillans of Elgin and the Townsleys of Clachan and Whitehouse in Kintyre, are two families destroyed by death on the road.

5. Certain medical problems are acute among some Travellers. For centuries marriages between relations have been the norm rather than the exception. This has polarised the hereditary strengths and weaknesses of the group. Some families are large – but there is also relatively high infertility, and many couples have married too late to have children.

In the face of these major population and social problems, adoption became, or perhaps it continued, as a common fact of life. It was used by the Travellers as a deliberate mechanism to preserve families and to bolster the group's minority status. It did not perpetuate the north Highland Traveller way of life but it is a phenomenon of great human interest because, for centuries, across Europe, the Gypsies have been feared and demonised as 'child stealers', and in Scotland, stories about Tinker theft, abduction and purchase of children have been an integral fact of popular folklore. Now it must be true that, during the last five hundred years, some children have been kidnapped by Gypsies and it is certainly true that some children/lovers have run away with the Gypsies – but the vast bulk of these stories are fabricated myths, reflecting fears not reality, myths based on an inversion of substance. Unwanted children have, almost by tradition, been *given* to the Travellers and Gypsies. In the days before abortions it was the best thing to do. Circumstance and need have encouraged Travellers to 'adopt' unwanted youngsters. It was a natural consequence of their nomadism, their numerical vulnerability, their traditional humanity and family centredness. Over the years, guilt-twisted remembrance has turned 'giving' into 'taking', agreed 'deals' into 'theft'. Child-giving is infinitely superior to murder – but psychologically equally disturbing to the settled population.

Children were adopted by the Highland Travellers as part of the natural culture of their extended family, as a means of sustaining group numbers, for companionship, for domestic help in the house, as nurses for the elderly, and out of personal love. Beyond all this, the adoption of strangers remains a sublime act of human kindness.

Appendix 2

A SECRET LANGUAGE AND COVER TONGUE

From the eighteenth century onwards, bilingualism was a tool of the Travellers' trade, the *ceardannan*, as horse-dealers, craftsmen, salesmen and news-bringers needed both Gaelic and English and, in addition the north Highland Travellers made use of an ancient, secret language, known as the '*Beurla Reagaird*'; a cover-tongue, used, in just the way Gypsies use Romany among non-Romany speakers. The *Beurla Reagaird* allowed Travellers to disguise intent – but it also had mystique, was socially reinforcing, and gave pleasure to hard lives. The *Beurla*

Reagaird is of historical interest because, although primarily used as a 'closed-shop' jargon, it retains 'literary' elements which relate it to the esoteric language of travelling poets, seers and shanichees in old Gaelic society.

Romany has a different character and accent in all the far flung corners where Gypsies have travelled but the language has remained mutually comprehensible. Romany is the prime means of affirming the current population spread of the Gypsy people, and of tracing their cultural, geographic and racial origins. If Romany proves the oriental origin of the Gypsies what does the *Beurla Reagaird* prove?

Most Travellers in the southern half of Scotland have a fair knowledge of the Gypsy cant. In the north, this 'English' cant is largely replaced by the *Beurla Reagaird*, a strange, pigeon-Gaelic-backslang which owes little or nothing to the Gypsies. It shares similari-ties with the Irish Traveller cant known as *shelta*. It only exists within Gaelic-speaking groups and in symbiotic relationship with Gaelic. A selected vocabulary of common *Beurla Reagaird* words still used in the north Highlands is set out below. It was supplied by Alec John Williamson, and written out by the Gaelic scholar, Dr John MacInnes.

English	Beurla Reagaird	English	Beurla Reagaird
Man	*Glomhach*	Window	*Winkler*
Woman	*Gearach*	Potatoes	*Cruinneagan*
Youth	*Liaogach*	Cheese	*Sairc*
Girl	*Peurtag*	Butter	*Iaogan*
Child	*Suaillean*	Meat	*Fean*
Father	*Daid*	Pocket	*Grobaid*
Brother	*Bual*	Shop	*Claban*
Mother	*Camair*	Tobacco	*Sin-tait*
Crofter/Farmer	*Glomhach Caud*	Grass	*Liomas*
Chief	*Cal Simidh*	Salt	*Lasgarn*
Huntsman	*Liaogach Charmadrachd*	Meal	*Nialain*
Policeman	*Glomhach Cau(d)*	Sugar	*Meli*
Minister	*Gasgarn*	Peat	*Noib*
Fool	*Gramaid*	Cart	*Hurly*
Devil	*Neabal*	Shilling	*Uillisg*
God	*An Dhailean*	Pound	*Lumb*
My God	*Mo Dhailean*	Pig	*Gnobag*
Myself	*Mo rainn-head*	Hen	*Caineag*
Eye	*Deircean*	Tin	*Giarcan*
Eyes	*Deirceanan*	Cow	*Blainteag*
Teeth	*Stireagan*	Sheep	*Liobhag*
Nose	*Groib*	Rags	*Fidileas*
Mouth	*Bilidh*	Stick(s)	*Sim*
Posterior	*Taur*	House	*Cian*
Hands	*Mailcean*	Mansion	*Cian tom*
Hair	*Logaidh*	Hotel	*Cian Riongail*
Moustache	*Beastag*	Church	*Craban*
Penis	*Giocan*	Knife	*Tearlasg*
Shoes/boots	*Luigean*	Sword	*Tearlasg Tom*
Clothes	*Cleitean*	Fish	*Sgian*
Milk	*Taileaman*	Blanket	*Filleag*
Eggs	*Gruideagan*	Pipe	*Cheamban*
Horse	*Giofan*	Herring	*Sgian*
Bread	*Turan*	Trousers	*Eanach-taur*
Road	*Eanach*	Skirt	*Suaircean*
Water	*Sgaoi*	Basin	*Simeasag*
Bottle	*Roonder*	Paraffin	*Uilidh*
Whisky	*Sgaio-head*	Pail	*Raig*
Boat	*Caran*	Tent	*Cian bin*
Fire	*Tur*	Cat	*Geaidlean*
Light	*Leasg*	Dog	*Geann*
Door	*Rotach*	Pay	*Torp*
Tea	*Sgladach*	Work	*Gothaich*

English	Beurla Reagaird	English	Beurla Reagaird
Medicine	*Giomasagan Glotair*	Killed	*Carmith*
Song	*Drocan*	In	*Stiort*
Sleep	*Corlam*	Outside	*Chaim*
Stars	*Leasg an Dailean*	Good	*Muin*
Moon	*Leasg Tom*	Bad	*Cean*
Rain	*Sgaoi*	Large	*Tom*
Pearl	*Eanach Tom Sgaoi*	A worthless dog	*Cleid*
Gold	*Grad Tom*	A worthless cow	*Sgrog*
Pipe/Pipes	*Cheamban*	A worthless horse	*Siuidean*
Speaking	*Gloramas*	A worthless sheep	*Briuidean*
Saying	*Ruanaich*	A worthless hen	*Grug*
Ask	*Geug*	A worthless man	*Cliob*
Go in	*Bag stiort*	A worthless woman	*Usgaid*
Go out	*Bag chaim*	A worthless cat	*Streech*
Go away	*Mearslaich*	A tall gangly man	*Sgiogardach*
Do it	*Nead*	A dangerous man	*Canlubach*
Look	*Deirc*	A fat woman	*Geomhrag*
Stop/Be quiet	*Guisean*	A crying baby	*Sgialltean*
Stealing	*Biorachdadh*	A small unpopular man	*Gruitean*
Eating	*Luis*	A useless man	*Cultar*
Drunk	*Sgiomaideach*	Mentally retarded	*Teall*
Courting	*Guilm*	A stupid idiot	*Daot*
Hiding	*Labachd*	An untidy woman	*Lurach*
Fighting	*Carmaid*	An over forward girl	*Blos*
Kill	*Carm*	An over forward boy	*Briogan*

English	Sentences in the Beurla Reagaird
The minister's coming	*Hars an gasgarn bagail*
The shepherd is approaching	*Glomhach na liobhagan bagail*
Go and steal some peats	*Biorach noib*
Take in the basin	*Bag Stiort an Diomasag*
Let out the dog	*Bag chaim an geann*
The bread (food) is good	*An turan muin*
The devil take your foolish talk	*Carm an neabal gloramas greamadach*
Control the dog there are sheep here	*Bag stiort an geann thars na liobhagan*
I paid the man	*Throp mi an glomhach*
Yes he is drinking	*Starais an rainn luisearachd*
Sticks for the fire	*Timichean an tur*
I saw a woman and a man going out with a cow	*Dheirc mi gearach is glomhach mearsalaich blainteag*
Be quiet man	*Guisean liaogaich*
The forester is approaching	*Glomhach nan timichean bagail*
See the drunk woman	*Dearc an gearach sgiomaideach*
Put a match to the fire	*Bag gasag an tur*
Dog at the hen house	*Geann bagail gu eanach nan caineagan*
People speaking on the road	*Noideachan ruanach an eanach*
Take to your feet man	*Bag na luigean liaogaich*
Go away	*Mearslaich*
Look at the child going to the river	*Dearc an suaillean bagail chaim an sgaoi*
Doctors or body-snatchers about	*Glotairean cean an arso*
The doctor's or body-snatcher's coach	*Hurly nan glotairean cean*
The doctors killed the child	*Charm na glotairean cean an suaillean*

English	Sentences in the Beurla Reagaird
Take the horse's pail in	*Bag stiort raig a' ghiofain*
Look at the man's worthless shoes	*Dearc luigean cean a' ghlomhaich*
Come off the road, people going to church	*Bag an eanach. Noideachan bagail na chraban*
Look at the horse grazing	*Dearc an giofan luis an liomas*
People coming	*Noideachan bagail*
Look out there's a policeman coming	*Deirc an glomhach caud bagail*
Man entering the pub	*Glomhach bagail na chian riongail*
A man looking at a horse	*Glomhach deirceil a' ghiofain*

Dr MacInnes, formerly of the School of Scottish Studies, Edinburgh University is the leading authority on the *Beurla Reagaird*. It is a very complex subject. I am deeply indebted to Dr MacInnes for the information he has given me. Elements from his research are integrated into the following brief summary of current thinking about the origins of the *Beurla Reagaird*.

As travelling merchants, the *ceardannan* (the word originally meant craftsmen), played a vital role in Gaelic society. They were part of, but clearly separate from, the settled population. There was a certain contempt for them, a fear of them, they were treated like Ishmaelites. Their distinctness is affirmed by Acts of the Parliament of Scotland, for example, which issued exactions for 'bards, sorners (beggars), and ithir siclike rinners aboot'. We hear of them travelling in bands and quartering themselves on sometimes reluctant hosts – eating them out of house and home and engaging in debates of wit and contests of verse, till vanquished, or harried, they moved on.

In Gaelic one grade of poet was designated *bleidire*, a word which includes the sense of 'wheedler, flatterer' within its wider meaning. In some Gaelic dialects the plural *Na Bleidirean* was used to describe travelling bards of this kind, and there can be little doubt that this kind of 'traveller culture' has fed down into the culture of the Gaelic Travelling People today. Their secret language, the *Beurla Reagaird*, relates in various ways to that bardic tradition, but their use of it has become increasingly practical – it enabled Travellers, for instance, to keep a crofter in ignorance as they discussed the good and bad points of a horse. But, however it is used, the *Beurla Reagaird* retains a root in the medieval Gaelic literary tradition.

Dr MacInnes states that when Dr Hamish Henderson, in the 1950s, first recorded the name of this language, he spelt it as *Beurla Reagaid* and others have followed him in that spelling. A native Gaelic speaker, however, hears the 'r' sound (or 'r-colouring') in the last syllable: it is *Reagaird* or *Reagairt*. There the connection with the Irish 'craftsmen's' secret speech '*Beurla eagair na saor*' – is unmistakable. And here we have *Beurla*, now used for 'English' (shortened form *Beurla Shasannach*,

'Saxon speech') preserving an old meaning. *Beul* is mouth: that which issues from the mouth, i.e. 'language', as in older Gaelic *Belre*. (In this connection it is interesting that when the chemist in Lairg asked Old Suzie Stewart 'Do you have Gaelic?' She answered 'Oh Mr Ross, you know Gaelic was my first English!')

Studies of Irish *Shelta*, a related but by no means identical argot, have drawn attention to those elements which connect it (and the *Beurla Reagaird*) with the linguistic activities of the early Gaelic poets and other learned orders. An eminent nineteenth-century Celticist, Professor Kuno Meyer, summed up the discussion and concluded 'that *Shelta* is a secret language of great antiquity and that in certain Irish manuscripts we have mention of it under different names, and that, though now confined to tinkers, its knowledge was once possessed by Irish poets and scholars who probably were its original framers'.

Shelta contains a number of Romany words. The *Beurla Reagaird* has very few. Some Gaelic-speaking Travellers, like Alec John Williamson, have a fair knowledge of the English Traveller cant but they do not confuse it, in use, with the *Beurla Reagaird* – rather it is used as an independent, occasional fourth language and the syntax of the *Beurla Reagaird* always follows the pattern of Gaelic and the phonology is largely identical.

Some words in the *Beurla Reagaird* are obsolete Gaelic, or literary Gaelic. *Caineag*, the *Beurla Reagaird* word for 'hen', was used originally, in Gaelic, to describe the fowl used to pay a tithe – thus it was often the poorest, scraggiest hen available. (Just the kind of hens likely to be passed on to the Travellers! And it is interesting how many phrases in the *Beurla Reagaird* describe worthless creatures.) *Gloramas*, the word for 'speaking' was originally a literary term. The word for girl *peurtag* may be a borrowing from English/Scots 'partridge'. Some words can be, in one way or another, connected with ordinary Gaelic: the Gaelic word for mother, *mathair* becomes *camar* in the *Beurla Reagaird*. Big, *mor* becomes 'tom'. *Glomhach* the word for man must relate to the Gaelic word for a youth, *oglach*. The Gaelic word *dean*, which means 'to make' is pronounced backwards in the *Beurla Reagaird* to become *nead*.

In summary, the core of the *Beurla Reagaird* is undoubtedly ancient, it is a creation of Gaelic-speaking people, and its major secret lies in its 'disguising of words by the introduction of arbitrary elements'.

The continuance of the *Beurla Reagaird* as a living 'sub-language' into the late twentieth century is another example of the general pleasure Travellers take in language. Because their culture is still essentially non-literate, their 'speaking' is more free to change and evolve than literary and bureaucratic speech and languages. Chance, mistakes and misconception often lie close to the heart of creative change. The Travellers enjoy manipulating words just as they like changing their names – less by marriage, than by habit and desire, by wilful wish to confuse and sheer participatory delight. They decorate, humour, vitalise and subvert conventional descriptions, rhythms and associations. Like cartoonists they leap on the odd and peculiar, they characterise and personify – as can be demonstrated with a short list of Traveller English-language nicknames:

Wooden Sleeves, Love-in-a Close, Twa Holes in a Blanket, The Big-ma-Hungry, The Waterbottle, Half-a-Shirt, Meg-and-the-Moneyfeed, Forty Pooches, Fish-Airse, Pishy Jean, Hieland Scrogg, The Sheep's Heid, Laughter, The Rockingham Tea-pot, Alec-was-his-Granny, The Little Dancer, The Four-eyed Blister, Crazy Horse, Lang Cauld and Hungry, The Galoot, The Wild Colonial Boy, The Scoots, Kettle-heid, The Half-Hangit Ministair, Burnt Bonnet, Cauld Stane, White Iron Kate, Wee Grassie Mouse, Quarry Yaks.

Such cover-names are often not known to their owners. They are used according to situation. They are part of the whole culture that preserves Traveller identity. They are products of communal living amidst a wider community in which elusiveness is useful. In Carrbridge in 1994 a man arrived at a ceilidh, a Stewart, and left five hours later, Jimmy Higgins, singing! Asked where he'd find a place to sleep for the night he replied 'I aye claese my een when I sleep – if I can lift me heid come the morn, I'll not complain where I foond it!'

Appendix 3

ROAD, TENTS AND CAMPSITES

Roads: the Sutherland Stewarts followed three major routes:
1. North along the old A836 to Tongue via Altnaharra, where they would branch either west to Durness or east to Strathie. This journey would be repeated several times a year. Only in the autumn would they proceed beyond Strathie to Thurso, for the big horse fair and market at Georgemas Junction.
2. North west from Lairg along the A838, past Loch Shin to Laxford Bridge, where they would branch out around Scourie and Kinlochbervie, and usually return via Durness, Melness and Tongue.
3. West on the A837 up Glen Oykel to Ledmore and along the north side of Loch Assynt, where they either turned north to cross the Kylesku Ferry, or continued west to Lochinver, Polbain and Auchiltibuie.

The Ardgay and Edderton Williamsons covered the same ground but their 'native heath' was recognised as being more to the south, covering all of Wester Ross and extending as far down as Skye in Inverness-shire.

These traditional routes follow ancient tracks through gaps in the mountains which are historically much older than the roads laid out by military builders like General Wade, and the drove roads along which Highland cattle were moved to the Lowland markets. The Travellers had to get where people were – in doing this they followed prime routes, first developed in the Neolithic period.

Campsites: the Travellers returned to the same campsites year after year. They were chosen according to the need for dry ground, fresh water, grass for the horses, and the proximity of a local population. Such sites were sanctioned, not by local councils but by traditional patronage, or traditional use. Shelter from wind seems not to have been a particular priority and, almost without exception, the campsites were vantage points, providing panoramic vistas.

Why should such picture-postcard sites be chosen? The aesthetic impulse lies deep in human consciousness. Like footloose tourists and modern holiday-makers the Travellers have always had an eye for a view. Instead of stopping the car, removing their clothes, or taking a snapshot, they set up camp, stayed for a week, bought and sold goods, played the pipes and told stories about heroes.

Mankind has a very deep instinct for place and for aesthetic placement. When Alexander Solzhenitsyn returned from America to Russia after twenty years of exile, he travelled from Vladivostok by train, slowly in stages, so as to truly 'live' his homecoming. On the banks of the river Angora peasant villagers set out a picnic above a great bend in the river. Standing with a sandwich in one hand and looking down on the hollow where a small hamlet nestled, he said 'In the old days people knew where to place a village in the landscape.' What was true of the old Russians, was powerfully true of the Highland Travellers.

Traditional campsites to the north from Lairg were: Tirry roads, Dalnessie, Rhian, Crask, Vagastie, Altnaharra, Grumbeg, Rhifail, Achnabourin, Apigil (for Bettyhill), Armadale, Lednagullin, Strathy, Melvich, Reay, Janetstown (Neil's Park Mr Macdonald) – for Georgemas Market.

Altnaharra, Loch Loyal, Brae Tongue, Kinloch, Melness Ferry, Melness Midtown, Hope, Mussel Burn, Laid, Rispond, Sangobeg, Lerinmore, Durness (Lerin), Coulin Hill, Rhiconich Hotel, Ardmore, Laxford Bridge, Achfary, Kinloch, Merkland, Overscaig Hotel, Fiag Bridge, West Shinness, Tirry.

Traditional campsites to the west from Lairg were: Gruids, Alister's Dyke/Rosehall, Tuitem, Oykel Bridge, Lubcroy, Altnacealgach, Ledmore Crossroads, Ledbeg/Lyne, Inchnadamph, Skiag Bridge, Unapool (Kylesku), Scourie, Kinlochbervie, Skiag Bridge, Little Assynt, Lochinver, Stoer, Drumbeg, Inverkirkaig, Inverpolly, Badnagyle, Polbain, Achiltibuie, Elphin Bridge, Elphin, Strath Canaird (for Ullapool).

The bow-tent remained the normal accommodation for the north Highland Travellers until they gave up the road (the last traditional journey in the north west being taken by the Ardgay Williamsons in July 1978). In southern Scotland a variety of tents of all shapes and sizes have been used by the Travellers but in the north there seems to have been a remarkable, conservative unity to the form of tents. They were big, stout and well-finished structures but at the same time relatively easy to put up, take down and stack on a cart. They were built like skin around a rib-cage, an armature of bowed hazel sticks. These were pre-stressed into permanent bows, against a wall, rock or trees, while the saplings were still supple. On site, these sticks were shafted into the ground and the tops bound together, usually along some kind of ridge pole, or poles, to create a firm but flexible skeleton. Over this tarpaulin covers were draped (or hides, skins, blankets, nets, plastic sheets or tattie bags). These tarpaulins were secured externally with heavy stones and, if necessary, ropes and strings. Drainage ditches were dug to run off water.

The tent-stones were left at the campsite in orderly heaps for subsequent use. Today, these stones provide the strongest physical evidence as to where camps once were. In modern times open fires were seldom lighted. Stoves were placed in the middle of any large tent, close to the 'split' doorway where the two canvasses joined. If fires were lighted, turfs would be carefully removed and replaced unless a river-bed provided a natural hearth. A proportion of tents flung up quickly look like wigwams, but most bow-tents squat in the landscape like tarpaulin igloos and have proved highly resistant to wind.

Habitations like the bow-tent provided the beginnings of European architecture. Siberian shelters constructed around found mammoth tusks in the palaeolithic period, have been reconstructed by archaeologists and they look remarkably like Traveller tents. Structurally, it is interesting to note that bow-tents make use of the round arch and the half-dome and employ an essentially modular system of construction, uniform struts being placed more or less equally along the ridging pole. This makes the tents at once rude but ancient 'pre-classical forms' and strangely modern – mixing hunter-gatherer low-tech mechanics with Roman dynamics. They have a lumpen, dead shark, rather ugly shape – but 'golden sections' flow naturally from the three-dimensional use of the square and circle forms on which these tents are based.

Are Highland Traveller tents products which can claim direct descent from learned precedents going back many hundreds, perhaps thousands of years? Or are they shacks, 'make-do arrangements' of the kind that poor people, refugees, New Age Travellers and SAS commandos fling up as need dictates? The answer is probably a mixture of the two – but the historical ancientness of Traveller culture is affirmed from so many different angles, that the likelihood of these tents being, at least partially, the direct heirs of prehistoric precedent is strong. One can ask why and when was such a precedent, in north west Scotland, broken?